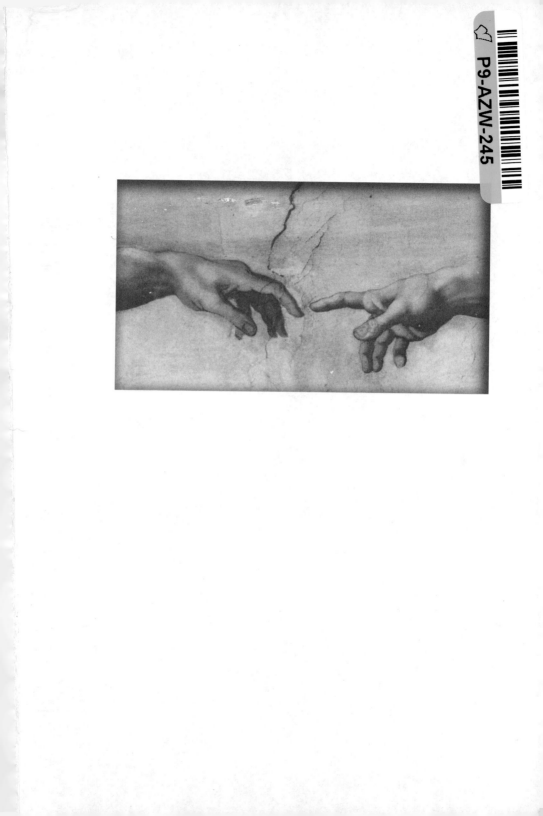

Dialogue

with

GOD

Mark and Patti Virkler

Bridge-Logos
Orlando, Florida 32822

Bridge-Logos

Orlando, FL 32822 USA

Dialogue with God

by Mark and Patti Virkler

Printed in the United States of America.

Library of Congress Catalog Card Number: 86-70744
International Standard Book Number 978-0-88270-620-7

Unless othrwise identified, Scripture quotations in this book are from the *New American Standard Bible*, © The Lockman Foundation, 1960 , 1962, 1963, 1968, 1971, 1972, 1973, 1975, 1977. Used by permission.

G163.321.B.m707.35250

*This book is gratefully dedicated to our friend
Rev. John Arnott, the apostle over the Toronto Renewal.
He is committed to seeing all believers experience the
Father's heart through hearing His voice.
His steadfast love and support have strengthened and
encouraged us deeply through the years.*

Contents

Introduction

This is the story of my search for the voice of God. For the first ten years of my Christian life, I lived in a box of rationalism I had built for myself. My life was governed by the rules and principles for successful Christian living that I discovered through my study of the Scriptures. My prayers were monologues, never managing to break through to "the other side of silence," to a place of two-way dialogue with God.

I always believed that Christians should be able to hear God's voice. I knew He wanted to guide us continually and that one of the ways He guides is by His "still, small voice." Jesus clearly stated that "My sheep hear My voice." Yet no matter how hard I tried, I never could hear that voice speaking to me. I read books and attended seminars. I studied the Word. I questioned those who were able to hear from the Lord. But my searching seemed to be in vain. It seemed to come so easily and normally to those who knew the voice of God within them. They were naturally intuitive and mystical and couldn't understand why I was having so much trouble with such a simple thing. They didn't know what to say to help me.

But the Lord had seen the desire of my heart to know His voice, a desire that could not be crushed even by repeated failures and disappointments. He gradually led me to the right resources to teach me the skills I needed: inner stillness; spontaneity; vision; journaling. When all the pieces were in place, I realized that I had received much more than I expected. I was looking for a voice; I found a Person. I was looking for guidance; I found a Shepherd. I was looking for the will of God; I found a relationship with the Son of God.

Since I have been able to discern the voice of the Lord in my heart, I have moved into a life of sweet fellowship with Jesus. I no longer live under law, for now I am governed by love. Rules have given way to relationship. Daily I am in immediate contact with my Lord, and my whole life has been changed. My personality, my family and my ministry have all been altered by the wisdom and compassion of Jesus now available to me. My heart has been convinced of the love God has for me and I will never be the same.

The deep love God expressed for His children and His great desire to communicate with each one compelled me to write down the skills I had learned. I shared the burden of the Lord that every Christian would enjoy the blessed communion with Him that I had found. I began sharing what I knew, teaching others how to hear God's voice and break through in two-way dialogue with Him. Many have joyfully entered this new way of living.

The Church is beginning to hear God's voice and see God's vision. The time for mourning has passed. The moment of renaissance and restoration is upon us. The prophets calling for repentance have done their work. The Church is awakening to her sins, her responsibilities and her kingdom authority. The kingdom of this world shall indeed become the kingdom of our Lord and of His Christ. He shall reign through us in every aspect of life on this earth.

It is my prayer that the Lord will anoint this book, using it to bring people like me into a new dimension of Christianity, a place of two-way dialogue with God. I pray that the love and acceptance you receive from the Lord may heal you of all fears and inadequacies, and transform your life. I pray that God's vision may be birthed within you, that you may discover your place in the kingdom of God. I pray that you may find life, as you talk with God "face-to-face, as a man talks with his friend."

1

Struggling to Hear God's Voice

A Divine Appointment

"Mark! Get up!"

The commanding voice woke me from a sound sleep and I sat straight up in bed. Though I had never heard it before or since, I immediately knew that I had heard the audible voice of God!

"What? What?" I said in confusion.

"Wake up! I am going to teach you to hear My voice!"

"Great!" I said, as I lay back down. "Okay, go ahead."

"GET UP! Go to your office. I am going to teach you to hear My voice tonight!"

Finally grasping the significance of the moment, I quickly obeyed. That night, as I knelt at the altar of our little country church, the Holy Spirit gave me the precious gift I had been seeking for so long and launched me into the calling that would become my passion for the rest of my life. He drew together all I had learned during a year of intensive study on prayer and hearing God's voice, and showed me how it all fit together into four simple keys that were revealed in Habakkuk 2:1,2.

How I Got Here

When I accepted the Lord at age fifteen, my immediate hunger was to learn God's Word or, as I liked to put it, to become a biblical man. This hunger was deep and insatiable. Three years later, with great eagerness I enrolled at Roberts Wesleyan College to study for a Bachelor of Arts degree in religion and philosophy.

I found college exciting because I was learning the Bible inside and out. My hunger to become a biblical man was slowly being satisfied. I read and studied the Bible through and through, outlined and made graphs of each book, and taught it weekly as a youth pastor. This was the days before the Bible-on-cassette was available, so Patti made our own recording of her reading through the New Testament that I listened to while I worked.

Practical, biblical, logical—those words have always appealed to me. Having grown up on a dairy farm in a conservative rural community, my approach to life had always been practical, down-to-earth and sensible. When I first accepted Jesus, I joined a very conservative Baptist church and felt an immediate call on my life to become a pastor. Until then I had always intended to be a farmer; I enjoyed the practical lifestyle of dairy farming, especially seeing something tangible accomplished at the end of a long day's hard labor.

It was no surprise, therefore, when I found a passionate desire within me to make the Bible real, practical, and down-to-earth in my life. As I studied and taught, I began to see that the voice of God, or the "word of the Lord" as the prophets called it, was very real, and a continuous theme in Scripture. I noticed that from Genesis to Revelation, men and women heard God's voice speaking to them, and a hunger grew within me to hear God's voice in my own heart. A strong desire to become a spiritual man and to understand the ways of the Spirit began to burn as I recognized that I could only be a biblical man if I, too, could hear the voice of God.

So I began searching for God's voice within my heart. I waited expectantly for the inner audible voice of God to speak to me and say, "Hello, Mark. This is God." He would have a deep bass voice, of course. Maybe there would be lightning in the sky, the wind would blow, and the windows would shatter. I would then jump in instant obedience and do whatever He wanted me to do.

But nothing happened. I listened and listened, but I could not discern any "voice of God." All I heard were thoughts rummaging through my mind until I eventually wandered off in aimless daydreams or, even worse, fell asleep.

It was extremely frustrating! Prayer simply didn't work for me and I couldn't understand why not. I thought that maybe if I read more of the Word it would help. Then I'd be able to hear God's voice, I reasoned. So I devoured the Bible, reading whole books in a single sitting. But I still couldn't discern that quiet inner voice.

I read in Isaiah 58 that if we would fast with the right spirit, we could cry out to God and He would answer. We would *hear Him say*, "Here I am" (Is. 58:9). Jesus' teaching also indicated that fasting would increase your spiritual power and authority. So I decided to try fasting to see if it would make me more spiritually receptive. I fasted for days and even weeks at a time, but I still couldn't hear a voice within my heart.

I hoped that when I graduated from a Christian liberal arts college that somehow, along with my diploma I would be endowed with the ability to hear God's voice. But I received my degree and still could hear nothing other than my own wandering thoughts. There just was no inner voice! No matter what people said or the Bible taught, I could not find a voice.

As I moved into pastoral ministry, I hoped and prayed that the voice would come with my ordination. I mean, how can you possibly be a pastor without hearing God's voice? It would be an especially embarrassing situation to be pastor of a full gospel charismatic fellowship! Just think: Someone was sure to give a message in tongues and if no one else gave the interpretation, it would be my responsibility to maintain proper order by giving it myself. But how could I speak a prophetic word if I couldn't hear from God? My church would find out I was a fraud! I would be ruined! Surely, God in His mercy did not want that to happen to me. Surely, He would use the opportunity of my ordination ceremony to break through the silence into my heart. Please, God? But my ordination came and went and still there was no voice. By now I was getting discouraged. I had tried everything I knew and still, nothing.

I went back to the Scriptures to make sure that the people of God truly heard His voice. Yes, God unequivocally reaffirmed that in every covenant from Genesis to Revelation He had spoken to His children. Here are a few of the hundreds of verses of Scripture that confirmed this truth to my heart:

And they [Adam and Eve] heard the sound of the Lord God... (Gen. 3:8).

Now the Lord said to Abram... (Gen. 12:1).

The Lord said to Moses... (Ex. 4:21).

Now the Lord said to Aaron... (Ex. 4:27).

And it shall come to pass, if thou shalt hearken diligently unto the voice of the Lord thy God... (Deut. 28:1 KJV).

The Lord spoke to Joshua... (Josh. 1:1).

Then the Lord said to me [Isaiah]... (Is. 8:1).

The word that came to Jeremiah from the Lord, saying... (Jer. 7:1).

The word of the Lord came...to Ezekiel (Ezek. 1:3).

I [Jesus] can do nothing on My own initiative, as I hear, I judge... (Jn. 5:30).

And the Spirit told me [Peter] to... (Acts 11:12).

[Paul] having been forbidden by the Holy Spirit to... (Acts 16:6).

I [John] was in the Spirit on the Lord's day, and I heard behind me a loud voice like the sound of a trumpet, saying, "Write in a book what you see..." (Rev. 1:10,11).

But you have come to Mount Zion and to the city of the living God...and to Jesus, the mediator of a new covenant...See to it that you do not refuse Him who is speaking (Heb. 12:22,24,25).

I just could not accept the premise that God would stop speaking in this dispensation of grace, especially when there was such a deep hunger within me to hear. That longing had to be placed there by God.

Around that time, God graciously placed in my life a co-elder in our local assembly who was able to clearly hear the voice of God and speak it forth in beautiful prophecy. I marveled at the purity, power, and accuracy of the way he spoke the word of the Lord. I decided to ask him what he did to hear the voice of God. I thought he could give me some clues that would finally throw open the door for two-way prayer in my own life.

I tried to evoke every bit of direction and understanding I could from him. He patiently shared his own experience, but he wasn't able to help me. I finally realized that he is naturally intuitive and that hearing God's voice comes easily to him. I am too analytically inclined to understand the naturalness of the intuitive flow. For me, the spirit world was only found by following a detailed map of instructions. Instead, he told me what so many already had: "You just know that you know that you know." Have you ever heard that explanation? I want you to know, if you don't know it doesn't help to be told that you know! I left even more frustrated than when I came. I also had extinguished almost all possible leads.

In total desperation, I examined the only remaining possibility I could think of: I checked to see if I was truly saved. It didn't take much contemplation to decide that I was. I had definitely repented and confessed my sins. I had invited Christ in and asked Him to become the Lord and Savior of my life. The elders had laid hands on me to receive the Holy Spirit and I had been baptized in water. I believed the Bible to be the unerring Word of God, and held to all the truths of evangelical theology.

Okay—I was definitely saved. Well, what in the world was the problem? Maybe I was just trying too hard and being too practical about the whole thing. Maybe I was expecting too much of Christianity. Maybe I should just be content like so many other Christians seemed to be. I had the Bible—maybe I didn't need His inner voice after all. I was weary and at my wit's end. I had tried everything I knew, and nothing had worked. I listened as hard as I could and still had no inner voice in my heart. It just was not there. I was not going to enter deception and pretend it was there—if it wasn't there it wasn't there.

A short time later a nationally known Bible teacher whom I deeply respected was speaking at our church. I plied him with questions afterwards. "How do you hear the voice of God in your heart?" I asked. His answer astounded me: "What people call the 'voice of God' is merely the subterranean rumblings of the spiritual mind." In other words, there is no such thing!

Part of me wanted to believe that. After all, it wouldn't be a weakness in my life not to have something that didn't exist, would it? But then I thought about the co-elder in my church who could prophesy so beautifully and others whom I'd heard speak forth the Word of the Lord. And I knew that the hunger in my heart would not be satisfied with anything less than a full two-way relationship with Almighty God.

I thank God that even when we are unaware of it His hand is leading us. Through all my hunger and searching He was leading me one small step at a time.

Most of the steps were not even noticeable at the time, just seemingly insignificant events or fortunate circumstances. Yet today I can look back and see how the hand of God moved. Through all my failures and depression and confusion, He was always working all things out for my good.

The Four Keys

The beginning of the revelation came in a quiet way. My wife, Patti, and I drove to a nearby town to attend some tent meetings and after the service browsed through the book tables. A book by Michael Scanlan on inner healing caught my eye, since it was a new ministry at the time and I knew almost nothing about it.

I bought the book and was very blessed by what I read. I thought of the many people I knew who had deep hurts and had not been helped by counseling. Perhaps this was the answer for them, I thought. Shortly thereafter Patti and I attended a retreat on inner healing by Fathers Dennis and Matthew Linn. Although we spent a lot of time dealing with theological questions, it was there that God affirmed in me the need for dream and vision in the adult Christian life.

I spent much of the next several months studying everything I could on prayer. I read about twenty-five books and everything I could find in Scripture concerning prayer. I experimented with different kinds of prayer. Near the end of that year, the Lord awakened me from sleep with the sound of His audible voice. That night God opened up Habakkuk 2:1,2, in which the prophet described what he did when he went before God to hear His voice, and in those verses He showed me several revolutionary keys that I had never seen nor heard taught before. Let me show them to you briefly now, then I will spend several chapters delving into each one individually, showing precisely how they can be developed and used in your prayer life.

> *I will stand on my **guard post**...And I will keep **watch** and **see** what He will **speak** to me...Then the Lord...said, **Record** the vision....* (Habakkuk 2:1,2 emphasis added)

Obviously Habakkuk could discern the sound of the Lord's voice in his heart. He said, "Then the Lord said." Also, throughout his writing, Habakkuk recorded what God spoke to him. Therefore, he knew the sound of God's voice.

The first key to hearing God's voice, then, is learning *what His voice spoken within sounds like*. Rather than being an inner audible voice, I discovered that God's voice in our hearts generally sounds like a flow of spontaneous thoughts. Yes, God graciously spoke to me in an audible voice that one night, but that is certainly not the norm. In fact, it is more likely an indication that I was too thick or too stubborn to get His message any other way! Like Paul on the road to Damascus, I had to be "hit upside the head" in order to hear what He had to say to me.

The Lord will take drastic measures if necessary, but He would rather we learn to discern Him speaking as spontaneous thoughts from within our hearts. I will spend an entire chapter expounding on this idea, backing it up biblically and experientially, and then discussing the effect this truth has on our lives.

The second key found in Habakkuk is in the phrase, "I will stand on my guard post." Habakkuk knew how *to go to a quiet place and quiet his own thoughts and emotions* so he could sense the spontaneous flow of God within. Most of us know we are supposed to quiet ourselves, but it is just so hard to do. Later on, I will present numerous biblical tools for quickly quieting our hearts and minds before God so that we can begin to sense the active flow of His Spirit within.

The third key is found in Habakkuk's phrase, "I will keep watch to see." I asked myself why he said it that way. Why didn't he say, "I will *listen* to hear what He will speak to me." It makes more sense to me that one would listen to hear spoken words than watch to see them.

By the time this question was answered in my heart and mind, God had opened up an entirely new revelation (to me at least) concerning the place of dream and vision in prayer. I had never even thought of looking for vision as I prayed. I had never considered presenting the eyes of my heart to God and asking Him to fill them, looking to see what He wanted to show me. However, as I began to search the Scriptures, I found that *dream and vision* were a regular part of all the prophets' prayer lives. I will unfold this revelation with Scriptural support and a careful examination of how dream and vision actually work in prayer.

Finally the fourth key demonstrated in Habakkuk 2: Then the Lord said, "Record the vision." What an incredible idea — actually *writing out my dialogue with God.* And yet I soon saw that the whole book of Habakkuk is the story of a man who wrote down his prayer and the answers he received back from God. And it was God Who commanded him to write it down.

I had never heard a sermon on the value of recording our dialogue with God; it had never even crossed my mind that I might write down my prayer and God's answer. I have come to call this process "journaling," and as I looked for a basis for it in Scripture I found not just one or two verses on journaling, but hundreds of *chapters* demonstrating this process. Many examples are found in the Psalms, the prophets, and the entire book of Revelation.

It always shocks me to find the Church spending so much time discussing doctrines based on just a few verses of Scripture only to neglect a doctrine that is commanded in Scripture and demonstrated in several hundred chapters. It makes me think we are out of balance sometimes. I will devote an entire chapter to journaling, examining the whole process biblically and showing what tremendous value it has in helping us hear God's voice. I will also describe how it works practically.

Safeguards

Now, before we go any further, we need to discuss some safeguards for this journey into the world of Spirit impressions.

When we talk about hearing the voice of the Spirit of Almighty God, people sometimes fear that they could get it mixed up with the voice of satan or the voice of their own hearts' desires. If that happened and they acted on it, it could bring real destruction into their lives, they fear. Too often, the solution they think best is to not seek the spiritual life at all—to simply live out of biblical law and ignore the possibility of hearing from God personally.

This is certainly one alternative, and many people have obviously taken this path, but it is clearly not the way of the abundant life Jesus promised us. Instead, God has given us several safeguards in Scripture that, if we will follow them, we can live as Jesus did, comfortable and confident we are protected and in the Father's care in both the spiritual and physical worlds.

The Scriptures

Probably the greatest protection we have on our spiritual journey is the Word of God. A good knowledge of the Scriptures can save us from many errors and heartaches. At the Bible School where I taught, we required a certain level of biblical knowledge as a prerequisite to this teaching on hearing God's voice. When I teach in other churches, I recommend that those attending the course have at least read through the New Testament and be currently reading in the Old Testament.

This is not to say, of course, that God does not speak to new Christians who have not yet read the Word. Of course He does! But if they do not couple their prayer time with an intensive study of the Word and a relationship with a spiritual counselor, they will quickly run into danger.

There are two basic ways in which the Scriptures can help and protect us. First, every revelation must be tested against the written Word of God. If the revelation violates either the letter of the Word or the spirit of the Word, it is to be rejected immediately. There is no place for rationalizing, twisting or explaining away the truth of the Bible. There can be no strange, personal interpretations of some obscure verse. The Word of the Lord will stand forever, and any word to us from God will be in total agreement with both the letter and spirit of the Eternal Word.

We must not only test God's voice in our hearts against the Bible, but see any revelation as built upon the Scriptures. The Lord told Joshua to meditate upon, confess, and act upon the law of God day and night so that He could give him success. If I have filled my mind and heart with the Bible, the Holy Spirit will draw forth the precise verses, stories or principles I need in a given situation. The spontaneous flow of illumined Scriptures will bring wisdom and insight far greater than my own mind could deliver if only I will pause and allow myself to be dependent on God.

The Body of Christ

The second important Scriptural safeguard from error and spiritual harm is a humble, teachable spirit. So often the ones who claim to hear from the Lord are arrogant and self-righteous. Their attitude is, "God told me and that's all there is to it." But God resists the proud and gives grace to the humble. Such an arrogant spirit will eventually cause them to fall into deception. All revelation should be tested. God does not speak to us so that we may lord it over anyone else. Rather, we ought to be known as the meekest of men.

We are a part of the Body of Christ. The full revelation of Jesus does not reside in us individually but only as we come together as a Body. We all need to be committed to a local expression of the Body of Christ, and anyone who wants to delve into the spiritual dimension of life should have a relationship with a spiritual counselor they respect.

We cannot survive if we try to walk alone. The Lord will show you with whom you are to establish an accountability relationship, if you ask Him. This is a powerful protection for your life: "In the multitude of counselors there is safety" (Prov. 11:14 KJV). I will discuss the concept of spiritual counselors in greater detail later on.

Humility

There are other basic safeguards as well. God gives revelation only for the areas in which He has given authority and responsibility. A wife will normally receive revelation for her home or her outside job. A husband will receive wisdom for his family and functioning in his business. A pastor will receive revelation for the church over which God has made him responsible.

Along with God-given authority comes God-given revelation to wisely exercise that authority. Therefore, you should expect revelation only in those areas for which you are legitimately responsible. Stay away from ego trips that seek revelation for areas in which you do not have authority. Don't look for a "word from the Lord" to the President or other world leaders. Don't even look for a revelation for your employer or pastor, unless you are responsible to him as a close friend or counselor. Revelation is given only for God-ordained areas of authority and responsibility.

Testing

Also, we should be sure that all revelation we receive is leading us toward greater wholeness and the ability to love and share God more perfectly. If at any time our attempts at dialoguing with God become destructive, we must stop at once and seek out our spiritual counselor.

You may be frightened by such a warning, and even tempted to ignore the spiritual world altogether, rather than risk the dangers. But only those who think they can make it all alone, those with a "just Jesus and me" attitude, need be concerned. If you are applying safeguards such as those I have mentioned and are sincerely seeking God's voice, you can confidently approach life in the Spirit.

Before continuing to read this book, I strongly encourage you to carefully examine your life to make sure these guardrails are intact. If they are not, please lay this book down, and take the time necessary to establish them in your life. Then come back, pick it up again, and go on.

The revelations the Lord gave me will be a great blessing to those who are walking righteously before God, but they could as well open up the foolish man to satan's wiles. The Christian who has placed God's safeguards around himself need never fear deception, but all must be aware of our enemy, who "prowls about like a roaring lion, seeking someone to devour" (1 Pet. 5:8).

The year I spent learning to hear God's voice has paid off with tremendous fruit. I learned that I needed to still my own mind and listen to the flow of God's inner spontaneous thoughts. I learned that I needed to open my heart to the flow of dream and vision that God placed within. And most of all I learned I needed to journal, to write down my dialogue with Almighty God.

I first made sure that the safeguards were in place. I knew the Word. I was willing to submit all inner revelation to the letter and the spirit of the Bible. I was willing to walk in relationship with the Body of Christ and with the counselors God had given to me. I made sure that all revelations led toward greater wholeness and the ability to love and share God more perfectly. Then I was ready to go on the greatest adventure of my life.

The Desire of God's Heart

Why didn't God give up on me long ago? Why does He keep leading me to know His voice? And why is it that I want so desperately to hear His voice? In fact, why is this the almost universal cry of Christians around the world and down through the ages? In their desperation to hear from God, men and women have stripped their lives of every other comfort and distraction. They have given up all their worldly goods to live in starkest simplicity so that nothing could come between them and their God. They have made vows of silence so that the only voice they might hear would be the voice of God. Why have godly men and women throughout history been so consumed? Why was I so consumed?

Quite simply, it is because the deepest desire of God's heart is to have communion with His children. From the beginning of time His desire has remained the same. He calls us all gently, but persistently. He even lets us experience the dissatisfaction that life without Him brings. Though our spirits are cluttered and our minds confused, still we sense deep within us a longing for a special relationship, the special kind of love that will satisfy our hearts.

In the Garden

"Adam! Adam, where are you?"

When we hear those words we think of the sorrowful day when man's fellowship with God was broken. But let's think for a moment what it was like before that day. How many other days did the Father come to the garden in the cool of the day just to take a walk with the man and woman He loved so much. How often did He call, "Adam, Adam!" How many times did Adam respond joyfully, "Here I am, Lord!"

Can you see the three of them, perhaps hand in hand, slowly wandering through the lush flowers, sometimes stopping to pick a juicy fruit? Adam must have talked about his responsibilities of the day: how his pruning helped the peach tree, and the strawberry seeds he had planted that were giving luscious red fruit. Father listened, a gleam of pride in His eyes.

Eve talked about her animal friends: the tricks the monkeys were doing and how the squirrels scolded them so furiously. Soon they all laughed at the picture she had painted with her words. As the sun set, they may have fallen into a companionable silence, enjoying the brilliant display of colors even more because they were enjoying it together.

That is communion. That is the sharing of love we were made to enjoy. Father wants us to come to Him with our joys and successes. He wants us to share our laughter with Him. And He wants to enjoy our pleasure in His creation. He wants to be our best friend, our companion, our lover.

How His heart rejoices when we take time to relax from our labors and devote ourselves wholly to conversing with Him! It was for this that He created us. He longs for someone with whom He can share His love. God is love, and as a song says, "Love isn't love 'til you give it away." God longs for us to come so that He may give that love to us.

For a long time I viewed a leisurely stroll in a garden in the cool of the day as essentially a waste of time. I wanted to be producing something. I didn't have time to spare for such unnecessary extras. But the Lord began gently and lovingly teaching me that a leisurely stroll and sharing love with someone are not unnecessary extras; they are the culmination of His purposes. That is what He desires. That is the purpose of creation and life.

He created me for the supreme purpose of sharing love with Him. He created me with the capacity to love so I could return His love. I had lost sight of this somewhere in the hustle of life. I thought that producing *things* was more important than producing *love*. As God reminded me of creation, He called me to repent of idolizing work and asked me to put love center-stage again. I heard. I listened. And I repented and was healed.

His Chosen People

God has tried to restore the communion He enjoyed with Adam and Eve in the Garden of Eden. He established a covenant with the people of Israel in which He promised to be their God, and that they would be His people. At the mountain of God, He offered them His voice. He wanted desperately to talk with His children. After all, His whole purpose in creating them was so He could enjoy fellowship with them.

In Deuteronomy 5:22-31 Moses recounted what happened then. God offered His voice, but told the Israelites it came with fire, a common biblical symbol of purging and purification. Rather than embrace God's outstretched hand of love and fellowship, and endure the accompanying purging process, they came up with an alternative solution. Moses, the Israelites said, why don't you "go near and hear all that the Lord our God says; then speak to us all that the Lord our God will speak to you, and we will hear and do it" (Deut. 5:27). Rather than enjoying a face-to-face relationship with God as Moses did, they were content with a list of laws to live by (Deut. 5:31).

God has impressed deep within my heart that either I will accept living out of a relationship with Him or I will live out of a list of laws. Having already tried to live out a list of New Testament laws, I concur with Scripture: The end of the law is death. Trying to keep laws, no matter how good they are, ends up producing death processes of guilt, condemnation, depression, discouragement, and heaviness within me.

It finally began to dawn on me that if I am led by the Spirit, I am not under the law. If I will walk in fellowship with Almighty God, I will find myself spontaneously living the demands of the law. Life would be so much easier this way, don't you think? The burden of trying to keep a host of commandments would no longer be on us. We would be living out of a person, the person of Christ.

I have now come to the point where I can sense the Father's initiative within and flow with it. I have moved from law to grace—continual, moment-by-moment grace.

David

God has continually offered communion and fellowship to His people, and they have continually broken His heart by refusing Him and choosing instead to live under law. Still, occasionally down through the history of the Old Testament someone was not content to live under rules and sought instead the relationship for which he was created.

Probably the man who achieved the highest level of communion with God in the Old Testament was David. He was not one to keep his thoughts or feelings under wraps. When he heard Goliath challenging the armies of Israel and their God, he didn't care who knew what he thought about it or what the consequences were. When the Ark of the Covenant was returned to Jerusalem, David was not shy about expressing his joy, and he danced with so much excitement and exuberance that his wife became embarrassed.

David approached his relationship with God with the same fervor and emotional freedom. No matter what he felt, he went straight to the Lord and openly and passionately expressed his feelings. When the guilt of his sin was heavy upon him, David poured out his heart to God:

> *Wash me thoroughly from my iniquity, and cleanse*
> *me from my sin. For I know my transgressions, and my*
> *sin is ever before me. Against Thee, Thee only, I have*

sinned, and done what is evil in Thy sight...Hide Thy face from my sins, and blot out all my iniquities...Deliver me from blood guiltiness, O God, Thou God of my salvation (Ps. 51:2-4,9,14).

When the danger of his situation overwhelmed him with fear, David cried out to his deliverer:

I cry aloud with my voice to the Lord; I make supplication with my voice to the Lord. I pour out my complaint before Him; I declare my trouble before Him...I cried out to Thee, O Lord; I said, "Thou art my refuge, my portion in the land of the living. Give heed to my cry, for I am brought very low; deliver me from my persecutors, for they are too strong for me" (Ps. 142:1,2,5,6).

When the injustice of his enemies became more than he could endure, David very honestly and vehemently called out to the Judge of all for justice and vengeance:

O God of my praise, do not be silent! For they have opened the wicked and deceitful mouth against me; they have spoken against me with a lying tongue...Appoint a wicked man over him; and let an accuser stand at his right hand. When he is judged, let him come forth guilty; and let his prayer become sin. Let his days be few; let another take his office. Let his children be fatherless, and his wife a widow (Ps. 109:1,2,6-9).

When joy and peace flooded David's soul, the earth could not contain his praise:

Praise the Lord! Praise God in His sanctuary; praise Him in His mighty expanse. Praise Him for His mighty deeds; praise Him according to His excellent greatness...Let everything that has breath praise the Lord. Praise the Lord! (Ps. 150:1,2,6).

How does our Father feel about such an unbridled relationship? Acts 13:22 makes it clear: "I have found David the son of Jesse, a man after My heart, who will do all My will." To say that God was pleased with David would be an understatement! God delighted in their relationship as much as David did. This is the kind of open and honest communication He longs to have with each of us. He wants us to come to Him with all of our lives: the joys and sorrows, successes and failures, highs and lows.

As I pondered David's relationship with God, the Lord began showing me not to stuff my feelings down into my heart and cover them over with a "Praise the Lord!" He taught me to be totally open and honest with Him. He wanted me to express all my fears and angers and hurts, to invite Him into them, and to hear all He wanted to say to me about them.

So I learned to express myself fully and freely before God, then to quiet myself in His presence, and to hear and record what He spoke back. He replaced my anger with His love, my depression with His joy, my death with His life. As I listened, I truly discovered that He spoke words of life.

Jesus

Jesus told us a little of what His relationship with the Father was like. In His high priestly prayer, Jesus prayed that we may be one in Him as He and His Father are one. He declared that He did not speak on His own initiative but on His Father's, Who abided in Him and accomplished all His works (Jn. 14:10). "I speak the things which I have seen with My Father" (Jn. 8:38). In fact, Jesus said He did *nothing* on His own initiative (Jn. 8:28). The unity and communion between Father and Son were so great that Jesus always responded according to the Father's promptings. He always knew His Father's will and He always obeyed. They were One.

Jesus prayed that we may be one with our Father also, that we may always hear and obey, that we may testify, "We do nothing on our own initiative, but as our Father speaks, His will is accomplished."

What an incredible way to live! Doing nothing on our own initiative—is such a lifestyle possible for man? Was Jesus demonstrating to us how man should live, or was He showing us how God would live in this world?

I conclude from the *kenosis* passage in Philippians 2:5-8 that Jesus emptied Himself and took the form of a bond servant so that He could be an example of how *man* should live in this world. Therefore I have accepted the challenge to seek to live as Christ lived. It is clear from John 5 and 8 that Jesus lived out of the Father's initiative, vision, and spoken word. Truly this is the fullness of what God has always desired.

However, this was so foreign to the way I lived that it looked like an almost impossible task. Could I actually come to a place where I did nothing on my own initiative; where I only spoke the words I heard the Father speaking within; where I only did those things I saw the Father doing? Could I really cultivate this kind of openness to God's voice and vision?

With the keys God was unfolding before me concerning prayer and from my attempts to hear His spoken voice, I was convinced it was possible to live by divine initiative as Jesus did. Therefore I purposed to learn to be constantly tuned to God's voice and vision. I knew I was drawing away from my culture by seeking this way of life, but I believed that Christians are called to live as Jesus did, and I was willing to pay the price to change.

It took a long year to begin to establish these fundamental changes in my life. These are not changes you decide on one day and find fully in place the next, especially if you're analytically inclined like I am. It has taken many years for Jesus to work this kind of alteration into my lifestyle, and it must continue to be a daily decision to maintain this way of life. I have found that God must take many of us through the same slow, painful breaking process He took me through. However, each of us who has taken a step of growth in the Lord Jesus Christ can gladly testify that the price has been well worth it.

Mary and Martha

Jesus and His disciples were invited one day to Martha's house for dinner. Making a meal for a crowd in those days was a very complex and time-consuming matter. You couldn't just take a roast out of the freezer, thaw it in the microwave, and pop it in the oven. You had to kill the calf, dress it, and roast it over a fire. You didn't bake frozen bread or whip up a cake mix. It took time and energy to prepare the breads and vegetables and sweets.

So, when Martha invited Jesus and His friends home she was willing to sacrifice herself for their comfort. Her sister Mary lived with her, so at least she would have help keeping the servants moving and assisting with all the preparations. After Jesus arrived, Martha made sure her guests were comfortably settled, then excused herself to get to work, surely expecting Mary to follow.

She selected the fatted calf herself and watched long enough to be sure it was quickly being prepared. As she hurried back to the house, she looked around for Mary to ask her to help with the bread, but Mary was nowhere in sight. Perhaps she was at the neighbor's, borrowing something, Martha thought. As her hands worked quickly, her mind raced even faster, making lists of things that had to be done.

As she passed the door, Martha thought she heard Mary's voice. She stopped and looked in the room where the guests were lounging. There, sitting at Jesus' feet, was Mary! Just sitting there! Martha couldn't believe it. "Here I am, running all around, tearing my hair out to get a good meal for them, and she's just sitting there! How dare she! She has no right to leave me with all this work! Wouldn't I like to be in there too, relaxing and hearing Jesus speak? Then what would they do? Pretty soon they'd all be grumbling because they were hungry and dinner wasn't ready. It would serve them right! And how can Jesus just let her sit there? He knows I'm in a rush. Why doesn't He make her help?" On and on she fumed as she doubled the speed of her work.

Finally she was ready to explode. Angrily she marched into the house, her hands sticky with dough and her dress sprinkled with flour. Walking straight up to Jesus she demanded, "Lord, do You not care that my sister has left me to do all the serving alone? Tell her to help me" (Lk. 10:40).

She must have been totally unprepared for His response. The look of love and compassion in His eyes probably made her want to cry. He said, "Martha, Martha, you are worried and bothered about so many things; but only a few things are necessary, really only one: for Mary has chosen the good part, which shall not be taken away from her" (v. 41,42).

Do you hear what Jesus said? Only one thing in life is necessary: communion with Him! When I really understood what He was saying, my whole being protested: No, Jesus, that's not true! Lots of things are necessary in the Christian life. There's producing and serving and evangelizing and writing and teaching and caring for the poor. They are all necessary! How can You say they are not?

Probably I was hit so hard by Jesus' words because I was like Martha, constantly driven to serve and produce. I knew if I accepted His words, my whole life would need readjustment.

Gradually the Lord began to show me the problem with my thinking. It is true that service, productivity, and evangelism are important, even very important. But they must never become goals in themselves. If they do, we have moved back from relationship to law. Such things are important only so far as they are products of communion.

When I am listening to the Lord, He gives me instructions and ideas that increase my productivity a hundredfold. As I hear from Him the kind and place of service He has created me for, I find fulfillment and success with every effort. And when I follow His leading in evangelism, the catch is so plentiful that the nets almost break. But all of this happens only if the one necessary thing in life—listening to Jesus—has first priority.

I did not marry my wife so that she would serve me. I married her so that we could be together, enjoy each other's company, and share our lives. What I want most from my wife is not her service or her obedience but her love. Jesus is the Bridegroom of the Church. He is not married to her primarily so that she may serve Him, but to share His love.

Paul

Paul was one of the greatest apostles and missionaries that ever lived. He probably was involved in the salvation of more souls than any other apostle. Yet when he expressed the deepest cry of his heart, it was, "Oh, that I might know Him!" (Phil. 3:10). Paul said that the thing he wanted most in life was not to win more souls, though he did that; nor to establish more churches, though he did that, too. What he cared about more than anything else was an intimate relationship with Jesus. He wanted to know Him and be with Him and hear from Him. Paul longed to love Him more and more each day. And as a result of time spent communing with the Lord, Paul went out and changed the world.

We, too, cannot try to change the world and then become intimate once the work is done. All service, all productivity, all evangelism must flow out of communion.

The Church

God spoke to man once again in the New Covenant and offered us a full relationship with Him.

When I accepted Jesus as Lord of my life, I received "eternal life." If I thought very much about what that meant, I assumed it was something like a membership card that I would give to St. Peter at the pearly gate and thus be admitted into heaven. Eternal life meant I would live forever.

What a surprise when I found out that Jesus had something different in mind: "And this is eternal life, that they may know Thee the only true God, and Jesus Christ whom Thou hast sent" (Jn. 17:3). Eternal life is *knowing* God the Father and His Son.

The Greek word for this "knowing," *ginosko*, is a very strong word. It may be defined as being intimately acquainted with someone in a growing, progressive relationship. *Ginosko* is used in the Septuagint translation of such passages as Genesis 4:1, "Adam *knew* his wife Eve; and she conceived..." (KJV, emphasis added). It involves the most personal, intimate relationship between husband and wife. This, then, is eternal life; to be intimately involved in a growing relationship with the Father and the Son. Eternal life is a relationship!

Many people look to heaven primarily as an escape from the cares and trials of this world. That is not really what heaven is all about. God gives us eternal life in heaven so we can continue our intimate relationship with Him forever. It would not be heaven without the close communion with our eternal Lover that begins in this life and grows sweeter with the passing

25

into eternity. Heaven comes to earth in our relationship with the Father and Son! Heaven can begin for you the day you move from law to love, from rules to relationship—the day you truly begin to *know* God!

Jesus came to offer us eternal life, a return to the garden where our Father is still walking, still loving, still longing for sweet communion with us.

Hebrews 12:18-25 is a word to us, the Church. The writer compared the Israelites' fear at the fiery mountain, where God once offered relationship, to the glory of Mount Zion. In verse 25 He said, "See to it that you do not refuse Him who is speaking." Once more God is speaking. Once more He is offering relationship. He is saying, "Please do not do what the Israelites did. Please do not refuse My voice. Please do not return to the Law. Please do not reject Me once more."

We are faced with the same choice. Will we accept the voice and the fire that comes with it? Will we live in relationship and daily conversation with God? Or will we turn away in fear and remain in bondage under the law which can only work death in our lives? Let us not refuse Him Who is speaking.

His Bride

And I heard, as it were, the voice of a great multitude and as the sound of many waters and as the sound of mighty peals of thunder, saying, "Hallelujah! For the Lord our God, the Almighty, reigns. Let us rejoice and be glad and give the glory to Him, for the marriage of the Lamb has come and His bride has made herself ready" (Rev. 19:6,7).

The climax of history is a wedding! All of creation, all the universe, all of life is building toward the ultimate expression of the Creator's love: the marriage of the Son. And right now we, the Church, are engaged to be married. What do engaged couples usually do? They spend lots and lots of time together, sharing their love, sharing their lives, sharing everything.

When my wife and I were dating in college, we spent hours sitting under a big maple tree on campus just talking. I have no idea what we said that kept us there for whole afternoons. We just talked on and on about ideas and feelings, dreams and fears, important things and things that were only important because they were shared. Because we loved each other, we wanted to share every part of our lives.

We are engaged to be married to Jesus. His heart is longing to share His ideas and feelings, His dreams and His love with us. Doesn't your heart respond to that love with the same desire? Don't you want to share your whole life with your Betrothed?

Our Response

I made a decision when the Lord revealed these things to me: Love is more important than work. Love, not productivity, is the center of the universe. I have begun to slow down and enjoy life, every single minute, and to share it in love with Father and those around me. And if no one is around me, I'll just love life, and living, and the beauty of His creation.

And what about work? Well, God has told me again and again that He can do more in a moment than I can do in a month. Do you know, He's right? As we've communed together, He's made me incredibly productive, more than I ever have been when "I" have pushed.

Now I enjoy life more. I enjoy my wife, my children, those to whom I minister and those who minister to me. I will never return to "workaholism." Love will always be the center of life for me.

Why don't you stop right here, put this book down and express your love to Jesus? In some way tell or write of your love for Him and your gratitude for all the blessings He has given you. Thank Him for all the things that He has revealed to you and for His beautiful creation. Just love Him for all He means to you.

When you are finished, wait for His reply. Write down any thoughts that come into your mind. He may want to say He loves you too. He may tell you how precious you are to Him. He may give you guidance or peace about an area of concern. Whatever He wants to say, give Him the chance to say it. He's been waiting for you. Won't you respond?

2

The Spoken Word:
Tuning to Spontaneity

KEY #1

God's voice in our hearts sounds like a flow of spontaneous thoughts. Therefore, when I tune to God, I tune to spontaneity.

The first key to clearly discerning God's voice in our hearts is to determine what His voice sounds like. Our God is a communicating God Who longs to make His thoughts and His will known to us. He has given us the *Logos*, the written Word, to teach us the laws that govern life on this earth and show by example the results of keeping or breaking those laws. God also speaks to us through the counsel of spiritual friends and advisors. And He uses circumstances to guide us in the way He wants us to go. All of these are vital means through which God communicates His will to man.

There is still another line of communication open to the children of God. There is a knowing, like men and women in the Bible, that "the word of the Lord came to me." There is a voice of God that we can hear—not necessarily audibly—but nonetheless clearly.

Many Christians long to have this kind of communication with our Lord. Some of us have been told, however, that it isn't available to us. We were told that "Bible characters" were in some way different and more favored, that God has chosen not to speak to us by name in this Church Age. By believing this, we have been robbed of the sweet communion for which we were created and redeemed.

The prophet Elijah was one to whom the word of the Lord came. Yet James 5:17 makes it clear that he had a nature like ours. God doesn't play favorites! I believe that every child of God can experience the same fellowship that Adam and Eve enjoyed in the garden and Moses experienced in the meeting tent.

Jesus declared, "My sheep hear My voice" (Jn. 10:27). I believe that is true. He is always speaking and His sheep do hear His voice. Unfortunately, our culture has so affected our minds that we often do not recognize that it is our Shepherd Who is speaking. Our Western civilization has become so rationalistic, humanistic, and scientific that we have left no place for the spiritual to break in on the visible world. But if we quieted our frantic thoughts long enough to hear His words, we would probably exclaim, "I just had a brilliant idea!" or "The answer just came to me!" When man is the center of the universe and the source of all knowledge, "I" must be the originator of all my thoughts.

I have found in my own life and in the lives of those I teach that a little education, a little training, and a little stepping back from the sophistication of adulthood can make it possible not only to hear and know God's voice, but to actually carry on a two-way dialogue in intimate communion with Him.

You may be saying, "But how can *I* recognize God's voice?" Probably no question plagues Western Christians more. For years I searched for the answer. I studied everything I could find in the Bible that indicated how New Testament believers received guidance. I read every book I could find on the voice of God and the gifts of the Holy Spirit. I reasoned that in order to be used by the Spirit in the gifts, particularly the vocal ones, I had to be able to recognize God's voice. Although many wrote about the nature of the gifts, nothing I found clearly taught me how to be used in their operation.

So I listened, as I have said, for the still, small voice, but all I heard were regular thoughts running through my mind. In desperation, I cried, "Where are You, God?" Finally, during a year of searching and studying, the Spirit brought revelation truth to my heart. He showed me that God's voice is sensed as a spontaneous idea appearing in my mind. The key word is *spontaneous.*

The voice of God is Spirit-to-spirit communication, the Holy Spirit speaking directly to my spirit. It is sensed as a spontaneous thought, idea, word, feeling, or vision. Thoughts from my mind, on the other hand, are analytical and cognitive. I reason them out; one logically follows the next. Thoughts from my heart are spontaneous. It is an intuitive process.

Now I think you would agree that if this is a true definition of what God's voice actually sounds like, I have just provided a very simple answer to a very difficult question. Everyone has spontaneous thoughts every day. Are these all God's voice?

I am *not* saying that every spontaneous thought is the Holy Spirit speaking to you. I *am* saying that spontaneity is heart-level communication, and that analysis and reasoning are mind-level communication. Therefore, if I want to tune from my head to my heart, I tune from cognitive, analytical thoughts to the flow of spontaneous thoughts.

When I finally get to my heart, however, I find there are still three "voices" I can hear which need to be distinguished. I can hear those of my own heart, the Holy Spirit's, or satan's. I still have to do some judging and discerning, therefore, but at least I have moved from my head to my heart. That in itself is a major accomplishment for many of us in the Western world. We will talk in depth about testing this spontaneous flow later on.

First, I want to back up the definition I have given you with appropriate Scriptures, and some confirming experiences. One of the literal meanings of *paga*, the Hebrew word for intercession, is "a chance encounter" or "an accidental intersecting." Genesis 28:11 gives an example of *paga* used in its literal sense. Jacob was fleeing to his uncle's house, and he "came upon by chance" (*paga*) a certain place and spent the night there. He was just traveling along and "stumbled upon" this place to spend the night. He hadn't made reservations or included it in his itinerary. He was just walking along and there it was.

Now I don't know about you, but "to strike or light upon by chance" seems to me to be a very strange definition of prayer or intercession. If I were to tell you that intercession was a chance encounter or an accidental intersecting, you might scratch your head and wonder what I'd been drinking! How is prayer or intercession a chance encounter or an accidental intersecting? Let me show you from something you have probably experienced.

Do you remember a time, perhaps when you were driving, when suddenly someone's name popped into your mind and you just knew you were supposed to pray for him? You hadn't been thinking about that person at the time. The thought just "came out of nowhere." But you accepted it as God prompting you to pray. That was intercession. That was *paga*. When a "chance" thought intersects our reasoning processes, that "chance" encounter is really a divine encounter. God is speaking quietly and easily into our heart.

This is the voice of God: a chance idea that intersects your mind, not flowing from the normal, meditative process, but simply appearing in your heart. This is God's voice—an idea from God lighting upon your heart and being registered in your mind as a spontaneous thought.

It was such an exciting revelation to me to realize that I had already heard God speaking to me! Though I had never heard an inner "voice," I had been aware of ideas lighting upon my mind. They had come simply as spontaneous thoughts. This finally taught me what to listen for to hear God's voice. *When I am listening for the Lord's voice, I am listening for spontaneous thoughts.* I have found that if I write out these intuitive thoughts, I am amazed at their wisdom when I reread them. I am now convinced that I am hearing God's words to me.

God's voice often sounds like a flow of spontaneous thoughts. This is not to say, of course, that this is the only way God can speak to me. At the beginning of this chapter I listed several other ways to know God's will. Occasionally He even speaks in an audible voice. However, I have found that God's voice normally sounds like a flow of spontaneous thoughts that light upon our mind.

I have discovered certain characteristics of God's interjected thoughts which help me recognize and have confidence they are truly from Him:

They are like my own thoughts, except that I sense them as coming from my heart rather than my brain, in that they are spontaneous, not analytical or cognitive. It has taken a definite and deliberate refocusing for me to turn from living in analysis and logic to living in spontaneity. This has been a goal of my life for the last few years. It used to be while as I was driving, my mind would be busy hashing over the day. Everything anyone had said to me was run through the computer, analyzed, and processed. I lived in constant analysis. But not anymore. Now as I am driving, I worship. I share love with Jesus. I sing Him a love song and allow Him to speak back to me in spontaneous thoughts. I have worked on changing my life so that I am normally tuned in to love and the great Lover of my soul.

I have found that if I remain tuned to spontaneity when I need to think things through or reason them out, the Lord can better interject wisdom and insight. At first I thought that if I "wasted" time loving, I wouldn't be prepared with the answers I needed when I arrived at work. He has taught me, on the contrary, that while I am loving Him He rewards me with productivity, creativity, authority, favor among men, faith, and wisdom.

God's voice is often light and gentle and easily cut off by any exertion of self. If I interrupt the spontaneous, intuitive flow with my own analytical thoughts or my own will, He will not try to shout above the noise or regain my attention. He will simply be still and wait until I am again ready to listen.

I found a tendency to sermonize to be a weakness I had to overcome when I was learning to listen to God. One time the Lord began to speak to me about the need to die to self, to take up my cross. Immediately I thought, "Oh, I know a lot about that! I've preached some good sermons on that very subject!" And I began to write out everything I knew and believed about dying to self. Then I realized what I was doing. My mind had taken over and I was tuned to reason rather than spontaneity. As soon as I became aware of it, I stopped my own thoughts and moved back to intuition.

I said, "Okay, Lord, why don't You pick up where You left off? Why don't You tell me what You wanted to say about dying to self?" He did! What He had to say was a little different than what I had believed and taught and it brought adjustment to my life and ministry.

If you find yourself interrupting the Lord, don't whip yourself or wallow in guilt. Just say, "Whoops!" and return to spontaneity and intuition.

God's voice will easily come as God speaking in the first person. For example, He might say to me, "I love you, Mark." It does not have to be that way, however. Essentially the choice is up to you. It is your leap of faith in accepting the words as being from God that will make the difference. Remember, he who comes to God must come in faith.

God's voice often has an unusual content, meaning it is better and somewhat different than my own thoughts. It is wiser, more merciful, more discerning, and more concerned with motives. As Jesus so often did while He walked as a man, God may seem to ignore the question asked and address the real heart of the issue.

At first I had doubts about my journal and was tempted to throw it all away as merely a product of my own mind. But as I reread it, I realized that I don't look at life the way the Person speaking in my journal does. I look at the surface. I hear only people's words and react only to their actions. In my journal a desire to see into the heart, to understand the motives and to heal the hurts was expressed.

God's voice often causes a special reaction within me. There is often a sense of excitement, conviction, faith, vibrant life, awe or peace that accompanies receiving God's word. Many times there is a quickening in my spirit or a sense of sharing a burden with Jesus.

God's spoken word carries with it the fullness of strength to carry it out. The yoke of the Lord is easy and His burden is light. His will is not to put us under bondage, but to bring us into satisfaction and joy. Even if He asks a hard thing, He gives the power to do it. If we say yes to Him, His grace flows through us to accomplish His will. His Spirit goes out with His word to fulfill His purpose.

Your spiritual senses will be trained as you use them, and as time goes on you will more easily and frequently hear God speaking.

At first, you need to learn to distinguish God's interjected thoughts from the cognitive thoughts that are coming from your own mind. My guess is that you have already experienced God interjecting thoughts into your mind. For instance, have you ever been struggling with a difficult problem when all of a sudden the most creative solution you could imagine popped into your mind? If you have, you probably took credit for coming up with the idea and patted yourself on the back, saying, "Not so dumb after all!" What I've come to see is that such spontaneous, creative solutions to difficult problems that just drop into my mind are not mine at all. They are God's. He is speaking them within me. Rather than take credit for them myself, I now give the glory to God.

I have found that almost everyone has had another type of experience also. Have you ever been in the middle of prayer and had some garbage thoughts defile it? Most people have also taken credit for these thoughts, believing they are their own and feeling guilty and embarrassed.

I want to suggest to you that they are probably not your thoughts at all; it is satan seeking to break up your prayer time. Again, you shouldn't take credit for them, nor feel guilty or ashamed. I simply tell satan that I am in the middle of prayer and in Jesus' name to take his garbage thoughts and leave. As I turn my thoughts back to Jesus I sense an immediate release flowing through my heart and mind.

I have learned to take credit neither for the *spontaneous* good nor evil thoughts that flow within my heart. I give God the credit for the good ones and I give satan the blame for the evil ones.

The Power of *Rhema*

The Scriptural evidence of the power that accompanies God's word spoken by His Spirit into and through us is truly amazing. Let's look at a few examples.

Rhema Releases Productivity

One morning Simon was washing his nets on the shore of Lake Gennesaret. He was tired and discouraged after fishing all night and catching nothing. Caught up in his own thoughts of failure and depression, he hardly noticed the Man preaching nearby nor the crowd almost pressing Him into the lake in their eagerness to hear His every word.

Suddenly Simon's attention was captured as the Teacher walked over and climbed into his boat. Simon was about to demand that He get off his property, but the Man spoke to him, and requested that he put out a little way from the land so He could better speak to the people. Just as he was about to rudely refuse, Simon looked at the crowd so eagerly following this Man. "I wonder what the attraction is," he might have thought. "Maybe I should find out. I've nothing to take to the market today anyhow. Why not?" So he did as requested.

The time seemed to fly by as he sat in the boat, listening to the Teacher. Such words He spoke! Could they really be true? Could there really be a place in the kingdom of God for one such as he? Could Yahweh really love one as rough and loud and impulsive as he?

All too soon the Teacher finished speaking. He turned to Simon and said, "Go out into the deep water and let down your nets for a catch." Brought sharply back to reality, he replied in disgust, "We worked hard all night and didn't catch anything." Then, thinking again of the power of the words he had just heard, he added, "But at Your bidding (*rhema*), I will let down the net." Simon signaled his crew, and they threw the nets over. Suddenly, as if at some unseen signal, fish swarmed into the nets. Soon the nets were full to the breaking point. They frantically called their partners in another boat to come help. Soon both boats were so full of fish they began to sink.

What made the difference? Why did they labor fruitlessly for long hours and then catch more than they could handle? The difference was *rhema*. I can do what I think needs to be done, when I think, where I think, and the way I think. I can work hard, exhaust all my energy and resources, and still accomplish very little. When I begin a day, I can look at all of the needs clamoring for my attention and wear myself out trying to meet them all. Or, I can start my day in prayer, and receive God's direction as *rhema*, telling me where to devote my time and energy. If I do that, I can walk through my day in peace, free from guilt and hassle, and accomplish far more than I ever could under my own initiative. *Rhema* gives us timing and it gives us location. *Rhema* gives productivity.

Rhema Is Life

We have already seen that we must make a choice between living in relationship or living under law. The letter of the law kills but the Spirit gives life. Jesus said, "It is the Spirit who gives life...the words [*rhema*] that I have spoken to you are spirit and are life" (Jn. 6:63).

When someone speaks *rhema*, you can feel the lifting in your spirit, the life flowing through you. The *Logos* can be given as law that brings us into bondage and death, or it can be preached in the power of the Spirit bringing us into freedom and life. The difference is often simply one of emphasis, a lack of clearly proclaiming that the power of the resurrected Christ does the work. If what is preached are rules that must be obeyed to achieve right standing before God, the Word is reduced to law. But when the same Word is opened under the anointing of the Spirit, it shows us the glory of Christ within us and releases us from the power of sin and death.

Rhema Gives Authoritative Teaching

When Jesus taught, the Jews were amazed because He spoke with such authority. Where did He get this power? It was not His own divine right, for Philippians 2 makes it clear that He emptied Himself when He became man, laying aside all privileges and powers of Deity. So what is the secret to the authority of His words? John 14 clearly tells us that He did not speak on His own initiative, but that the Father was abiding in Him. The words Jesus spoke were *rhema* to Him, *rhema* received as He spent time in the presence of the Father. Because He spoke out of the Father's initiative, His teaching was powerful and authoritative.

The same holds true for believers today. When in counseling or teaching I speak forth the *rhema* I have heard from God, there is authority and power to change lives. This is the "anointing," the "divine unction." *Rhema* results in authoritative teaching.

Rhema Results in Fullness of Desire

"If you abide in Me, and My words [*rhema*] abide in you, ask whatever you wish, and it shall be done for you" (Jn. 15:7). If we are living in relationship, hearing the voice of God and obeying it, we will always receive what we ask for. This reminds me of Psalm 37:4, "Delight yourself in the Lord; and He will give you the desires of your heart."

The first half of each verse is the key to the second half. If our delight is the Lord, if our greatest pleasure is being with

Him and pleasing Him, then the desires of our heart will be only what give Him pleasure. If His *rhema* abides in us, the fire will do its work in us. We will be cleansed and purified of all desires that are not His and what we wish will only be His will. St. Augustine enjoined believers to "love God and do what you please." This was not a license to sin but a recognition that if we truly love God, what we please will be to do His will.

Rhema Brings Faith

I have left until last what is perhaps the most important, most significant result of *rhema*. Romans 10:17 is a well-known yet little understood verse. "So faith comes from hearing, and hearing by the word [*rhema*] of Christ." Faith is the result of divine initiative. Faith is fired in our hearts when we hear the spoken word of Christ to us.

You have probably experienced it. You were facing a trial or problem. You wanted to trust God. With your mind you knew His promises and knew He could keep His word. Yet in your heart you wondered if He would do it for you. Suddenly, one day as you were reading the Word or praying or listening to a sermon, a specific word spoke to you and you knew that you knew that God was going to come through for you. Faith was no longer a mental activity or a spiritual discipline. Faith was alive and vibrant. No longer was there a striving to believe; you entered the blessed rest of confidence in your God. *Rhema* resulted in faith.

When you are doubting and your faith is weak, rather than going to the *Logos* alone, you need to go to prayer and ask the Father to speak His word into your heart. When He speaks, faith will explode within you. When you don't know where to go or what to do next, you need to hear *rhema* from God. To move powerfully in faith, you must move in response to *rhema*: the witness of the Spirit within you.

God Gave You a Mind…

You may be wondering if I am going to recommend throwing our minds away since spontaneous heart thought is that part of us through which the voice of God so often flows. Not at all! God has given us both our hearts *and* our minds. We are not to despise or overuse either. They are both gifts from Almighty God, and they both have a place.

In our culture we have essentially idolized the mind and scorned the heart. Many of us need to repent of that idolization and scorning, and to ask God to balance them out in our lives. That is precisely what I have had to do. Repentance provides the foundation for change, and God has the ability and desire to balance each of us.

Let me show you briefly two different approaches to receiving pure revelation from the throne room of God by comparing Luke's method with John's.

Luke appears to have been the more analytical one by nature. He tells us how he received his Gospel: "It seemed fitting for me…having investigated everything carefully from the beginning, to write it out for you in consecutive order…" (Lk. 1:3). This doesn't sound like an intuitive, heart-functioning person to me. As a matter of fact, it sounds totally analytical. And yet Luke's Gospel is pure revelation.

John used a completely different approach. He seems to have been more the mystic: "I was in the Spirit on the Lord's day, and I heard behind me a loud voice like the sound of a trumpet, saying 'Write in a book what you see…'" (Rev. 1:10,11). That sounds like an intuitive, visionary approach to receiving revelation! Yet both of them received and wrote pure revelations that stand to this day.

So, as you can see, there are at least a couple of ways to receive revelation from the Holy Spirit. Luke's method for hearing from the Lord will likely appeal to the person who is more analytical by nature. The person who is generally intuitive will probably relate more to John's process.

We may have a hard time accepting and honoring an approach different from our own. The analytically-inclined person may say, "Why don't you come down to earth, get your feet on the ground, and quit being such a flake?" The intuitive type may retort, "Why don't you get your head out of the books and just allow yourself to be led by the Spirit? Why can't you just go with the flow, rather than having to reason it out all the time?"

We must learn to honor the fact that God grants pure revelation to both. I am most comfortable using Luke's approach. I study things out carefully and then ask the Holy Spirit to put it all together in the way He wants. But I also believe that in order for me to receive pure revelation I must use more than just my analytical abilities. I must allow intuition and spontaneity to flow into the process also, or else I will only come up with a product of my own analytical reasoning.

For example, when I used to work on sermons, I locked my brain into gear and researched Scripture, developing an outline to preach from as I went along. If some spontaneous thoughts came along, I kicked them out and said, in effect, "Get away from me, I'm working on my sermon!"

As I look back on it now I realize I was really rejecting the spontaneous voice of the Holy Spirit Who was trying to direct me as I prepared to feed His flock. Now I have learned to allow intuition to flow into my analytical thought processes as I work on a sermon or a book, and I am convinced that I now much more perfectly communicate the pure voice of God.

God will tell you which direction you lean toward and where He wants to take you. If you are overly analytical, God may be calling you to begin developing your intuitive side. If you are very intuitive, He may be calling you to develop your analytical abilities.

I asked the Lord one day, with a slight tone of complaint, why He had me teaching people on hearing the intuitive voice of the Holy Spirit when I was certainly not intuitive by nature. Why not have someone who was naturally gifted in this way take the message and go with it? His reply was, "Mark, if we are going to teach an analytical culture how to be intuitive, it must be done by one who is himself analytical and has moved into intuition." "Good point!" I said.

The corollary, of course, is that many of those I teach, especially those who are naturally intuitive and visionary, will go far beyond me in discerning and experiencing God's voice. My response is, great! Will you lend me your giftedness when I need it? I am glad that we are not in competition in the Body of Christ, but that we serve one another with our gifts. I will lend you my gift of teaching. I ask that you lend me your gift of revelation and discernment, that God may be glorified in His Church.

I want to close this chapter on learning to tune to spontaneity by talking about a principle that has been instrumental in setting free hundreds of God's people. (I will share additional principles in later chapters.)

Praying with an Idol in Your Heart

Ezekiel 14:4 says that "any man of the house of Israel who sets up his idols in his heart, puts right before his face the stumbling block of his iniquity, and then comes to the prophet, I the Lord will be brought to give him an answer in the matter in view of the multitude of his idols." This brings into focus a startling truth concerning an inappropriate method of prayer, which I am afraid has been practiced by many.

When I come to the Lord in prayer, I am to be a living sacrifice. I am to have laid down my will and be totally abandoned to God's will concerning the issue about which I am praying. If that is not my posture, I am to pray for God to form that posture within me before I begin praying. If I pray about the issue while I still have a definite direction about it in my own heart, that direction of my own interferes with the signals coming from the throne of God and causes me to believe that God is confirming the direction I felt, whether He actually is or not.

In other words, if I pray about a thing, and the thing is more prominent in my vision or my consciousness than the Lord is, the answer that comes back will be from me, rather than from the Lord. On the other hand, if the Lord is more prominent in my consciousness than my vision of the thing I am praying about, then the answer will come from the Lord and it will be pure revelation, not contaminated with my desires.

The principle here is that the intuitive flow comes out of the vision I am holding before my eyes. I am commanded to fix my eyes on Jesus, the Author and Finisher of my faith. If I do, the vision will be pure.

An example of a seer getting his vision clouded and receiving damaging direction can be found in the story of Balaam in Numbers 22. Balak had sent messengers to Balaam, asking him to come and curse the Israelites. When Balaam sought God about it, God was very clear: "Do not go with them; you shall not curse the people; for they are blessed."

Balak again sent messengers, more distinguished than before, with the offer that Balak would honor him richly and do whatever he asked if he would only come and curse the Israelites. Apparently gold and riches were on Balaam's mind because he said, "Though Balak were to give me his house full of silver and gold, I could not do anything." However, he invited them to stay, saying, "I will check with the Lord again."

Since he so desperately wanted the option to receive the honor, gold, and riches, he went again in prayer to the Lord, this time with an idol in his heart. As could be expected, the Lord gave him the answer in view of the idol in his heart. He said, "Sure! Go ahead!" However, God was angry with Balaam and sent an angel with a sword to block his path (Num. 22:22).

When we pray with an idol in our hearts we may get an affirmative answer from the Lord, but it will bring us to destruction. Therefore, when we pray, we must be certain that our vision is purified and that we see Jesus as One Who is much larger than the thing or issue for which we are praying. Only then will our answer be pure and life-giving.

Logos and *Rhema*

As a concluding note to this chapter I want to mention that Paul Yonggi Cho has suggested that *rhema*, translated "word," is used by New Testament writers to describe God's spoken voice within your heart. After careful consideration, I agree with him. If you would like to explore this idea further, the first three appendices may help. Appendix A is "*Logos* and *Rhema* in the Greek New Testament," Appendix B is a list of the seventy uses of *rhema* in the New Testament, and Appendix C is "Understanding the Power of *Rhema*."

From this point on I will refer to God's inner voice as the *rhema* word. This is just one of its uses, but it provides a simple way for us to encapsulate the concept.

It was extremely difficult for me to begin moving out of cognition into the spiritual dimension and intuition. But as I have continued in this walk, the way has become easier and easier. It is almost "first nature" to me now. God has totally refocused my life. He can do the same for you.

Let me encourage you now to pause and take about five minutes to experiment with what you have learned in this chapter. Take out a paper and pen, and, using vision, see Jesus with you in some comfortable scene (possibly from the Gospels). Write down, "Lord, what do You want to speak concerning the things I am learning?"

Then focus the eyes of your heart on the vision of you and Jesus together, and tune to spontaneity. In simple faith begin writing down the thoughts that begin flowing within your mind. Don't challenge or doubt them for the time being. Just receive them in simple child-like faith and record them as they flow.

Remember this is only an experiment. After four or five minutes, when the flow is over, go back and test what you have written. Does it line up with Scripture? Does it sound like what God might want to say to you? In this simple exercise many of you will find that you are beginning to dialogue with God!

3

Becoming Still: Quieting Our Thoughts and Emotions

KEY #2

I must learn to still my own thoughts and emotions, so I can sense God's flow of thoughts and emotions within me.

So often when I come to the Lord in prayer I find that all of the rush and activity of my life follows me into my prayer closet. All of the noise and flurry of everyday life screams for my attention, while pressures and responsibilities call from within. I would like to be able to immediately find sweet communion when I shut the door to my room, but I find that it cannot be forced or rushed.

Have you ever gone into your prayer closet with only fifteen minutes to pray and experienced your mind racing, your emotions changing widely? Have you ever told your racing mind, "All right, you have exactly three minutes to simmer down, so I can begin sensing the quiet inner impressions and thoughts of the Holy Spirit?"

If you have, you have discovered that pressuring yourself to become still is a total waste of time. It's like trying to make yourself go to sleep at night as you toss and turn on your bed. The more pressure you use, the more wide awake you are. Similarly, the more I try to force my own busy thoughts and emotions out of my heart and mind so I can sense God's spontaneous flow within, the more agitation I feel.

On several occasions I have left my prayer closet totally discouraged because I was unable to get beyond my own raging self to the Holy Spirit's gentle inner impressions. I came out after twenty minutes knowing I had not contacted God at all in my spirit. I found this extremely frustrating. When I have so little time for prayer to start with, I am incensed by having to waste time in simply trying to get past myself.

Later I will share with you an excellent biblical technique that God has designed for us to quickly quiet ourselves in His presence. This is not the end of prayer nor a goal in itself; it is, however, the necessary first step so the rest of my prayer time can be spent in dialogue with Almighty God.

Be Still, and Know...

Psalm 46:10 encourages us, "Be still, and know that I am God" (KJV). There is a deep inner knowing in our spirit that each of us can experience when we quiet our flesh and our minds. Even when walking in outer turmoil, we can experience peace.

The New American Standard Version gives several synonyms or alternate readings for "be still" in Psalm 46:10. It may be understood as "cease striving, relax, or let go." Each of these phrases gives an excellent description of what takes place inside me when I come to this place of stillness.

Another way to see it is having an attitude of playfulness. Life for me used to be work—lots of hard work. Even when I played, it was work. I was serious and intense about everything I undertook. But the Lord showed me that it is He Who does the work. It is He Who accomplishes the task. My part is to be caught in *His* movement and flow with it. I must let go of my intense striving and relax into His perfect ability.

One of our students had similar struggles, and recorded this in his journal:

"Father, what do You say I need today? I'm so torn on what to focus on. More fear of the Lord, more love, more repentance, more healing and deliverance, etc? I just don't know how to come to You."

"Yes, all of those are needed in greater measures. But the greatest is for you to quietly sit at My feet and to learn of Me. You must not be frantic in your approaching Me and My presence. As mentioned earlier, simply come and sit in My presence. Draw from Me. Be still, relax, cease striving and know that I am God!

"Be in the receiving mode. One cannot receive when running about frantically in the natural until there is a stopping, and open arms, etc. So, in the spirit, Stop! Put out your arms and receive. Do not try to get more fear of the Lord or try to muster it up. The same goes for deeper repentance, etc. Do not go about frantically trying to stir up or force yourself into greater repentance. It is needed in much greater measures and it will come and is coming.

"Turn your eyes upon Me. Fix your gaze upon Me. See Me. Focus and set your mind and affection on Me and I will do in you all that is needed. Come. Rest. Receive. Allow Me to embrace you and to shower on you over and over and over again. You cannot learn everything all at once. Do not be so hard on yourself. Receive of Me day by day. Little by little, truth by truth, revelation by revelation. BE STILL and know. It is in stillness that the hearing comes. It is when you are quiet and in a state of rest that you can hear and receive from Me. Be still!"

Remove Outer Distractions

But how can I come to this inner stillness? The first step must be removing all outer distractions. In Mark 1:35 we read that Jesus went to a lonely place to pray. The prophet Habakkuk went to a guard post when he wanted to hear from God. And in 1 Kings 19 we find Elijah alone in a mountain cave, frightened and depressed, when the word of the Lord came to him.

I found when I first began seeking inner stillness that I needed to find a quiet place where I could be alone and undisturbed. So I learned to rise before the rest of my family and allow the quietness of early morning to help bring peace within my spirit. I soon discovered I had to take the phone off the hook during my quiet time or I was sure to be interrupted. I struggled with this, until the Lord convinced me that I was not indispensable and life would go on quite well without me for an hour or so!

During the first few weeks of seeking inner stillness, I found that I could only become attuned to intuition first thing in the morning. Since analytical thought had been such a powerful idol in my life, I found I had to carefully avoid becoming involved in analytical thinking before prayer, because I'd then be caught in it for the rest of the day. But if I began worshiping as soon as I awakened, sang through my shower, and maintained that attitude until I reached my study, I was able to stay spiritually attuned throughout my quiet time. If I moved into cognitive reasoning, however, it was very difficult for me to return to intuition.

As I continued, it became easier. Eventually my little daughter, Charity, began getting up with me. Since my wife, Patti, had usually been up with the baby during the night, I wanted to let her sleep. As I became more comfortable with quieting myself inwardly, I was able to see that Charity was cared for and yet come to stillness within myself. You, too, will find that you will cultivate the skill of quieting your heart and mind before the Lord as you practice it.

Get Comfortable!

As I tried to focus my heart and mind on Jesus I found another distraction: my body. If there was tension or discomfort in any part of my body, I became very conscious of it when I sought to be still. For me, kneeling is not the posture most conducive to prayer. My goal in prayer is to be totally God-conscious, and if my knees ache or my feet are asleep, my attention is divided. If kneeling, or any other physical posture, draws my attention to bodily discomfort, then it has hindered my prayer. Of course, if I become totally relaxed in body and spirit, I end up asleep! I have found that the best position is sitting in a comfortable chair at my desk, with a Bible and pen and paper nearby. David also sometimes sat as he prayed (1 Chron. 17:16).

Remove Inner Distractions

Quieting the outside distractions is the easier part of coming to stillness; as I approach quietness, I usually find my mind raging with voices, thoughts, pressures, and tensions that demand my attention. The loudest ones seem to say, "You forgot to change the oil in the car" or "You didn't call your parents yet." All of my unfinished business and my forgotten responsibilities vie for my attention as soon as I become still. I have ignored them, and when they see a chance for recognition, they take it! If I try to push them back down, they only scream louder. If I focus attention on them, I am overtaken until I do their bidding. So what can I do? I simply write them down. I listen to their demands and assure them of my future attention by carefully listing them. This seems to convince them they will be taken care of, so they quiet down.

The next voice that often breaks through is my conscience. If the Lord has spoken to me and I have not yet been obedient, I hear my conscience clanging out, "Guilty! Guilty!" But should I cringe before it, wallowing in my guilt? No! If I am going to have fellowship with Jesus, I must not focus on my ugly shell, but on His marvelous grace. So when I have sinned, I confess my guilt and accept His complete forgiveness. I move beyond myself and my weakness into an awareness of Him and His greatness.

We are either going to gaze upon ourselves and our sin and weakness, or upon Christ and His glory and grace. The Bible teaches that we will be transformed into what we gaze upon: "But we all, with unveiled face beholding as in a mirror the glory of the Lord, are being transformed into the same image from glory to glory, just as from the Lord, the Spirit" (2 Cor. 3:18).

If I have decided to fix my eyes upon Him (Heb. 12:2) and see myself clothed with His righteousness (Gal. 3:27), I then discover myself being drawn into His presence, His glory, and His righteousness. It is so important that we carefully choose our focus. We will either focus on ourselves or on Christ, on our sin or on His righteousness. I have chosen to focus on what the Bible says is true, and I have discovered that I am then quickly ushered into His presence. I encourage each of you to carefully select your focus as you enter into prayer. The wrong vision brings death. The right vision gives life.

The goal of being inwardly still is not a total emptying of my mind or a cessation of my thought processes, but rather a refocusing of them. When all the other voices within me have been dealt with, I must find a way to tune out thinking/reasoning and tune in intuition.

Refocus on Him

The most effective biblical tool for heightening the spiritual sensitivity of most people is music. When Elisha wanted to hear the voice of the Lord, he asked for a minstrel to come and play for him (2 Kgs. 3:15). Often when I need to know He is there, I will sing a song of worship and adoration. Thousands of people around the world have been impacted by the simple practice of "soaking" in the Lord's presence, merely being still on the outside and allowing music to carry them into their hearts, where He is waiting.

Paying attention to the song in your heart, especially upon awakening, can be a clue to the message your spirit or the Holy Spirit Who is joined to your spirit wants to give to you, or may be an expression of what your heart is feeling. Songs of praise and worship can be extremely valuable in focusing your heart and soul on your Lord, especially if you engage the eyes of your heart to see what you are singing about.

Other times I have found a single cry within my spirit that I have allowed to come forth in song. One morning, I lay prostrate at the altar of our church, broken in spirit, overwhelmed with my sin and failure, feeling very far from God. As I began to play my autoharp only these words could express the longing I felt within: "Lord, arise! Lord, arise within me and cleanse me! Arise and heal me! Lord, arise!" I sang the words over and over because they expressed all that I was feeling. After five or ten minutes, the darkness began to flow out of me. The Sun of Righteousness rose within me, and faith, hope, love, joy, and the sweet knowledge of His presence filled my heart.

This exchange of light for darkness, faith for doubt, and hope for despair is not just academic knowledge but experiential reality. The Psalmist tells us that the one who abides in God's presence speaks truth in his heart. It doesn't matter what my heart is feeling, I must truthfully present myself and all my feelings to the Lord as I enter His presence.

Two other helpful biblical techniques I have found for becoming still are vision and love. I look with the eyes of my heart to see in the Spirit a vision of Jesus and me talking together, and the vision has the power to carry me beyond analytical thought. As I see Jesus with me, I express to Him all of the love I feel for Him, and as my love overflows I am drawn into the stillness of His presence.

Breath and spirit are indicated by the same word in both Hebrew and Greek. I can use my breath to bring my spirit into stillness. As my breath goes out, I confess all my sin and guilt. Slowly I breathe in the cleansing Holy Spirit. As I repeat this exercise, my body and soul come into a peaceful awareness of the presence of the Lord.

The goal in achieving inner stillness is to know deep within ourselves the movement of God. "Be still and know that I am God." "Rest in the Lord and wait patiently for Him" (Ps. 37:7). When I become still, I sense a shift within me and begin to experience the active flow of the Holy Spirit's feelings, ideas and visions.

One of the founding religious groups of our country was the Quakers. They understand the need for ceasing their own activities to have time to hear God. A vital part of their time together is spent in silence, each individual quieting his own thoughts to become aware of what the Lord is speaking within him.

When I live on the surface, aware only of external circumstances and responding to them as though they were all of reality, I am torn apart. My personality, my view of life, and my spirit become fractured and out of balance. But as I become still and regain my consciousness of the Lord living within me, peace, wholeness and unity are restored to my being. Because

Jesus lives in me, I find love, faith, power, and all the resources I need to have victory.

Becoming still is not *doing* something; it is being in touch with the Lord Jesus Christ within. I do not struggle or force myself to be still. It is a letting go, a relaxing, a ceasing to strive. To be still is to experience Jesus Christ in this moment. He is I AM. To live with the God of now, I must live in this moment. I am not mourning the past or worrying about the future—I am enjoying Christ in the present moment. I am letting salvation come to this present point in time. I am sharing this particular moment with the One I love.

Eastern Religion? The New Age?

You might be questioning the similarities between the Eastern mystical religions, such as yoga, transcendental meditation or Zen, and what I am advocating. Or perhaps you have been taught to fear all inner stillness as a tool of the New Age to allow demons access to your mind. It is true that the avenues of approach to the spiritual world are similar. It is true that some cults have spirit-to-spirit encounters. However, they are contacting the evil one and demonic spirits; we have communion with the Holy One. Avenues of approach are not in themselves good or evil. They are merely tools. It is the one we contact through these methods who is Good or evil.

I have taught students who were deeply involved in Eastern religions before meeting Jesus Christ. When they turned away from the demonic spirit world, they usually turned away from all spiritual experiences. I find this tragic, for Christianity above all religions should be alive with a vibrant relationship with the Holy Spirit.

In later chapters I will go into greater detail on testing and submission to the Word and relationship to the Body of Christ.

But for now, I want to be clear that Christianity is not simply an intellectual understanding. It is a daily, dynamic, ongoing relationship with the living Lord. Spiritual encounter is God's gift to His people. Satan is the great copy-cat and he has attempted to steal away this precious gift. The demonic religions have offered a counterfeit of the spiritual reality intended for the Church. And we, the Church, have rejected the reality out of fear of the counterfeit.

We forget that the presence of the counterfeit is proof of two things: First, there is a real item that is very similar to the counterfeit. No one would make counterfeit $21 bills. Who would take them? The counterfeit is one proof that the real exists. I believe that communion between my spirit and the Holy Spirit is the reality that "spirit guides" seek to counterfeit. Second, the presence of a counterfeit shows that the real item has value. No one is going to take the time to make counterfeit $1 bills. They are not worth the effort. Similarly, satan's demonic counterfeit of spiritual encounter makes it clear that true Holy Spirit encounter has great value.

Let us not withdraw from the real just because satan has made a counterfeit. We certainly must use care and not stand alone when we are dealing with spiritual experiences, but we need not run away from them. God provides us with ample safeguards in His Word and His Church, if we will humbly submit to them. It is time the Church stopped running away when satan raises his ugly head! It is time the Church stopped giving him whatever he touches! The Church must stand up in the authority of Jesus Christ and declare, "This is God's, and, satan, you take your hands off of it!"

Inner stillness and spiritual encounter are God's gifts to the Church. Man was created with an awareness of the spiritual world and a need to be in contact with it. He can never be satisfied with the material world alone. If we do not offer our people, and especially our youth, Holy Spirit reality for their daily lives, they will seek it elsewhere and be trapped in satan's lies.

A Testimony

I want to close this chapter with the following testimony. It is from a young man whose background caused serious doubts as to whether the whole concept of being able to dialogue with God was the truth of God or the deception of satan. Hopefully this testimony will encourage others who question as he did. His testimony will also introduce us to the concept of vision, which we shall cover in detail in the next chapter. The following testimony is used by permission from Paul Edwards, former director of Teen Challenge, Buffalo, New York, and currently on staff at Elim Bible Institute.

"As I think of how I first reacted to this concept of dialoguing with God, I have to laugh. I thought that this was heresy and trying to bring Eastern Religion into Christianity. But so much of my reaction was related to my past instead of to prayer and a thorough search of the Scriptures.

"Maybe if I related to you a little of my past you would understand my initial reaction. As a college student in 1970, I began a search for peace and purpose in life. This search led me into Hatha Yoga, meditation, chanting, Silva mind control and drugs. As I began this search I felt that God was my answer and meditation was the way to find God. In the beginning this seemed to work, but the more I meditated I began to touch evil and confusion instead of touching peace and God.

"After a number of years of this I came to the end of myself and ran right into Jesus. He had been there all the time. I received Jesus as my Savior and He filled me with the peace that I had always been looking for. But also, in the process of committing my life to Jesus, I turned from anything that even faintly appeared to be mystical, labeling it as satanic.

"So when I first heard about dialoguing with God I went and talked to Mark Virkler to 'straighten him out.' But as we talked, he challenged me to pray and search the Word to see if my fears and objections were Scriptural or just reactionary.

"As I sought the Lord, the Lord showed me that dialoguing with Him was a true concept that satan had just stolen and counterfeited. Since that time God has opened up to me a greater use of vision in prayer for my ministry. Here is a small example from my journal, written at a time in my life when I was praying about leaving my position as a Teen Challenge director:

"'Father, please give me more peace, joy and Your character. I really don't know what You want me to decide. So much of how I feel is wrapped up in this ministry. I need to have Your character qualities in order to make the right decision.'

"As I prayed, I saw in my heart Jesus' hand reach down and hand me a piece of bread, and He said, 'Eat it, for it is peace.' Then He handed me a jewel box that He said contained joy. He said, 'Open it.' And inside was a red ruby and He told me to eat it, for it is joy.

"Then the Lord's hand opened a small door that had fire in it, and He told me to look closer. As I looked inside I saw the fire, but in the midst of the fire I saw a small bridge through the fire. And then I noticed I was inside standing on the bridge and as I walked on this thin bridge the Lord handed me a sword to steady myself. Holding on to this sword helped me balance so I wouldn't fall.

"Then the Lord told me to look closer at the bridge itself; I saw that it was alive, and then I recognized the bridge was Jesus. On the other side of the flames there were stairs that I knew led up to the presence of God.

"Then I saw no more but the Lord spoke to me in my heart. 'Paul, character is developed by trials and trusting in Me to uphold you and take you through anything. Just as you looked at the flames and feared you would fall, when you refocused your attention on Me holding you up and the Word giving you balance, you received fresh strength. Notice how My peace and joy was fed to you to prepare you to go through this trial. Always remember I am your peace and your joy.'"

4

Seeing in the Spirit the Dreams and Visions of God

KEY #3

As I pray, I fix the eyes of my heart upon Jesus, seeing in the spirit the dreams and visions of Almighty God.

The third key the Lord opened up for me involves the use of vision in our prayer lives. Remember that Habakkuk *"kept watch to see"* what God would speak to him (Hab. 2:1). In some way Habakkuk was using vision as a part of his spiritual encounter with Almighty God. In Habakkuk 1:1 the prophet said, "The oracle (burden) which Habakkuk the prophet *saw*" (emphasis added). Many of the prophets also spoke of the burden and words that the Lord spoke within their hearts being formed in visions (e.g., Is. 1:1; 2:1; 6:1; 13:1; etc.).

This struck me as an entirely new concept: God uses visions regularly to speak His words within our hearts. I had never even considered the use of vision as an important aspect of my communication with God. At first I wasn't even sure why not. When I stopped to consider it, I found hundreds of verses from

Genesis to Revelation which demonstrated that in every covenant God has chosen to reveal Himself within our hearts by use of dream and vision.

In Appendix E, I have listed references to dream and vision throughout Scripture, and by no means is that list exhaustive. I recommend that you take a couple of hours sometime and read carefully through these verses to gain for yourself a basic appreciation of the way God uses dream and vision. This will give you the best grounding for the things I will say in this chapter.

As I considered the issue of vision theologically and philosophically, I realized there was no reason not to expect God to continue to speak to His people through dreams and visions, especially because He told us, "In the last days...I will pour forth of My Spirit upon all mankind; and your sons and your daughters shall prophesy, and your young men shall see visions, and your old men shall dream dreams" (Acts 2:17). Dream and vision are inseparably linked with the moving of the Holy Spirit in the last days. In this great latter-day outpouring of the Spirit upon the Church, we can expect that dreams and visions will be restored to God's people.

I have taught the four keys I'm presenting in this book in weekend seminars across the nation, and have found that many others struggle, as I initially did, with the concept of vision in their prayer lives. We live in a culture which idolizes rationalism; to believe that an ongoing visionary encounter with the living God is possible almost requires a total break with the culture. However, Christians have never been afraid to be different as long as they are sure they are standing on solid biblical grounds. The Scriptures in Appendix E show the prominence vision has always had in the prayer lives of the saints, and offer a biblical perspective on vision in the context of the life of the Church.

Is It Important?

In a seminar I conducted in Cincinnati, I asked all the participants to spend some time asking God about using the eyes of the heart to see Him and hear His Word. One response I received is from the Reverend Stan Peters, President of the Greater Cincinnati School of the Bible:

"Lord, what about the eyes of my heart? How important is this to You and me—to our relationship and our walk together?"

God's response was: "Ask a blind man if he would like to see the robin he can hear. Ask him if he would like to see his mother, his father, his sweetheart.

"I tell you he will scream and shout and tell you that he wants to see!

"You too need to be healed just as the physically blind, and be able to see Me clearly so that we can walk in perfect union and love. How can two walk together unless they agree? Do you agree you want to see?"

Stan's response was "Yes, Lord!" To which the Lord replied, "Then you will! I love you, Stan."

Another response came from Fred VanAllmen:

"Lord, how important are the eyes of my heart? Have I already used them? How should I use them?"

"They are so important. With earthly eyes all you see are a man's clothes and face. With the heart's eyes you see inside him. You see more of the whole picture. You see all the circumstances involved in any situation. You are better off with your heart's eyes than your human eyes. You can see Me with your heart's eyes. And you can see Me in everyone. And others will see Me in you...."

Both of these excerpts from their journals have been used with permission. They illustrate what I believe God is saying to His Church concerning restoration of the use of spiritual vision in our prayer lives. Therefore I will define in this chapter what we mean by vision, various types or levels of vision, a biblical foundation showing the use of vision from Genesis to Revelation, and how to prepare yourself to receive the divine flow of dream and vision. I will also examine ways of developing the eyes of the heart and how to present them before God to be filled. I will then close by showing how to test vision, and give an example of the healing power of vision as used in an encounter with God.

Seeing the Movement of God

When I speak of dream and vision, I am not referring to personal daydreams, but rather to seeing the movement of God in the spirit with the eyes of my heart. Prophets were called "seers," men and women who saw in the spirit the movements of Almighty God (1 Sam. 9:9). There are two worlds and two sets of eyes. Paul prayed that the eyes of the Ephesians' hearts might be enlightened, so that they would know spiritual realities (1:17,18). If we want to live in the spiritual world, aware of and responsive to the Holy Spirit's actions, then we too must use our spiritual eyes.

Vision can be beneficial in many ways. It can be used in communion with Jesus, as I see the reality of Him sitting next to me and speaking words of life. It can be used in ministry to others, as I ask Jesus to show me how He wants to touch someone's need. I can then respond to the vision He gives by speaking it forth, even as Jesus taught us to pray: "Thy kingdom come. Thy will be done, on earth as it is in heaven." The Greek verb in this phrase is in the imperative mood, issuing a command. Likewise, when Jesus looked at sickness, He saw through it to the divine health that is part of the kingdom of heaven, and commanded it, saying "Be healed." And the people were healed.

Types of Visions

There are at least five types of visions. Each category is equally valid. Each must also be tested against the Word of God.

The first type is received as a dream or a vision in the night. Paul received such a vision in Acts 16:9. He had been trying to preach the gospel in several cities, but had been prohibited by the Holy Spirit. For some reason, he was unable to receive the leading of the Lord through his usual ways. In the night, God gave him a vision of a Macedonian man calling for help, thus guiding Paul in his next step of ministry.

While I am sleeping, my heart is awake and very capable of receiving messages from the Lord. He may picturesquely and symbolically show me the condition of my spirit, my fears, angers, and hurts. He may reveal to me, often in figurative pictures, situations that need my prayers. The Lord and I can even carry on a conversation like Solomon in 1 Kings 3 and Daniel in Daniel 7.

Several years ago, I dreamed that I saw Jesus standing in the church I had attended as a child. I approached Him and asked the question that was constantly burning in my heart: "How can I learn to hear Your voice?" He responded, "You are on the right path. Keep going and don't give up." This experience greatly encouraged me and gave me hope to continue my quest. Many of my students have similarly dialogued with the Lord in their dreams which has convinced them of the value of dream experiences.

A second kind of vision is received while in a trance. Peter had such an experience in Acts 10:10-16. In this vision, the Lord symbolically told him that the Gentiles were no longer "unclean," and prepared him to minister to Cornelius, the centurion. For many years, this was the only kind of vision I recognized. But as I have come to know more about God's love for me and His desire to have communion with me, I have become convinced that trances are not His first choice. Generally, trance-visions seem to come when He cannot get through to us any other way.

Another form of vision involves seeing outside ourselves with spiritual eyes. For example, in Acts 7:55,56 Stephen gazed intently into heaven and saw Jesus standing at the right hand of God. He was looking out, but he was seeing with more than physical eyes; he saw with spiritual eyes into the spiritual world.

When I speak of vision in this book, I am not referring to these three kinds of visions: dream, trance, and seeing outside ourselves. There are two other types of vision which are more normative and less spectacular. God desires to be natural with us, though we usually associate His voice with rolling thunder and parting clouds. He wants to speak to us just the way we are. Often such meetings are so ordinary and so natural that we are tempted to disregard them as only products of our own mind. The next two kinds of vision are gentle, simple, normal.

The fourth type is a spontaneous, unsought inner picture. It is received in the same way as God's voice. Just as I sometimes experience having a person's name light upon my mind and knowing I should pray for him, in the same way I experience seeing a person's face and feeling the call to pray. I might not be in prayer or worship before this type of vision; often it simply appears out of nowhere. The picture is usually light and gentle, and is seen within. From polls of my audiences I have found that most Christians have experienced this type of vision.

The final kind of vision is similar to the last, except that it is received while seeking the Lord in prayer or worship. As I am before the Lord, I ask Him if there is anything He wants to show me and I deliberately present the eyes of my heart to Him, expecting Him to fill them with vision and revelation. This vision is also light and gentle, and I have found that I can alter it, if I choose to. Of course, I don't want to modify it, because my desire is not to see dreams of my own making but visions given by the Lord. This type of vision is the primary one to which I will be referring throughout this book.*

Daniel the Seer

Is it right to believe that these gentle, spontaneous visions that simply arise in my heart during prayer are actually spiritual encounters with God? The Bible clearly teaches that they are. In Daniel 4:13,14, King Nebuchadnezzar encountered an angel in a vision in his mind: "I *was looking* in the visions *in my mind* as I lay on my bed, and behold, an angelic watcher, a holy one, descended from heaven. He shouted out and spoke..." (emphasis added).

Most of us would not assume that an encounter with an angel could take place in a vision in our mind. Yet the teaching of the Bible is very clear.

Consider also Daniel 7:1,13 and 15. Daniel encountered the Ancient of Days and one like a Son of Man in a vision he had in his mind: "In the first year of Belshazzar king of Babylon Daniel saw a dream and visions in his mind as he lay on his bed; then he wrote the dream down and related the following summary of it...'I kept looking in the night visions, and behold, with the clouds of heaven one like a Son of Man was coming, and he came up to the Ancient of Days and was presented before Him...As for me, Daniel, my spirit was distressed within me, and the visions in my mind kept alarming me.'"

* See also Appendix D for a list of twelve Greek New Testament words used to describe revelatory experiences.

We may encounter God the Father, His Son and His angels in visions of our minds as we meditate on the Word of God. These visions can and do come alive, and they *are* actual encounters between God and man. In utilizing our visionary capacity, we are presenting the eyes of our hearts before God, asking Him to fill them.

A Biblical Foundation

Dreams and visions were an integral part of God's communication with man throughout the Bible. In both Covenants, God has used *rhema* and vision to make contact with man.

Our capacities to hear and see on a spiritual level are the two primary spiritual senses used to interact with God. In Genesis chapter 12, God spoke to Abram, promising to make him a great nation. This was *rhema*, God's spoken word to him. Abram obeyed that word and went out in obedience to the Lord. Later God returned to Abram with a further word:

"I will make your descendants as the dust of the earth; so that if anyone can number the dust of the earth, then your descendants can also be numbered...Now look toward the heavens, and count the stars, if you are able to count them...So shall your descendants be" (Gen. 13:16;15:5).

The Lord gave Abram a picture of His *rhema* so that whether he looked up at the sky or down at the ground, he would always be reminded of God's promise to him. The next verse emphasizes the power of vision:

"Then he [Abram] believed in the Lord; and He reckoned it to him as righteousness" (Gen. 15:6).

What an amazing statement! The vision crystallized the *rhema* and produced faith in Abram's heart. As a result of vision, Abram's belief moved from his head to his heart.

Balaam was a prophet whose ability to hear from the Lord was so highly respected that even the king of Moab called for his help. Because (at first) Balaam would only speak what he had heard from the Lord, he was unable to curse the Israelites as the king requested. In Numbers 24:2-4 and 15,16, Balaam spoke of himself as "the man whose eye is opened...who hears the words of God, who sees the vision of the Almighty." He also received revelation through *rhema* and vision.

Vision played a major role in the ministry of Jesus as well. In John 5:19,20 He said, "The Son can do nothing of Himself, unless it is something He sees the Father doing; for whatever the Father does, these things the Son also does in like manner. For the Father loves the Son, and *shows* Him all things that He Himself is doing..." (emphasis added).

Three chapters later, He again repeated the words, "I speak the things which I have seen with My Father" (Jn. 8:38). Jesus declared that He could do nothing on His own. All His power and authority came from His Father's initiative. If He saw God laying hands on the sick and healing them, then He laid hands on the sick and they were healed. If He saw God cast out a demon, Jesus spoke to the demon and it left. His actions flowed only out of the movement of God the Father, which He saw through vision and heard through *rhema*.

I have purposed in my spirit that I want to live as Jesus did. I have made a quality decision that I will not live out of what my physical eyes see, but I will respond only to what my spiritual eyes see. "For the things which are seen are temporal, but the things which are not seen are eternal" (2 Cor. 4:18). I know that God loves me and will show me what He is doing if

I will just open my spiritual eyes to see. (We will talk about ways to do this later in the chapter.)

Not only did Jesus see vision within Himself, He also taught in picture language. Matthew 13:34 says, "All these things Jesus spoke to the multitudes in parables, and He was not talking to them without a parable." A parable is an image created with words. It shows us the world through the lens of divine imagination. When Jesus saw a field ready for harvest, it was for Him an image of the hearts of men ready to be brought into the kingdom. When He saw vines heavy with fruit, it was for Him an image of our fruitfulness if we abide in His life. Jesus taught the crowds by drawing pictures with His words that they might see spiritual reality.

Even more amazingly, Jesus not only saw images and taught in images, but in Colossians 1:15, Paul called Him "the image of the invisible God." Throughout the old covenant, God sought to reveal Himself to His people. He gave them laws and commandments, priests and prophets, and the tabernacle and the temple to reveal aspects of Who He was.

Yet the people didn't understand. *We* don't understand. How often we have thought of God as a merciless judge meting out chastisement and punishment for our sins and weaknesses. So God decided to clear up all the misconceptions and give us a picture of what He had been saying: He sent Jesus. No longer need there be any doubt about what God is really like, for we have the living image who reveals God to us. As we watch the way Jesus moved among men, we see that God is kind and gentle and merciful. The glory of God is revealed in His Son, the image and fullness of God.

I have already noted in another context the close relationship of dreams and visions to the working of the Holy Spirit in Acts 2:17: "And it shall be in the last days, God says, that I will pour forth of My Spirit upon all mankind; and your sons and your daughters shall prophesy and your young men shall see visions, and your old men shall dream dreams."

I believe we are living in a time of mighty outpouring of the Holy Spirit. And, according to Acts 2:17, I believe we should expect that a flow of prophecy, dreams, and visions will come with this outpouring. *Therefore I expect vision to be a normal, natural flow within the hearts of believers.*

The centrality of vision in spiritual encounters is also attested to in Revelation 1:10,11. These are fascinating verses, because they illustrate several of the principles that can lead us into dialoguing with God. John said, "I was in the Spirit on the Lord's day, and I heard behind me a loud voice like the sound of a trumpet saying, 'Write in a book what you see....'"

John was "in the Spirit": that is, he was still, in contact with the Holy Spirit within. He heard a voice: that is *rhema*. He wrote down the revelation: that is journaling, which we will discuss at length in the next chapter. And he saw vision. John even entered the vision, talked with angels, and was part of the activity he saw taking place in the spiritual world.

So, from Genesis to Revelation vision was used to make contact between God and man, crystallize *rhema*, illustrate spiritual truth, and increase faith. I still had a lingering question: Why did God choose to speak in pictures and parables to teach spiritual truth? In fact, why is the entire Bible a series of stories? Stories leave so much more room for misunderstanding and disagreement. It seems to me that it would have been much more efficient to give us a book of systematic theology. That's what I would have done. I would have laid out all of the major doctrines on a nice, neat graph. Then there would be no room for error, misunderstanding, or disagreement.

But God revealed to me that He had a very good reason for writing stories rather than pure theology or graphs: A picture, created with words, moves and stirs the heart. Analysis can only satisfy the mind. And God is most interested in touching our hearts. Therefore, much of what we know of Him is revealed to us through a series of images.

The Value of Vision

Dr. David (Paul Yonggi) Cho, pastor of the world's largest church, is a strong believer in the power of images. He has stated that the language of the Holy Spirit is dreams and visions, which means that when the Holy Spirit wants to speak to me, He will normally use dreams and visions. Dr. Cho further stated that his ability to be creative came when he began "incubating" dreams and visions.

His commission from the Lord is to be always "pregnant" with dreams and visions. One of those dreams was to increase the membership of his church—it has now grown to over 700,000 members, and he preaches to even more than that each week. Dr. Cho sees with his spiritual eyes a membership larger than his physical eyes see.

Perhaps there is no place where the value of vision can be more readily recognized than in the ability to be creative. God is obviously the most creative Being in the universe. He IS The Creator. The ability to create is born in a creative spirit. The Spirit of God brooded over the waters (Gen. 1:2) and He called into being things which had not existed. And behold, the worlds were formed.

You cannot create anything if you do not first have a picture, a vision of it. Long before a skyscraper rises from the ground, there is an architect who envisions it in every detail. When Michelangelo looked at the huge piece of marble, he did not see the rough quarry stone that everyone else saw; he saw within it the beautiful figure of a young man. As he chiseled away he did not create that figure, but rather released the magnificent statute of David which he had seen within the rock.

God has placed within all men a spirit. That is what distinguishes mankind from the animal kingdom: Man has a spirit; animals do not. All of mankind has the capacity to create, to one degree or another, by the spirit within him. But we were designed by God to lend this creative ability of our spirits to the Holy Spirit to fill. We are to ask the Holy Spirit to overlay us, to flow through us and help us yield our will to Almighty God. Rather than creating through any ability of our own, we are the vessels through whom God moves and does His works.

Abraham: The Birth of a Miracle

Abram is a classic example of God bringing a creative miracle through a man's spirit. First, God spoke a word to Abram:

"Now the Lord said to Abram, 'Go forth from your country, and from your relatives and from your father's house, to the land which I will show you; and I will make you a great nation...'" (Gen. 12:1,2).

Next, God planted a picture in Abram's heart. The Lord came to him in a vision (Gen. 15:1) and showed him the miracle being fulfilled. "And he [God] took him [Abram] outside and said, 'Now look toward the heavens, and count the stars, if you are able to count them.' And He said to him, 'So shall your descendants be'" (Gen. 15:5). Conception took place: the purposes of Almighty God were implanted in the heart of a man. A seed was placed in him that, when allowed to germinate and grow, birthed the creative acts and purposes of Almighty God.

It is certainly significant that the spoken word of the Lord within Abram's heart, coupled with God's divine vision, produced a tremendous level of faith in Abram, such faith that even God took special note of it: "Then he believed in the Lord; and He reckoned it to him as righteousness" (Gen. 15:6).

This is exactly what will happen for each person who communes with God and receives His *rhema* and vision. They will conceive the creative ideas of Almighty God in their spirits which will produce a tremendous level of faith within them. Through such communion with God, I have been changed from a fear-filled pessimist into a faith-filled optimist.

Abram pondered the *rhema* and vision in his heart and "with respect to the promise of God, he did not waver in unbelief, but grew strong in faith, giving glory to God, and being fully assured that what He had promised, He was able also to perform" (Rom. 4:20,21).

Abram then spoke God's word as he was commanded. God said to him, "No longer shall your name be called Abram, but your name shall be Abraham; for I will make you the father of a multitude of nations" (Gen. 17:5). The name "Abraham" means "father of a multitude," so God was asking him to declare what God had promised him every time he spoke his name.

Abraham acted upon the word and vision that was spoken within his heart and his wife Sarah bore Isaac, the child of promise (Gen. 21:1-5). What a wonderful example of how the creative purposes of God can be birthed through our spirits into our physical world!

I believe that every person who begins to dialogue with God with regularity will find a surge of creativity in his spirit such as he has never experienced before. I believe that as conversation with God is restored to the Church of Jesus Christ, She will become the most creative force in the world today. Nothing will be able to match it. Creative solutions to the world's difficult problems will be released through the Church, and the world will be healed in a way it has not experienced since the Son of God walked in the land of Palestine. I testify to the fact that since such dialogue and communion with God were restored to my life, I have experienced my most creative and productive years.

The humanists have recognized the truth that there is creative power in man's spirit. As Christians, however, we know the full truth: Man's spirit was made to be a womb in which the creative ideas and energies of the Holy Spirit could be planted, incubated, and in the fullness of time, birthed into His world. And we know that any honor and glory that come from our accomplishments belong only to Jesus.

When the Spirit speaks a word to me, He gives a picture to hold as a reminder of His words. When I prepare to teach, I ask the Spirit for a vision of what He wants accomplished. As I teach, I hold that vision before me and speak with the goal of seeing it fulfilled. As I write this book, I hold before me the vision of the Church of Jesus Christ transformed by a restoration of intimate dialogue with God.

To sum up, remember Abraham, the father of faith.

Stage One—Conception

1. He heard the voice of the Lord (Gen. 12:1-3).
2. He saw with the eyes of faith (Gen. 15:5,6).

Stage Two—Incubation

3. He thought with a heart of faith (Rom. 4:20,21).
4. He spoke the word of faith (Gen. 17:5).
5. He acted in faith (Gen. 17:23).

Stage Three—Birth

6. He received the promise of faith (Gen. 21:5).

Prepare to Receive

When I was about twelve years old, I threw away all imagination and vision. I was becoming a man so I put away such childish things. Dream and vision were unimportant; they had no value for me. I knew that only logic, analysis and cognition were useful in dealing successfully with the real adult world. Because I did not use these gifts, they soon atrophied and before long I couldn't see anything in the spirit, even if I wanted to. Therefore, when I became convinced of the importance of using the eyes of my heart, it was extremely difficult for me to begin moving in that realm. I found three basic prerequisites I had to fulfill in order to begin receiving communication from God through spiritual vision.

First, I had to be convinced of the value of living in dreams and vision. For me, that meant a thorough study of the Scriptures to find the place of visions and dreams in the Word.* Only after discovering the centrality of the eyes of the heart in spiritual encounter was I ready to begin looking in the spirit for the vision of Almighty God.

But after so many years of disuse, my visionary capacity did not naturally and immediately begin receiving images of the spiritual world. Therefore, the second thing I had to do was set aside time to deliberately offer the eyes of my heart to God. When I have quieted myself, I ask, "Father, is there anything You want to show me?" Then I look to see. (See, for example, Daniel 7:2,9,13 and 8:2,3,5.) I wait quietly and expectantly, my inner being completely focused on Jesus. Suddenly there comes an inner awareness and I begin to see the movement of God within.

When I first came to God seeking vision, I had to come in faith believing that He would speak to me through images, vision and inner pictures. Hebrews 11:6 declares that he who

*Refer to Appendix E.

comes to God must believe that He is and that He is a rewarder of those who seek Him. If I don't believe that God wants to communicate with me through visions, then I will not receive revelation from Him in that way. If I begin to receive an inner picture and immediately begin questioning whether it is from Him, the picture will disappear because doubt has cut off my receptivity. I will explain this more fully in later chapters, but let's agree here that we can communicate with the Lord only by faith.

Developing the Eyes of Our Heart (Ephesians 1:18)

The Bible speaks of having our spiritual senses strengthened through use. There are several things we can do to strengthen our ability to see in the spirit. Perhaps the easiest and most common way of availing ourselves of vision for spiritual purposes is to enter into a Bible story. Simply picture the action as it takes place. Ask the Holy Spirit to take over in the vision and show you what He wants to speak to you through the story. He will. Watch what He does. Don't just watch as an observer, but enter into and become part of the action.

The children's video series *Superbook* is an excellent example of this, as is the music of Don Francisco and Carman, two truly anointed performers and songwriters. Many of their songs are dramatic reenactments of biblical stories, often in the first person, as if they were actually involved in the story. By allowing our vision and emotions to flow with the action of the song, we can understand what it may have been like to live through those experiences.

I regularly poll the Christian audiences who attend my seminars, and I have found that about two-thirds of all adults normally picture a Bible scene as they read it. One-third do not. It comes as a shock to the two-thirds that there are people who just read stories analytically for the theological content.

Likewise, it is a great surprise to the one-third to find that so many of those sitting around them usually picture Bible scenes as they read them.

Since God tells us to come to Him as children, and, of course, one hundred percent of children see a story as they read it, I have decided always to read with vision from now on. This is one excellent way to restore the use of a "muscle," our visionary capacity, that for many of us is somewhat atrophied. I encourage you to use the eyes of your heart as you read the Scriptures (Eph. 1:18).

Don't forget that the Holy Spirit lives within you, and that you can ask Him to make the vision come alive with His own life and then let Him take you where He wills. God will encounter you in the midst of your Bible study with a flow of His divine life. Simply relax as you read. See the scene in your mind's eye and ask the Holy Spirit to take over. You will be surprised at how much vision will begin flowing within you. The Bible says we have not because we ask not (Jn. 16:24; Jas. 4:2b).

Seeing in Prayer

Another time for seeing in the Spirit is during prayer. As I quiet my heart, I ask the Lord to show me whatever He wants. I see Jesus right there with me, listening as I talk to Him. Often I see us in a biblical setting, such as walking along a beach or sitting at a well.

I do not force it, however, or try to paint in details that do not come naturally. The most important thing is the sense of His presence. My wife and I, along with many others, have noted that when we began using vision in prayer, we did not naturally see Jesus' face. His Presence impressed us. He is a being of love—agape love, incomprehensible love. Later on we did see His face, with striking eyes of compassion, but facial features are unnecessary, even unimportant, to this kind of prayer. His compassion and love, however, are significant. The important thing is that we come to meet with Jesus and then let the Holy Spirit take over.

I look intently at Jesus in my vision. I don't struggle or squint, or try to force something to appear. I simply look in faith, focusing my attention upon Christ within me. As the Holy Spirit takes over, I see Jesus begin to move and speak. His words are wisdom and life and His actions are love and peace. Like John the Revelator, I am in the Spirit; I look; and I see and hear.

I have found this particularly effective when I am interceding for others. I see them in my mind's eye and then ask Jesus to come and do for them whatever He wishes. I see Him meeting them and I speak forth whatever I see Him doing. He may lay His hands upon them and speak health. He may take them in His arms and bring them the comfort no mere human could offer. I experienced this while praying for an elderly woman before surgery. I began to pray for her healing, and in my mind's eye I saw her lying in her hospital bed. As I watched, I saw Jesus come and lift her into His arms and carry her home to be with Him. I prayed aloud what I saw, Jesus holding her in His arms and giving her peace as He took her home. Afterward I talked with her loved ones about the need to know the Lord's will, and that sometimes we have to release those dear to us into the blessed rest of death.

Through this incident and many more like it, I have become convinced that praying in the Spirit involves praying out of the *rhema* and vision that God gives us. He is never bound to act in a certain way by our prayers; He does, however, give us revelations and ask us to speak them forth.

Another time I was praying for our Congress. I asked the Lord to show me a vision of what He wanted to do in and through these men, whose thoughts and decisions are so important to our world. He showed me the room where they meet, each man in his proper place. Then I saw rays of light like bolts of lightning descending from heaven and touching each congressman. I began praying for God's light to fill each one, and that His wisdom and purity would flow through each of them. When I finished praying, the rays of light were still streaming down to touch each one. So I prayed again, and did not stop until the vision faded.

Seeing in Worship

Praise and worship took on new meaning and power when I began seeing what I was singing and allowing the Holy Spirit to control the vision. When I sing about bowing before Him, I see myself kneeling at His feet. When I sing about His sacrifice, I see the cross, and watch as He pours out His life for me. When I sing of His Lordship, I see myself joining the angels and multitudes worshiping before the throne. I may set the scene, but the Spirit will take over and show me the vision. Sometimes I see Him moving through the congregation, meeting people's needs. Sometimes He just smiles at me with a love I simply can't describe.

Another time, Patti was visualizing a song during a worship service and the Spirit gave her an incredible vision which lasted nearly a half hour! (That story is recorded in a later chapter.) As the congregation flowed from song to song, each one was incorporated into the vision and became a backdrop for the action taking place. Worship truly becomes a spiritual encounter when we allow the senses of our hearts to become involved!

Again, as I poll groups of Christians, I find that one-fourth of them *normally* use the eyes of their hearts as they worship, and picture the scene they are singing about, allowing the Holy Spirit to take it where He desires. I recommend that the rest of us who are not in that group begin presenting the eyes of our hearts before God as we sing. He generally does not fill what we do not present before Him. The prophets were "seers" because they were "lookers."

Seeing in Sleep

My study of dream and vision in Scripture made it clear to me that my dreams are a natural expression of the inner world. Dreams are not simply a mixed-up rehash of the day's events, but rather my heart's symbolic expression of what I am feeling deep within. They provide a natural and readily available avenue for spiritual encounter. When Solomon asked the Lord for wisdom, it was in a dream (1 Kgs. 3:5-15). Many of Daniel's prophecies were received in dreams (e.g., Dan. 7:1). And Paul's call to minister in Macedonia came as a vision in the night (Acts 16:9,10).

Having accepted dreams as a valid avenue of spiritual communication, I decided to begin listening to them. Of course, I could only remember one or two per year, so I didn't expect much to come of my decision. But there is something that happens when we begin to take our dreams seriously. Suddenly they begin speaking to us. The very night I made my decision, I had three distinct dreams that I remembered when I awoke. I have seen the same thing happen repeatedly with my students. When we recognize the value of dreams, they begin to speak to us.

For dreams to be useful, I first have to remember them. Then I have to understand them. Therefore, I try to record my dreams immediately upon awakening, as Daniel did: "Daniel saw a dream and visions in his mind as he lay on his bed; then he wrote the dream down and related the following summary of it" (Dan. 7:1). I then ask the Lord to give me the interpretation of my dream. I believe He will do it for you and me, just as He did for Daniel: "And it came about when I, Daniel, had seen the vision, that I sought to understand it; and behold, standing

81

before me was one who looked like a man. And I heard the voice of a man between the banks of Ulai, and he called out and said, 'Gabriel, give this man an understanding of the vision'" (Dan. 8:15,16).

Dream interpretation is a fascinating subject that you will want to explore further to deepen your communion with God. I highly recommend two books on the subject: ***Dream Interpretation*** by Herman Riffel and ***Dream Dreams*** by Steve and Dianne Bydeley.

One Screen—Three Projectors

One way to understand our visionary capacity is to think of it as a viewing screen that can be used by three projectors. One projector is satan's, one is mine, and one is the Holy Spirit's.

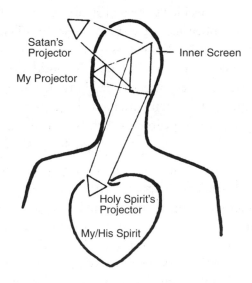

one inner screen—three projectors

It is a spiritual principle that whatever is not purposely presented to God is quickly filled by satan. Because the Church has not been taught how to present the eyes of our hearts to the Lord, satan has taken them over without our knowledge. Therefore, we find our imaginations often filled with evil, such as lust, worry, failure, and defeat. We can experience this so often that we may be tempted to curse our imaginations as instruments of the devil.

How often do we face a potentially explosive situation and say, "I can see it now. It's going to be awful! There will be a big fight and nothing will ever be the same again!" Or suppose your husband is late returning from work. What pictures do you see on that inner screen? An accident? An affair? No doubt it must be something terrible, and satan is more than happy to supply an endless assortment of unhappy possibilities.

We must cut off instantly any and all pictures shown on our inner screen from satan's projector. We should take every thought captive to the obedience of Christ (2 Cor. 10:5). Our ability to see in the Spirit is an incredible gift. Let's rise up in the authority of Jesus Christ and reclaim it for His purposes!

My Projector

I myself am the operator of the second projector. I have the power to use it for good or for evil. Jesus speaks of looking at a woman "to lust after her." I can't blame this on satan. It's my idea and my inner picture. I choose the attitude with which I look at the woman. I am looking *to lust*. I also paint the picture of her as I want to see her. Stroke by stroke, I create my little fantasy. This is using my own projector to create my little pictures on my inner screen.

I can also use my mind to present the eyes of my heart to the Lord. To do this, I can "prime the pump" by setting the scene, seeing the reality of Jesus present with me, and asking the Holy Spirit to fill the vision with His life. In so doing, I am not trying to prime God, but rather to poise myself properly before the Lord, so He can move freely upon me.

When I was a child, we had an old-fashioned hand pump near our door, a remnant from the days before indoor plumbing. The water from that well was the clearest, most refreshing water I have ever tasted. There was only one problem with that well: In order to get water out, we had to put water in. We didn't have to prime the pump because there wasn't any water. We poured the water in to prepare the pump to receive and draw forth the water that was already there. The little cup of water we poured in could be stale and tasteless, but the flow that came as a result of it was always fresh and pure.

Priming the pump in vision prepares me to see what the Spirit will offer. It gets me into a position to receive and draw forth the flow of living water. My own little image may be stale and impure, but that doesn't prevent the flow that springs up within my soul from being pure and life-giving.

John wrote in Revelation that he looked, saw a door, and heard a voice. Then, "Immediately I was in the Spirit" (Rev. 4:2). When I read that I wondered, "Where were you in verse one?" If I were writing the account, I would have said, "I was in the Spirit, I looked, I saw and I heard." But he wrote it the way he did to teach us something important. Listen to the sequence again. "I looked and behold, a door...I heard...Immediately I was in the Spirit."

John had been in the Spirit in chapters 1 - 3, seeing visions and receiving revelation. He must have taken a break at the end of chapter three and afterward wanted to return to the spiritual dimension. At the beginning of chapter four, John primed the pump by looking. No doubt he was asking, "Lord, is there something more You want to show me?" And God answered,

"Sure! Come on up!" Then John saw visions and actually entered the action, dialoguing with angels and heavenly beings.

This kind of revelation is not reserved for special saints! We are all kings and priests. God doesn't grant gifts because we are spiritual but because He loves us. And He has gifted us all with an incredible projector which we can use to prepare ourselves to receive the vision He wants us to have.

One of our students named Mike received the following encouragement from the Lord through journaling: "The outcome always is determined by the 'looking' or the focus of the eyes. 'While we look not at the temporal....' 'Moses endured as seeing Him who is invisible....' 'Looking unto the author and finisher of our faith....' 'I will look unto the hills whence cometh my help....' My Word goes on and on about trust and about the gaze of the soul and the focus of our eyes.

"You remember the old song you used to sing: 'Turn your eyes upon Jesus, look full in His wonderful face, and the things of earth will grow strangely dim, in the light of His glory and grace.' Turn and look. Turn away from all but Me. Look FULL in My wonderful face. Mike, My son, your looking must be FULL. It must not be the occasional glance. It must not be the odd or rare time when you're really desperate. It must be the purposeful and determined turning aside and the gazing and beholding of My splendor and glory. Looking FULL into My face."

The Spirit's Projector

The third projector belongs to the Holy Spirit. With His projector He carries us beyond our imagination into the spiritual dimension. In Revelation 4:2, after John had primed the pump by looking, the Holy Spirit took over and showed him visions that went on for chapter after chapter.

Poised Before Almighty God

I desire earnestly to live as Jesus did, out of the Father's initiative and doing only what He saw His Father doing. However, before I can live that way, I need to learn how to become a seer. In rationalistic cultures, where seeing with the eyes of the heart is generally looked upon with scorn, it takes a monumental effort to become at ease with seeing vision as Jesus did. It is an enormous step even to believe that such a thing is possible.

My experience, as well as the experience of many others, has convinced me that once we have grown accustomed to looking expectantly to the Spirit for a vision from the Lord, it appears readily. The simple act of looking in faith opens us up to begin seeing.

I am convinced that the spiritual world exists, whether I see it or not. In becoming a seer, I simply learn to see what is. In learning to see, I am learning to bring alive my atrophied visionary capacity and present it to God to be filled.

Once my visionary sense has been rejuvenated and presented before Almighty God, He offers me the opportunity to live like Jesus, drawing on the continuous flow of divine vision.

The prophets of Israel simply said, "I looked," and, as they quieted themselves before God, "they saw" (e.g., Dan. 7:2,9,13). I found that when I reclaimed the use of my visionary capacity, I, too, could simply quiet myself in the Lord's presence, look, and see the visions of Almighty God. I am a seer simply because I have become a looker.

If your intuitive and visionary functions have atrophied through lack of use, the process is not as simple as just looking and seeing. Vision must be exercised to restore its vitality. This involves three steps: repenting of sin (the sin of scorning one of God's gifts); asking God to breathe new life into this inner sense of seeing; and developing this sense which God is restoring. This development involves standing in the belief that God will do it, taking the first wobbly steps, and gaining strength. Through grace we will get to the point of walking with ease, where we are able to allow God to direct the pathway.

This is exactly what has happened with vision in my life, as well as in the lives of many others. Through the scorn that was heaped upon it and through continuous disuse, my visionary capacity atrophied and died. Therefore, when I began looking to see the vision God wanted to present to me, I saw nothing. I had so scorned my visionary capacity that it was unable to function when called upon to do so.

I began the process of restoration by repenting of my contempt for visionary experiences. I asked God's forgiveness for not honoring and using this gift He had created and given me. I also repented of idolizing the logic and analytical thinking that had swept over me as well as over my culture. I covenanted to honor and seek His vision as much as I had honored and sought analytical thought.

Then I asked God to breathe upon my visionary capacity and restore it, to bring it back to life and teach me how to allow Him to flow through it.

Finally I was ready to take my first few wobbly steps. As I sat in my study seeking God's face, I was drawn to a scene from John 4 in which Jesus sat by the well and talked with a Samaritan woman. Sensing that God wanted to sit and talk with me, I pictured the scene with a slight adaptation. Instead of seeing the woman talking with Jesus, I saw myself. As I peered intently into the picture and looked to see what might happen, it came alive through the Holy Spirit. Jesus moved and gestured, as any of us might when talking. With His movement, there came into my heart His words and directives for my life.

This was the first time I had ever sought vision in this way, and I was thrilled to see it so readily come alive and be taken over by the power of the Holy Spirit. I found as I repeated this experiment in subsequent days that God continued to move through these "self-initiated scenes," causing them to come alive with His own life and become supernatural visions direct from the throne of grace.

Objections

At this point I want to stop to answer some of the questions you may be asking. First, "Don't you limit God by forcing Him to fit into the scene you have set for Him to fill?" The answer is, "Absolutely yes!" Of course, God has some freedom as He takes over the scene you have set. He can move it to a certain extent in one direction or another.

However, if your scene is totally removed from the one God wants to show you, you will find that nothing happens. The scene does not come alive; it remains dead. God is not able to move in it. When this happens to me, my response is to relax and say, "God, how do You want to reveal Yourself in this situation?" With that, God implants a vision through which He can move.

A second question is, "Well then, why don't you just look for His vision, rather than begin by initiating your own?" As I have said before, that works fine for the naturally intuitive and visionary person. However, those of us with stunted visionary abilities will often need a learning tool to get started. Once accustomed to vision, though, this type of person will be able to discard the learning tool, and simply look and see.

"Are you saying that your self-initiated image is a divine vision?" Of course not! My image is my image; God's supernatural vision is His vision. We should never confuse the two. I never say that my "priming of the pump" is God's vision. It is simply my priming the pump. However, when that inner "click" is experienced and the vision moves with a life of its own that flows from the throne of grace, it then is obviously no longer my own. It has become God's. Mine is mine, and God's is God's.

Someone may ask, "Where does the Bible teach that we are to set the scene ourselves, in order for God to begin flowing in vision?" My response is, "Where does the Bible say that we are not to set a scene and ask God to fill it?" I do not think there is a clear teaching on either side, which means we will have to marshal some verses that we could interpret as supporting one of these viewpoints. Another option would be to allow each individual Christian the liberty of working out his own salvation in this area, since there is no absolutely clear biblical teaching on the issue.

The closest verses that could conceivably speak against setting a scene are those that speak of avoiding vain imaginations and not setting up any graven images. According to Webster, a graven image is "an object of worship carved usually from wood or stone." Obviously, the scene we set in our minds is not carved or worshiped. It serves simply as a steppingstone to the living flow of divine images. Webster defines "vain" as "having no real value; idle, worthless." I do not see a learning tool as something having no real value, or being idle and worthless. Learning tools are valuable, and have an active place in the learning experience. The fact that the Bible speaks of vain imaginations tells us that there is also an effective use of imagination. I believe that setting a scene for God to fill is one of these effective uses of imagination.

It must be remembered that consciously setting a scene is only a temporary learning tool, needed only by some individuals. The naturally intuitive person will not need this device. He will simply look to see, and the vision will be there. The analytically-oriented person will later put aside this learning tool, once he is able to open himself naturally and normally to vision.

It is possible that if we lived in a more biblical culture we would not have so many obstacles to overcome. If we normally discussed our dreams at breakfast with our families and sought God's interpretation, as Joseph did, we would find a natural skill built into our lives concerning visionary things. However, who in America takes their dreams seriously, and discusses them regularly in a family gathering? Practically no one. If we did, we would be viewed as strange. Is it any wonder that skill in, and openness to, visions are almost totally lacking in our culture?

As a Church, we need to repent for having allowed the rationalism of our time to distort our own perspective of a balanced lifestyle. Some people fear that there may be seeds of Eastern thought in some Church teaching today. Did we ever stop to realize that Jesus was not a Westerner, that God did not intend for us to idolize logic and scorn vision?

God is calling us to make Jesus our perfect Example, to aspire to walk as He did, to do nothing on our own initiative, but to live as Jesus did, by a constant flow of *rhema* and vision.

Will you search until you find the way to that lifestyle and experience? Will you continue on until you discover Him? "You search the Scriptures, because you think that in them you have eternal life; and it is these that bear witness of Me; and you are unwilling to come to Me, that you may have life" (Jn. 5:39,40).

Lord, we come to You. We repent of allowing our culture to dictate scorn for the visionary capacity which You have created and placed within us. We ask Your forgiveness and ask that You restore to our hearts a proper use of dream and vision.

Restore our ability to hear and to see. Draw each of us into all that You have for us.

Testing Vision

Many of us have been tempted to fold up our inner screen rather than risk receiving images from satan's projector. To do so, however, closes the door to one of our most powerful senses for encountering spiritual reality. I believe the Bible offers a better idea. Paul exhorted the Church to test all things, reject the evil and hold fast to the good. There are three basic areas that help determine the source of either *rhema* or vision.

The Spirit

First we need to determine the spirit of the word or picture. Each of the possible sources has distinctive characteristics. If the source is myself, the picture will be born in my mind, rather than my spirit. It will be a picture I have painted, stroke by stroke—a creation of my own mind.

If the source is satan, the picture will be an intruding image. It will seem out of place. I should ask myself if my mind was empty or idle. The old adage about the devil's playground still holds true.

If the source of the pictures is God, they will be a living flow coming from my innermost being. I can check to see if my heart was quietly focused on Jesus when the vision came.

I have also discovered that I can test the origin of a vision by placing, in my mind, the vision next to a picture of Jesus. If the vision is not from God it will be incongruous; it will not exist comfortably side by side with a picture of Jesus. This method of testing is like that presented by Charles Sheldon in his book *In His Steps*: to ask always, "What would Jesus do in this situation?"

Ideas in the Revelation

Another area we may test is the ideas put forth in the revelation (1 Jn. 4:2-5). We do so by examining the content. If the ideas are merely my own, they will be a painting of the things I have learned, an expression of what I have been taking in to my mind and heart. Therefore, if I have been feeding on evil and perversion, what flows out of me will be evil and perverted. If I have been feeding on the Word, the flow of images will be wise, pure and good.

Revelation from satan will be negative, destructive and pushy. It will be accusative and fearful. It will violate both the nature of God and the Word of God. Perhaps the clearest indicators of satanic influence are ego appeal and a fear of testing. Darkness does not want to come into the light. The excuses often go something like this: "You must not tell anyone what has been revealed to you. You have great insight that other people can't understand! You are different than the others, so you have been chosen to receive special revelation. Even your pastor doesn't have the insight and revelation you have received. So don't tell anyone!" If I hear that within myself or from other people, warning bells go off. Reject such ego appeals and any revelation that seeks to be kept hidden.

Any revelation from God will be open and eager for testing. It will be meek and humble, willing to be submitted to the Body of Christ. Truth seeks truth and is not afraid of the light. Divine revelation will also be instructive, up-building and comforting; I immediately reject any thought or picture which is not. The Holy Spirit is the Comforter, and His words bring peace. Satan is the accuser, and I will not accept his condemnation.

Of course, the Bible also says that satan comes as an angel of light. How do we discern him at those times? One way is through allowing "the peace of God [to] rule in your hearts" (Col. 3:15). I have on a couple of occasions received revelation in my journal which seemed good and true. However, I felt uneasy about it. It just didn't sit quite right. Not that there was anything biblically wrong with the instruction. It just didn't feel right. I took it to my spiritual counselors, and it did not win their wholehearted approval. (I will have more to say on the safety to be found in counselors later.) Coupling these two factors together, I decided that it was not from God, and that I would not act upon it.

Remember we have said that spiritual revelation comes primarily through *rhema*, vision, and burden. These three need to line up, particularly the burden of peace: a peace that passes all understanding (Phil. 4:7). I do not think satan can counterfeit peace. Therefore make sure that the peace of God rules (or plays the part of the umpire) in your heart.

Examining the Fruit

The final test of revelation is an examination of the fruit it bears (Matt. 7:16). The fruit of my thoughts and pictures will vary, depending on what I have been feeding myself. If my heart is full of evil, the fruit will be evil. If my heart is filled with the Word, the fruit will be good.

The fruit of satanic revelation will be fear, bondage, anxiety, and confusion. There will be a feeling of compulsion that I must do something right now. I will be driven to obedience. My ego is inflated. I think, "It's just Jesus and me, and we don't need anyone else." This results in "Lone Ranger Christians": unsubmitted, rebellious, in and out of fellowship with the Body of Christ. They are easy prey for the devil, and their delusion and deception will increase as long as they insist on standing alone.

Holy Spirit revelation quickens our faith, instills peace, and brings enlightenment and knowledge. The good fruit of the Holy Spirit will grow as a result of what we have seen and heard. We will increase in humility as we recognize the miracle that the Almighty, all-powerful God has chosen to have fellowship with us. We will be like Moses, who talked with God face to face just as a man speaks to his friend, and yet was the meekest man on all the earth.

The Healing Power of Vision

I would like to close this chapter on vision with the testimony of one of my students. At the end of a class on vision, I asked the class to join me in a visionary experience. I helped them set the scene: sitting at a well with Jesus, as in John 4. Here is the testimony of one woman's experience as she related it to the class the following week.

"Four months ago I experienced a great tragedy. I was expecting my fifth child. At five and a half months I went for my regular checkup and the doctor couldn't find a heartbeat. Within hours I was admitted to the hospital and my son was taken from me.

"I was emotionally destroyed and couldn't find peace. My nights were filled with horrible dreams until I could no longer sleep for fear of the torment that it would bring.

"When I was awake, my mind was filled with the sight of my son Jerome as I had seen him in the hospital, lifeless and small enough to fit in my two hands. I sought the Lord earnestly for healing and the ability to see past the pain to the gift that was in it. But healing did not come. I couldn't see Jerome in heaven; I could only see my own hurt. People kept telling me that time would heal the pain, but instead it continued to grow.

Last week, as I sat at the well, Jesus came and put His arm around me. All I could say to Him was, 'It hurts.' He said, 'I know,' and taking me by the hand said, 'Let's go for a walk.'

"He led me to a big shade tree in the middle of a grassy meadow. We sat down under the tree and He said, 'I want you to look up into heaven.' I looked up at the beautiful blue sky with fluffy white clouds and in the midst of them I saw an angelic form holding a baby. I quickly turned away, saying, 'I can't look.' He put His arm around me and gently said, 'I love you. It will be all right.'

"A few minutes later Jesus said, 'I want you to look up again.' The angelic form and the child had moved closer to me. Once more I turned away and cried, 'I can't look. This is too painful, Lord. I can't look.' Again His arm came around me as He lovingly said, 'I know it hurts, but I love you very much.'

"We sat together in silence for a few minutes until Jesus said again, 'I want you to look up.' The angelic form was right beside me holding the baby, who looked very much like my son Jerome. Jesus placed the baby in my arms and said, 'I want you to hold him and love him.' Although I know it was just a few minutes of time here in class, it seemed like I spent hours with him. I was able to do all the motherly things a mother would want to do: tell my baby how much I loved him; check all of his fingers and toes; nurse him; just hold him and love him. As I did all of these things, I could feel the healing taking place inside of me.

"Finally the Lord said, 'It's time to go.' 'I can't go yet,' I said, and He said, with such understanding love, 'That's all right. We'll stay a little longer.' He let me hold Jerome a while longer, then asked, 'Are you ready to go yet?' I said, 'Yes, I'm ready,' and I was able to place my son in Jesus' arms.

"Jesus said, 'Come and go for a walk with Me.' We stood and He handed Jerome back to me. We began to walk and had only gone two or three steps when it seemed we stepped from earth into heaven. He led me over to what looked like a bassinette, all white and covered with lace. It was just beautiful. Jesus told me, 'This is where your child lies.' I laid Jerome down in his bed and was able to say, 'Thank You, Lord.' 'We'll go back now,' He said. We took a few steps and were back on earth.

"It's been a week since I had this experience. Prior to it, when I thought of Jerome, I saw only that lifeless form. Now when I think of him, I see him in Jesus' arms, whole and complete. Now, although I feel the sadness of missing him, it is not with the same deep pain I had felt for months."

Epilogue: One week after receiving this vision, the Lord told Cheryl in her journal that He would give her another son. His first name would be Jason, which means "the healing one," and his middle name Matthew, meaning "God's gift." He also impressed Isaiah 61:1 into her mind: "The Spirit of the Lord God is upon me, because the Lord has anointed me to bring good news to the afflicted; He has sent me to bind up the brokenhearted, to proclaim liberty to captives, and freedom to prisoners."

Within a few weeks Cheryl realized that she was with child. The conception had occurred within a week of the vision the Lord had given her. Nine months later, Jason Matthew was born. God's promise of healing was fulfilled.

As we close this chapter on seeing in the Spirit the dreams and visions of God, let me suggest that you pause, take out a sheet of paper and ask, "God, what do You want to say to me concerning the use of the eyes of my heart? How have I used them? How would You like me to use them? What are Your thoughts concerning dream and vision?" Then relax and tune yourself to the spontaneous flow that will begin to bubble up within you. In faith, write down the thoughts that are coming to your mind. When the flow is over, go back and test them. Decide whether you feel they were from God. Share the results of your experiment with someone else. Find out their impressions.*

---

*For further reading, examine Appendix F, "Dreams and Visions Throughout Church History."

5

Journaling: Writing Out Our Dialogue With God

KEY #4

Journaling, writing out our prayers and God's answers, provides a great new freedom in hearing God's voice.

God is speaking to us all the time, but often we find it difficult to clearly distinguish His voice from our own thoughts. We doubt and question and never step out in faith to act upon His words. If there were a way to move beyond our doubts without throwing away our common sense, if we could receive in faith and still test the spirits, how much easier and greater would our fellowship with Father be! The simple technique I call journaling provides that way and has been the single greatest facilitator to my ongoing two-way dialogue and communion with God.

Journaling is simply writing out my prayers to God and what I believe His response is to me. It is a diary of my two-way dialogue with God.

When the concept of journaling was first revealed to me, I immediately went to the Word to see if it had any biblical foundation. By the time I finished my study, I was amazed at the Church's neglect of this biblical, helpful tool. The entire book of Psalms is really a journal. It is the record of man's prayers and often of God's responses. Repeatedly we hear David pouring out his heart to God, feeling alone and deserted and crying out for the divine presence. After such appeals the word *Selah* is often written in the text. *Selah* means a pause or a musical interlude. During this pause, David stilled himself and contacted his God. On the other side of the *Selah* there is a different, deeper level of faith. God had spoken to him and the entire tone of David's words reflected the result.

The books of the prophets are often a record of man's communication with the Lord or one of His messengers. Daniel received a dream and recorded it. He then asked for the interpretation and wrote down the reply. Habakkuk is another excellent example. The next chapter will be a more detailed study of his experience but we notice that in chapter one, Habakkuk cried out to God for understanding; chapters two and three are God's responses to his prayer.

The book of Revelation is another good example of biblical journaling. John recorded the visions he saw, the questions he asked, and the answers he received. "The Revelation of John" is the record of his spiritual communication.

Not all journaling was preserved as Scripture. A good illustration of the kind of journaling we are talking about is found in 1 Chronicles. When God gave the design of the temple to David, He gave it to him through journaling. "All this," said David, "the Lord made me understand in writing by His hand upon me, all the details of this pattern" (1 Chron. 28:19). However, this descriptive pattern was not laid out fully in Scripture. Our journaling that records our dialogue with God is similar to this. It is for a point of need in our lives and obviously will not be added to the Bible for future generations.

Benefits of Journaling

When I was first learning to hear the Lord's voice, I quieted myself within and without, pictured Jesus and waited patiently for an answer. A few words or phrases would often come to my mind, but my reaction was to immediately question whether they could be from God. I didn't want to be deceived by any counterfeits, so I wanted to carefully test everything I received. The only problem was that such testing is, in effect, doubt, and doubt jams my spiritual receiver. Therefore, I heard nothing more. He who comes to the Lord must come in faith. I had been in faith for about fifteen seconds, received three seconds of revelation and hung up the receiver through my doubt. This was a real problem for me. How could I receive in faith and still test what I was receiving?

Journaling provided the solution to my dilemma. Through journaling, I am able to write out my prayers and receive the Lord's answers in faith, writing down all He has to say. I can write paragraph after paragraph, even page after page. I can write for five minutes, ten minutes or even an hour. I do not have to be concerned with testing the revelation as I receive it because I have a clear, permanent record that can be examined and analyzed after the divine flow has ceased. Doubt can be set aside, without throwing away my common sense. My receiver can remain open and operative as long as necessary. Journaling has released me to enjoy a new dimension of communion with my Lord.

Another benefit of journaling is that it gives my busy brain something to do while I am receiving revelation. My mind is used to being in control of my life and it can become very upset when my heart starts to take over. It throws a tantrum and wants to know what's going on. It questions and doubts and does its best to stop my receiving the Holy Spirit's communication, wanting to return my attention to what it has to say. The use of vision helps control this onslaught, as does journaling. I can tell my mind to settle down and do something useful by recording the intuitive flow. By keeping my mind occupied, I can keep it from interrupting.

Habakkuk 2:2,3 indicates a third benefit of journaling. The Lord told Habakkuk to "record the vision...for the vision is yet for the appointed time...though it tarries, wait for it; for it will certainly come." God lives in timelessness, and sometimes He will indicate that what He says will happen soon. Our concept of soon, however, may be totally different than His. We think soon is tomorrow, or next week at the latest. He might mean next year! (Two thousand years ago He said, "Surely I come quickly" [Rev. 22:20]!)

If we have no record of His promise, our faith may fail and our hope disappear. When the appointed time comes, we will probably have forgotten much of His word to us. When we write down the revelation as we receive it, we can turn to it later whenever doubt creeps in. Through this, our faith will be renewed and our hope restored. And our record will stand as testimony of the faithfulness of God when He brings it to pass.

Journaling also helps us keep the message pure. Sometimes when the Lord is speaking, I get so excited that I misunderstand or misinterpret His meaning. I may want or expect a certain answer, and allow my desires to prevent me from clearly understanding what I hear. If I act on what I think I heard, I meet failure. But if I am able to return to my journal, I can find out why. The Lord will direct me back to what I originally received and I can see where I went wrong: the Lord did not fail me—I failed to understand Him. His words always come to pass; my interpretations do not.

Some Results of Journaling

As I dialogued with the Lord daily, our relationship deepened and changed. No longer did I think of God as the stern Judge waiting for me to make a mistake. I realized that He is tender and just and full of mercy. I began to understand His love, and as we spent time together I found myself becoming more like Him. I learned what true love is and began to express it toward my Lord and my family and friends. I learned to love because He first loved me. I experienced this one time while berating myself for my sin and telling God over and over how sorry I was. He simply said, "Mark, I've forgiven you." Finally, He said, "Mark, I've forgiven you—will you forgive yourself?" It hit me like a ton of bricks. Whipping and demeaning myself were not His plan at all. His desire is freely bestowed grace. I have found that nearly every other Christian who has tried journaling has also found that God is less judgmental than they thought Him to be.

I have also become more aware of my spirit and the movements of the Holy Spirit within me through journaling. I have begun to move from living out of my head to living out of my heart, from my soul to my spirit. I no longer need to live in fleshly reaction—I can move in response to the Lord's promptings from within. I am not successful all the time, but my ability and potential for growth have made a quantum leap.

In my journal, I find that God always talks to me about my attitudes. He speaks of my anger, my scorn, my judgment. He tells me to honor, to love, to receive. He's much more concerned about the attitudes that cause my sins than about the sins themselves, and He wants very much to heal those attitudes. He hates sin, but He always works to root out its causes, not just to end our wrong actions.

Journaling has helped bring greater balance into my life as well. Most of us tend toward extremism in some areas. Our eccentricity is often based on valid ideas or experiences. For example, in the Church there are all kinds of extremes, each built on a genuine truth. But often, because a particular group becomes excessive in its teaching or practice of this truth, other believers reject the truth along with the people.

I tend toward certain extremes because I want to have my spiritual journey neatly laid out in nice clear goals: step one, step two, step three. When something works for me, I have a tendency to seize it as a sure-fire technique. Vision is one such area. I am excited about the power and value of vision in spiritual communion. Therefore, I am tempted to present it as a formula for success.

Before teaching a class on vision one day, however, the Lord spoke to me: "Remember that vision is more than technique. It is Me, living, moving and doing things. It is seeing Me in motion. It is the fascination of watching with the eyes of the heart. Therefore, make it more than a tool. It is an encounter with Me. It is Me, nothing more, nothing less, just Me! Remember that the purpose of all of life, and of this course, is to bring people to Me. Do not become so technique-conscious that you forget the supreme purpose of it all: to be together with Me. I love you, Mark." Journaling is helping to bring balance to my analytical and intuitive natures, as well as to many other areas of my life.

Journaling can also help clarify our focus. When we are involved in a situation, we tend to lose our perspective and begin to focus on the wrong things, viewing people and events negatively, as if there were a deliberate attempt to hurt and destroy us. Hearing from God through journaling can help adjust our focus and see things as they really are.

This happened with a couple in my class who came to me with a problem. Their daughter had begun to develop poor attitudes and her grades were beginning to drop. In reaction, her parents had begun to nag and criticize her. They showed her very little love and soon their times of family prayer ceased. They began to view Cathy as their enemy, rather than flesh of their flesh.

We prayed together and I encouraged them to try journaling about the situation. As they did, the Lord gave Tom a vision. He saw the Lord come to him, put His arms around him, and tell him how much he was loved. Then the Lord instructed him to do the same to Cathy. Tom and Susan were asked to express Jesus' unconditional love and to live according to kingdom principles. They realized that Cathy was not their enemy, but a child of their love.

As they began to communicate to her through Christ, rather than try to handle the situation on their own, a dramatic change took place. Cathy's attitude improved. Her schoolwork became so much better that she received stars for excellence. Even her teacher commented on the change. They realized that it was just the beginning and continued thereafter in fellowship with the Lord. They restored family devotions and said prayers together with earnest sincerity, rather than out of habit. Tom and Susan received their daughter back because the Lord clarified their focus and restored a proper perspective.

A Few Practical Matters

Since I am meeting the Creator and Sustainer of my life in my prayer, I try to journal when I am in prime condition, rather than when I am overcome by the worries and cares of the world. For me, this time is early in the morning. There is a quiet then that helps me come to stillness. This was especially helpful when I first began to dialogue with God. Now that I have become more conscious of the stirrings in my spirit, it isn't difficult for me to commune anywhere. Jesus abided in the Father's presence even when the demands of five thousand people pressed in upon

Him. As I was beginning and learning, however, I wanted everything going for me I could find. Some people discover the middle of the night is best for them. Whatever time you choose, it should allow you to offer the best of yourself to the Lord.

When I began journaling, I used a simple, spiral-bound notebook. Now computers have become a wonderful asset to me since I find it easier to type than write, and typing allows me to close my eyes and stay focused on the inner vision as I write. One student found that his best time was as he traveled in his car. He keeps a tape recorder with him and prays aloud, then speaks out what he senses from the Lord.

The method is not important, except that it should reflect the value my journal has to me. I try not to write on napkins or scraps of paper. That would indicate that I didn't really place much importance on it, unless of course that was all that was available. If so, I transfer the words to my proper journal as soon as possible.

My written journals have "PRIVATE MATERIAL" written in large letters on the front and back. They are kept secluded, and some entries are even written in code. Computer journaling is password protected. As I bare my soul to the Lord and He counsels me, we deal with struggles that no one else knows about.

One such area for most people is sexuality. In my pastoral ministry, it has become clear to me that man is both intensely spiritual and intensely sexual. God wants to heal our sexuality. I realized as I kept my journal that the Lord and I were spending a great deal of time on that subject, so at the end of my first year I went back and tabulated exactly how much attention we had given to it.

I was shocked to count over fifty pages on sexuality. I hadn't thought I was in that bad shape! There were fifty pages on who I am as a sexual person and how to handle the pressures within.

As I spoke at a seminar concerning the private nature of such sections of our journals, and the need for privacy and codes, one man jokingly suggested putting someone else's name on the cover! I don't think I'm willing to advocate such an extreme measure, but I do know that as God heals our deep hurts and inner struggles, the material will be very private.

I begin each entry with the date and include everything that is important to my spiritual life. Besides my communion with God, I record my dreams and their interpretations, visions and images the Lord gives me, and personal events or feelings that touch me deeply. I talk about my angers and fears, hurts, anxieties and disappointments, joys and thanksgivings. My journal becomes a diary of my spiritual journey, the mountains and valleys, successes and failures. It becomes a personal memorial of my Lord's love and faithfulness every step of the way.

If there are people or issues God is calling me to pray for regularly, I will list these in the last couple of pages of my journal or in a special file, and refer to them often, praying through the lists as the Lord directs. Rather than being bound legalistically to these lists, I feel free to move through them as the Holy Spirit leads.

Journaling has provided a way for me to receive the edification, exhortation and comfort of the Holy Spirit. He has offered me the healing love and affirmation needed to lead me toward wholeness and self-acceptance. Particularly during the first several months, the entries in my journal were about my relationship with Jesus and my relationship with myself. I did not try to move into the spiritual gifts until I was convinced of the reality of my dialogue with God and comfortable in my ability to discern the Lord's voice.

Only after my spiritual senses had been sharpened through months of use did I begin to act upon words of wisdom and knowledge for others. I have found through my students that if we begin to cultivate the gifts too soon, before we have developed skill and confidence, the mistakes made can set us back so severely that it is difficult to press on. As a result, we can forfeit the great blessing of a deep love relationship with Jesus Christ, and the wholeness He wants to give us.

There were times during the first few years of journaling when I was tempted to give up and throw it all away. Sometimes I couldn't seem to get through to Jesus. Other times the words seemed to be more from myself than from Him. And sometimes I acted upon what I believed was a word from the Lord, only to be disappointed when the result was not what I had hoped for.

Each of us reaches such plateaus in our spiritual life. But when we are tempted to stop trying, we must keep pressing on. We must be committed to going on, even when we feel we are without faith and it doesn't seem worth the effort. Because I kept on with my journal even when I didn't really feel like it, I am now able to live out of an inner dialogue. I recognize my Shepherd's voice and can receive it in faith, even without always writing it down. Of course, I do continue to journal but it is no longer as necessary as it was when I was first learning.

We need to accept the fact that whenever we learn a new skill, we will try and fail a number of times before we become proficient at it. It was true of learning to talk, learning to ride a bike, learning to spell, learning to speak in public, and pretty much everything new. There is no such thing as being perfect from the first try and never making a mistake. Therefore, I think we need to take this attitude to journaling. There will be times of stumbling, falling, and getting back up again. And that is okay! There is no other way to learn a new skill. And this takes some of the pressures off the journaling experience.

A lady at one of my seminars was not receiving anything during the journaling time. She said afterward that she didn't want to write anything down until she was absolutely sure it was the Lord. I encouraged her to relax and try to be free to make some mistakes. She did, and found to her amazement that God was indeed speaking to her through her journal. Practice does make perfect, but if we are too afraid to practice, we will probably never become perfect.

Another person was reluctant to write down what she was receiving because she was not a good speller and her grammar was imperfect. I promise you—God doesn't care! Grammar and spelling are irrelevant in your journal! This is not a test! Don't let something as unimportant as your language skills keep you from a fulfilling relationship with your Lord!

So relax; get comfortable; put a smile on your face! Don't take yourself so seriously, and begin the experiment. You will be amazed at what begins flowing within you. God is there for all to receive, especially His children. Let's become as children and go for it. I promise that you will not be disappointed.

Journaling is a learning tool to help us develop our skill in discerning inner sensations. It aids us in becoming more sensitive to the spontaneous flow of thoughts in our hearts. Once skilled in identifying and capturing this flow, most people find communion with God easy even without journaling.

As we walk and talk with God throughout the day we gradually begin abiding in Christ. After I had learned to dialogue with God, He called me to learn to abide in His presence even when I was not journaling. Not that I have stopped journaling, but now I realize that encounter with God goes far beyond the limits of my journal. It can occur anywhere, at any time, through many means. Journaling is just one of those ways, but it was the technique that opened up the way to a deeper relationship with the Lord.

Automatic Writing?

Let me close this section with two common questions. One is, "What about automatic writing? Isn't that demonic and essentially the same thing as journaling?"

Yes, in my estimation, automatic writing is demonic. However, it is not the same experience as journaling. It is satan's counterfeit to the true experience we see demonstrated in the Bible. In journaling, an idea is birthed in the heart, registered in the mind, and then written with the hand. In automatic writing, a spirit simply takes control of an individual's limp hand, and begins moving it around. Neither the heart nor the mind is used in this experience. Nor is the person focused on Christ, but simply open and passive, available to whomever or whatever. He is therefore a prime candidate for demonic influence.

To Whom Do We Pray?

I have also been asked, and I have asked the Lord, to whom are we to pray? Is it the Father, or is it the Son? Technically, I believe we are to pray to the Father, through the Son, by the working of the Holy Spirit. The entire Trinity is thus involved in our prayer.

On the other hand, John 15 calls us to abide in Christ, to live in Him. I believe that a part of living in Jesus involves dialoguing with Him, and that when I look for a vision of the Godhead, He is the image that often appears (Col. 1:15). I find that when I pray with authority I tend to address the Father, and that when establishing intimacy and friendship I generally commune with Jesus. When in corporate worship, or beginning a class, I often speak to the Holy Spirit, inviting Him to manifest His presence among us.

I have asked the Lord about this, and He has confirmed that it is most proper to pray to Him, through the Son, by the working of the Holy Spirit. However, He has also said that since the three are one, He will also honor my prayer when Jesus and I talk. After all, Jesus only speaks the words which the Father has spoken (Jn. 8:28,38).

In considering 1 John 1:3 and 2 Corinthians 13:14 we find that the Bible tells us we may fellowship with the Father, the Son, or the Holy Spirit: "Indeed our fellowship is with the Father, and with His Son Jesus Christ;" "The grace of the Lord Jesus Christ, and the love of God, and the fellowship of the Holy Spirit, be with you all." And really, that is the essence of journaling—to have fellowship with our triune God.

Now, why not try journaling? Take a pencil and paper and quiet yourself before the Lord. Talk to Him about what is on your mind. Let Him speak back and record what He says. If you don't sense a response, ask Him a specific question. Relax and in simple, childlike faith, write down what seems to be there. You will discover that it is Him.

Habakkuk is an example of a prophet who used all four keys in clearly discerning God's voice.

1. He tuned to inner spontaneous impression.

2. He stilled himself before the Lord.

3. He used vision.

4. He wrote out his prayer and God's response.

Habakkuk: Putting It All Together

Allow me to more fully share with you my first journaling experience in 1979. I was facing a problem with a rebellious teenage girl who was living with our family. Judy (not her real name) had been breaking the house rules and I felt it was time to confront her. I planned to tell her that these were the rules and if she wanted to live with us, she would have to follow them. If she didn't like it, she would have to leave. She was still at school so I went to my study to pray while waiting for her.

The concept of journaling had just been introduced to me so I thought I would give it a try. I had grown up on a dairy farm where there were several wells, so the setting in John 4 was comfortable to me. I pictured myself, like the woman of Samaria, sitting with Jesus on the edge of the well, our feet hanging over the edge. I looked at Jesus and He had such a loving presence. I only saw Him from the shoulders down, but I could clearly sense His love and acceptance.

I had the impression that I should pray about specific things, so I asked, "Lord, what about Judy?" I closed my eyes and looked intently at the vision of Jesus, and as I watched He moved, like you do when you are speaking. At the same moment, a thought came into my mind: "Love unconditionally!" I thought that sounded good, so I opened my eyes and wrote it down. I closed my eyes and looked at Him again. "Lord, do You want to say anything else?" I asked. This time He did not move, but again a spontaneous thought entered my mind. "She is very insecure."

That was all I received, but as I looked at Him again I thought, "This is remarkable!" Those thoughts had not come from me. I had my own ideas on how to handle Judy: firmness and love, but mostly firmness! My journal was saying to express mostly love. I'm not saying that this is always the right way to handle rebellion and disobedience, but for that particular girl, in that particular situation, it was the right thing to do.

So I acted on the word I had received. Instead of blasting her with condemnation, I had a very loving talk with her. I expressed our love and acceptance and concern for her. And there was no explosion or negative reaction such as might have come if I had handled it my way. Judy remained with us for over a year longer, growing as part of our family. What I had seen as rebellion, Jesus, looking deeper, had seen as insecurity.

As I saw the results of acting on the words in my journal, I began to think it must be God speaking through it, so I began experimenting. Each morning during my devotions I spent some time praying with journaling. And day by day I received such wise words, words concerned with motives and attitudes rather than surface issues, that the conviction grew that I was indeed hearing from God.

During those first couple of weeks I took much of what I was receiving in my journal and shared it with my wife and my co-elders, asking if they thought it was the Lord. They all confirmed that they felt it was. I believe this outside confirmation is absolutely essential, particularly when we are just beginning to hear God's voice in this way. I ask that as each of you begin journaling, you share your initial entries with at least two spiritual people whose advice and counsel you trust. These people do not have to be pastors, but you should feel comfortable looking to them for spiritual leadership.

By submitting your journaling for outside confirmation, you will quickly gain confidence in this new venture. As time goes on and you become experienced, you will only need to share journaling that calls for major directional moves. I'll cover this in more detail in the chapter on spiritual advisors.

Needless to say, my first few days of journaling stand as one of the dramatic milestones of my spiritual life. It was unbelievable! I was actually beginning to dialogue with Almighty God! My years of searching were being rewarded. At last I had found the voice of God within my heart. Along with my salvation and baptism in the Holy Spirit, this was one of the most significant turning points of my entire Christian walk. I sensed in my heart that this would totally revolutionize my Christian experience. Writing from this vantage point of many years later, I can confirm that every area of my life has been radically affected by my ability to dialogue with God. I now live guided by the inner voice of the Spirit of God within my heart. He gives me direction on a daily basis.

Habakkuk's Experience

Habakkuk was a prophet who not only heard the voice of God, but also told us how he did so. I am a "how-to" man, so I was especially blessed by what I read. I found that Habakkuk used each of the elements that we have been discussing in the last four chapters.

In chapter one of his little book, the prophet cried out to God about the injustices of the world around him. In chapter two, verses one through three, he prepared himself to hear the Lord's reply:

> *I will stand on my guard post*
>
> *And station myself on the rampart;*
>
> *And I will keep watch to see what He will speak to me,*
>
> *And how I may reply when I am reproved.*
>
> *Then the Lord answered me and said,*
>
> *"Record the vision*
>
> *And inscribe it on tablets,*
>
> *That the one who reads it may run.*
>
> *For the vision is yet for the appointed time;*
>
> *It hastens toward the goal, and it will not fail.*
>
> *Though it tarries, wait for it;*
>
> *For it will certainly come, it will not delay."*

We considered these verses briefly already, but I want to examine them more fully now, because they are such a fitting summary of all I have said.

First, Habakkuk had a place to get alone and quiet himself when he wanted to hear from God. This is Key #1: going to a quiet place and learning to quiet ourselves in the presence of our Lord. I learned to get away to my study and still myself in the Lord's presence. The best way for me to do this is by worshiping with my autoharp and singing in the Spirit. This quiets my outer being, and my inner self becomes poised before the Lord. I urge you to use whatever is most conducive to quieting your own spirit before the Lord. Some other ideas include listening to worship music, devotional Bible study, walking through nature, and sitting by a stream, to name just a few.

The second key is that Habakkuk kept watch to see what the Lord would speak to him. How many of you noticed he said that wrong? Wouldn't it make much more sense to say, "I listened to hear"? However, Habakkuk's insight opened up a whole new dimension to seeing in the spirit for me. I learned to look with the eyes of my heart as I prayed to see what God wanted to show me in the spirit. I used my imagination, inwardly picturing myself talking with Jesus in a comfortable setting. And sometimes I just looked to see, and immediately the Spirit's revelation was there. It doesn't matter who initiates my vision, just as it doesn't matter who initiates my prayers or my worship. What is important is that I contact the Spirit Who is joined to my spirit and follow Him where He leads.

The use of vision has several powerful effects on my heart and mind. First, it raises my faith, which opens me to the inner flow. Second, it keeps my mind occupied and out of the way. My mind is quite prone to jump into the middle of my prayer time and distract me. Better to get it to work with me as a facilitator rather than against me as a deterrent to my prayer life.

The third key Habakkuk gives us is that he tuned himself to the Lord's voice. He knew what it sounds like: "Then the Lord answered me and said…." Obviously Habakkuk could discern the Lord's voice in his heart, which we have seen generally sounds like a flow of spontaneous thoughts. Therefore, when I tune to the sound of God's voice I tune to spontaneity. The Lord begins to speak to me by His Spirit (1 Cor. 2:9,10), which is in union with my spirit (1 Cor. 6:17). His words are registered in my mind as unmeditated, spontaneous thoughts and impressions. I am able to distinguish His spontaneous thoughts from my own analytical thoughts, and so, we are able to converse.

The fourth and final key we observe Habakkuk demonstrating is writing down his dialogue with Almighty God. "Record the vision and inscribe it on tablets, that the one who reads it may run." As we saw in the last chapter, journaling is a dominant theme of Scripture, with hundreds of chapters demonstrating the process, and God over and over commanding it. Therefore, I began journaling. Writing helps keep my mind busy and useful, and gives me a record to help me keep my focus and provide a reminder of God's words to stimulate my faith and obedience later on.

In this way, the Lord showed me that the process I was experiencing in my morning devotions was very biblical, and easily demonstrated in the prophet Habakkuk's prayer life. In addition, John used the exact same process in Revelation 1:10,11. Habakkuk and John used four elements to dialogue with God:

1. Becoming still;
2. Tuning to spontaneity and *rhema*;
3. Using vision;
4. Journaling.

I, too, have found all four elements vital to my communion with the Lord. Just one, or two, or even three are not enough. I urge everyone who wants to move into this dimension of spiritual encounter to *commit yourself to experiment using these four elements* for a period of time. As a package of four together they work very well—so well that I can promise they will work for you!

Helpful Hints

Let me give you a couple of other thoughts that may help as you begin journaling. When I come to prayer desiring to hear God's voice, I no longer look and listen to the things that are outside me—I look inwardly to my spirit. I do not expect to hear God outside me, speaking from heaven, but rather from within me, speaking from my heart.

If I pause in my journaling and wait for a new thought or the right word, my mind is very quickly tempted to step in and fill the space with its own meditated, cognitive ideas. If allowed to do so, it may rush ahead of the Spirit, and result in impurity of revelation. Rather than let that happen, I focus my mind on a vision of Jesus. As I do, and for a moment wait quietly, His thought or word soon comes.

When you finish a journaling entry, you may notice that the spontaneous thoughts in your journal are similar to the thoughts you had before you began. I do not reject my journaling when that happens, and automatically assume that it was just me. Instead, I realize that because of the ease of communication, because the Holy Spirit is joined to my spirit, I was already picking up God's thoughts before I began journaling. (That is assuming, of course, that the journaling entry passes the tests given earlier in this book.)

Sometimes the Lord's word doesn't come to pass the way I expect it to. When this happens, I have found that I can ask Him why not and that He will tell me. The two most common reasons are that I have misinterpreted what He said, or the free will of another person was involved in the situation.

Don't Ask for Dates!

Another big step of clarity in my journaling came when I stopped asking God for dates of when things would happen. I have found that the dates I thought I received in the past were always wrong, and I think they came more from my own heart than the mind of the Lord. As I sought for understanding on this issue, I have come to two conclusions. First, the desire for specific knowledge such as dates can be related to the human tendencies that lead to witchcraft. It is a desire for knowledge that is not available through normal human senses. It can be a craving for power or control. God is much more interested in nurturing our faith in Him, and His response to specific questions about the future will more often than not be, "Trust Me."

On the other hand, the Bible does say that the Lord does nothing without revealing it to His prophets (Amos 3:7), so there are some people who will receive accurate information about the future from the Lord. These will almost always be individuals who have the *office* of prophet in the Church, individuals who are especially gifted by God as seers. Though we "can all prophesy" (1 Cor. 14:31), we do not all have the office of prophet, and therefore our skills and abilities will not all be the same.

Journaling is becoming a very popular exercise, especially in the secular world. It is an effective means of drawing out whatever is inside of you. Because of this popularity, some people in the Church resist it and reject its value to the believer. I think, however, that knowing that journaling is a way to reveal our inner man should make it especially valuable to the Christian, because Jesus Christ lives within us! Through journaling we are able to contact Him in a new way, drawing on His character and His Spirit to mold our lives. What an exciting opportunity!

It Takes Work

When Oral Roberts, the popular American healing evangelist, was asked how to go about learning to hear God speak, he replied, "Wanting to badly enough to work on it." In other words, you must have an earnest desire to hear the Lord's voice. If you can take it or leave it, if the longing for communion doesn't burn within you, there are enough roadblocks to prevent you from getting through to the other side of silence. For example, things deep inside us we didn't know were there will surface. If we are not willing to face them, we will reach a dead end. We must be committed to choosing communion rather than law, relationship instead of rules, supernatural life above natural.

The inner world is complex, and learning to relate to it will take time and effort. Most of us spent at least twelve years in school learning to successfully function in the physical world. Are we willing to devote one or two years to be trained by the Holy Spirit? The Lord called me to devote one year of my life to learning to hear His voice. That was all I tried to accomplish in my spiritual life during that year. All my efforts were focused on that one goal. And at the end of that year, the Lord commissioned me to take the next full year to learn to abide in His presence. Because I recognized the Spirit's voice, I was able to learn to remain tuned to it and function out of His intuitive direction as I walked among men.

Just as learning to walk entailed stumbling, falling, and trying again, so too does the spiritual walk. As each of my children began the process of learning to walk, I was amazed at their determination. No matter how often they fell or how many bruises they collected, they would not give up. Walking was better than crawling, and they didn't stop trying before they had it mastered. We will have to have the same conviction that relationship is much better than law if we are going to pick ourselves up when we make a mistake.

Confirming Testimonies

While searching for the key that would help me discern the Lord's voice, I read many books on the subject. At the time, I wasn't able to recognize the clues given in them. But after I was moving in spiritual dialogue, I returned to those books and repeatedly found confirming testimony of my own experience. This was very important to me, because I do not want to be guilty of teaching anything that cannot be confirmed by respected leaders in the Church. I found three points established by many sources:

1. God's voice often comes as a spontaneous thought or impression;

2. The inner eye is used by God to give us pictures;

3. Writing down these things is often important.

Following are a few representative statements drawn from Douglas Wead's excellent book entitled *Hear His Voice*: "An impression came to me...." "In my mind I saw a girl sitting at the table...." "I jotted down my thoughts."

In an article in *Charisma* in October 1981, Larry Tomczak was asked how spontaneous revelation actually comes. He replied, "1) Pictures. God often spoke to prophets through *pictures* or *visions*. He may *plant* a picture in your mind.... 2) Scripture. God speaks through specific Bible verses which come to mind. He may *impress* a part of a verse or even a reference upon your mind. 3) A word. God may bring to your mind a specific word or piece of advice that did not come as a result of a detailed thought process. It was more *spontaneous* and given *as if dropped into your mind.* The thoughts that come from the Lord in this way are usually *unpremeditated* and spontaneous in character and come more *in a flash*, without a logical sequence; whereas, when we are consciously thinking, or even daydreaming, we usually connect our thoughts with one another" (emphasis added).

John Patrick Grace quoted a number of respected Christian leaders in his book, ***Hearing His Voice*** (Ave Maria Press, 1979). Oral Roberts stated that sometimes God's voice comes as "an inner audible voice." Sometimes it comes as "words imprinted more quietly on my spirit." And sometimes it is simply "deep impressions." Dr. Roberts has received numerous visions from the Lord, and has copied down the words he received when instructed to by the Lord.

Francis MacNutt declared, "The way my guidance comes…is intuitive. Gut feelings. Instincts." Ben Kinchlow, of the Christian Broadcasting Network, said, "When God speaks to me in the Spirit, His voice translates itself into thought concepts that I can conceive in my mind. So when I say, 'I heard the Lord,' or 'The Lord spoke to me,' I mean He spoke to me through a feeling in my spirit that was translated into a thought in my mind. And the thought immediately brings with it what young people call 'a rush.' It's something that hits you as right."

According to Glen Clark, founder of Camps Farthest Out, the lost art of Jesus is His use of imagination. He wrote in ***The Soul's Sincere Desire***, "Jesus looked at reality through the lens of divine imagination. The imagination is the power we all possess of seeing harmonies, unities and beauties in things where the non-imaginative minds sees nothing but discords, separations, ugliness. The imagination of man is but the window or door which, when thrown open, lets the divine life stream into our lives."

Words such as these by respected men of God with a well-known ability to hear God's voice give me encouragement to continue using the tools of spontaneous thought, vision and writing as means of establishing communion with the Lord.

I want to challenge you to begin using these four elements in your prayer: becoming still; tuning to spontaneity; vision; and journaling. Try them at least twice a week, as an experiment, for the next three months. Go in faith, and allow God the opportunity of speaking to you in the first person. Set aside your doubts for just three months, then go back and examine the results. I am convinced that if you do you will be persuaded that you are truly contacting the Holy Spirit and dialoguing with Almighty God.

Will you give Him a chance to be your Friend?

6

Biblical Patterns for Approaching God

The tools of becoming still, tuning to spontaneity, seeing God's visions, and journaling brought great release in my communion with the Lord. Through them I was able to dialogue with Him most of the time. However, there were still occasions when I couldn't seem to get through to the Lord. I just wasn't able to make spiritual contact. I was confused and couldn't understand why this should be so. I knew I should tune my heart to His voice, but no one ever told me where to find the tuning dial! After struggling a long time, the Lord reminded me of the approach He laid out for those who seek His direct presence. This approach is pictured in the Tabernacle of Moses.

The Tabernacle is a very important subject in the Bible. There are more than fifty complete chapters speaking only about it. That is more than the total number of chapters in the gospels of Matthew and Mark together! That tells me that the Tabernacle is very important to God. It was vital to the Jews as a representation of God's presence and His plan for Israel to approach Him. It is significant to us too, as a copy, a shadow, and a pattern of heavenly things, as Hebrews 8:5 indicates. The Tabernacle also illustrates the preparations we need to make if we want to enter God's presence. My study of it, therefore, provided me with the tuning dial I had long sought.

The three parts of the Tabernacle each correspond to the three-fold nature of man. The Outer Court signifies the body, the Holy Place illustrates man's soul, and the Holy of Holies represents man's spirit. Within the Tabernacle there were six pieces of furniture and I have found that each represents an aspect of my approach to God.

The Outer Court

The Outer Court was a large open area surrounding the tent which housed the Holy Place and the Holy of Holies. It received the natural light of the sun and moon. This Outer Court corresponds to man's body, where we receive knowledge through our five physical senses.

In the Outer Court there were two pieces of furniture: the brazen altar and the laver. The brazen altar stood directly in front of the gate. It was there that lambs were sacrificed to atone for the sins of the people. This altar could not be bypassed. When seeking the presence of the Lord, we have to stop at the brazen altar and perform the proper sacrifice.

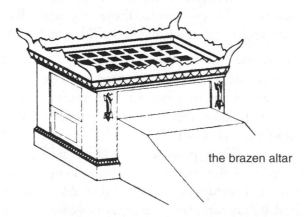

the brazen altar

*Permission to reproduce the drawings in this chapter has been graciously given by the G. T. Luscombe Company. They sell a set of twelve full-color transparencies of the Tabernacle and its furniture which can be ordered from your local Christian bookstore or directly from G.T. Luscombe Company. Inc. (P.O. Box 622, Frankford, IL 60425).

The brazen altar represents the cross, directly inside the gate of salvation. It signifies both our initial commitment to make Jesus the Lord of our lives, and the daily offering of ourselves as living sacrifices, holy and acceptable unto God (Rom. 12:1,2). Just as He offered Himself as a sacrifice for us, Jesus now asks us to offer ourselves for Him. Paul said, "I have been crucified with Christ" (Gal. 2:20).

Often we are tempted to shy away from the brazen altar. We want to avoid it if at all possible because it is hot! It means death to our flesh. It means laying down what we want and desiring only His will. This must be experienced daily. We cannot go around it. If we come to our journals and have not laid down our wills, the only voice that will come from our spirits will be our own. We will only hear our heart saying what it wants. We might then hold up our journals and say, "See, God said I could have three Cadillacs!" But it will only be our voice, not the Lord's. We must recognize the lordship of Jesus Christ in our lives if we want to experience true fellowship with Him.

The second piece of furniture in the Outer Court was the laver. This was a circular bowl where the priests washed themselves after sacrificing the lambs. It had two levels so they could wash their hands and feet. The material used was the highly polished brass that women used for mirrors.

the laver

The laver represents the Word of God. In Ephesians, Paul spoke of our being washed by water with the Word. The *Logos* has a cleansing effect upon our lives. Defilements of the flesh are washed away when we act in obedience to the clear commands of Scripture. It doesn't take any special revelation to understand and obey God's commandments. We don't need to call a prayer meeting to discern the meaning of "Do not commit murder." In the Outer Court God speaks to us through our natural senses. Our minds are well able to understand the commandments of Christ, and as we obey them our lives are cleansed and become more like our Master.

James likened those who hear the Word and do not obey it to a man who looks at his face in a mirror and soon afterward forgets what he looks like. That is why it is significant that the laver was formed from the mirrors donated by the Israelite women—it represents to us the Word, which reveals the defilements within us. Just as a mirror is useful only if we act on what it reveals, so we must act on the Word of God if it is to be effective in our lives.

The Holy Place

Within the perimeters of the Outer Court stood a beautifully woven tent that housed the Holy Place and the Holy of Holies. The Holy Place corresponds to our soul. The walls were several layers thick. The innermost layer was of fine, twisted linen of blue, purple and scarlet, with pictures of cherubim woven into it. This was covered with a curtain of goats' hair. Over it was a covering of red-dyed rams' and porpoises' skin. No natural light was able to penetrate the tent.

Within the Holy Place were three pieces of furniture: the table of shewbread, the seven-branched lampstand, and the altar of incense. The table of shewbread stood to the right as one entered the Holy Place. This table was only two and a half feet high and completely overlaid with gold. Twelve small cakes of unleavened bread and utensils made of pure gold were placed on it. The cakes remained on the table for one week, after which they were eaten by Aaron and his sons.

As the flour was finely ground to make the unleavened bread, so our wills must be finely ground as we totally commit ourselves to the Lord. Eating together, like the priests, represents the fellowship and communion we find within the Body of Christ. "As iron sharpens iron, so one man sharpens another" (Prov. 27:17). Our Christian relationships grind down our wills. Self and self-will give way to the give-and-take of a committed love relationship between brothers.

Jesus wants our strong self-will destroyed and our hearts committed to His lordship. Only when we have surrendered our "right" of self-determination, and when our desire is truly only to do His will, can we hear His voice with purity of heart.

The ornately crafted seven-branched lampstand stood directly across from the table of shewbread, on the left side of the Holy Place. It was formed from beaten gold and its flames were fueled by oil. This lampstand provided the only light for the Holy Place.

table of shewbread

the lampstand

The lampstand represents our mind, which is illumined by the Holy Spirit as we study the Word. The beaten gold indicates the cultivation of our minds. As the gold was formed and shaped into the proper design, so our thought patterns are formed under the illumination of the Holy Spirit. He can speak through them, aligning and perfecting them.

The book of Luke was written in this way. Luke stated, "Inasmuch as many have undertaken to compile an account of the things accomplished among us...it seemed fitting for me as well, having investigated everything carefully from the beginning, to write it out for you in consecutive order...so that you might know the exact truth about the things you have been taught" (Lk. 1:1-4). In other words, Luke carefully studied everything he could find about Jesus, analyzed and organized it under the illumination of the Holy Spirit, and wrote down the result of his work.

I usually prepare my sermons this way. After carefully searching out every Scripture on a subject, I organize the material into an outline. All of the investigation, analysis and reasoning are done in dependence upon the Spirit. He breathes into my mind His wisdom and knowledge.

The illumination of the Word has happened to almost every Christian. While studying the Bible, a verse suddenly seems to stand out, its meaning and application to life crystal clear. In the same way, we can learn to depend on the Spirit's breath in all of our thought processes. He can guide our reasoning and help us form godly, wise conclusions. As we submit our minds to Jesus Christ, the oil of the Holy Spirit illumines every thought. I have learned to allow intuition and spontaneity to flow into my reasoning processes, thereby allowing my heart and mind to work together, like the seven-branched lampstand.

The final piece of furniture in the Holy Place was the altar of incense, which stood directly in front of the door to the Holy of Holies. Each side of the altar had equal dimensions and it was overlaid with pure gold. Incense was offered twice daily on this altar, so that the fragrant smoke was constantly rising into the nostrils of God.

The three faculties of the soul are the mind, will and emotions. The table of shewbread illustrates Jesus' lordship over our will. The lampstand represents His lordship over our mind. And the altar of incense stands for the lordship of Jesus over our emotions.

The four-square aspect of the altar indicates an emotional life that is perfectly balanced. Such an emotional balance is difficult in the face of all the pressures of life. We often swing from optimism to pessimism, from faith to fear, from joy to despair. There is really only one way that our emotional life can be brought to, and remain in, balance. That way is Jesus, and our approach to Him is through worship, praise and thanksgiving.

Paul told us to give thanks in everything. In every situation, God is worthy of our praise. And through the continual offering of a sacrifice of praise, our emotions will be brought under the control of the Holy Spirit. Only He can bring us to balance.

the altar of incense

The psalmist declared that we should enter God's gates with thanksgiving and His courts with praise (Ps. 100:4). Worship, praise and thanksgiving are necessary parts of our approach to God. The horns of the altar, which were the highest points in the Holy Place, were the same height as the furniture in the Holy of Holies. Worship thus lifts us and moves us into the Holy of Holies, which represents man's spirit. Praise and worship are the best way to quiet our hearts and touch Christ within.

The Holy of Holies

A beautiful veil separated the holy place from the Holy of Holies. The Ark of the Covenant was the only piece of furniture in this inner room. There was no provision for light in the Holy of Holies. Like our spirits, it was completely dark unless the glorious light of the Lord's Presence filled it.

The Holy of Holies represents our spirits, where we can have direct communion with the Lord. In the Old Covenant, only the high priest was permitted to go through the veil, and only once a year, on the Day of Atonement. When Jesus died on the cross, the veil separating us from God's direct presence was torn from top to bottom, opening the way for each of us to have moment-by-moment fellowship with Almighty God.

The Ark of the Covenant was a chest made of acacia wood overlaid with pure gold. Within it were placed the tablets on which the Ten Commandments were written, Aaron's rod that budded, and a jar of manna (Heb. 9:4). The cover of the Ark was called the mercy seat. Over it, two cherubim fashioned of pure gold stood facing each other, their wings spread upward to cover the mercy seat. Moses and Aaron knelt before the Ark and God spoke to them from the mercy seat between the cherubim. Thus the Ark provided a *picture* of God's presence for the priests to focus upon as they came to meet with Him.

The manna in the Ark was a reminder of God's supernatural provision. As we wait in the presence of the Lord and receive direct revelation from Him within our spirits, supernatural life and strength flow up from deep within, strengthening us to face victoriously the trials of life. His divine life flows through us and out from us to meet the needs of a hurting world.

Aaron's rod that budded was a divine attestation of his God-given authority. God's word gives us authority. When we meet face to face with our Father as Moses did, when we hear His Spirit speak to our spirit, and when we speak forth what we have heard, our words ring with divine authority.

The Ten Commandments represent the law of God, the standard of holiness needed to meet with Him. When we come to God, we come to perfect holiness. But remember what has been placed above the law: the mercy seat. Jesus Christ has made atonement for our sins. Through His blood we are cleansed and made pure so that we can have fellowship with the Holy One. We receive access to boldly come before the throne of grace.

The book of Revelation was written out of a Holy of Holies experience. While in the Spirit, John received direct spiritual revelation as visions he then recorded.

ark of the covenant

We have seen that the Lord can speak to our natural senses through the clear commands of Scripture. As we offer our minds to Him, the Holy Spirit can illumine our thoughts, giving us supernatural wisdom and insight. And we can receive direct revelation from the Holy Spirit to our spirits. Each of these experiences is extremely valuable. We do not set aside the Bible because God speaks to us Spirit to spirit. If anything, our love for the Word will grow as we spend time with the Lord, and we seek to learn more about our Father and to test His revelation.

There is nothing about having spiritual encounters that makes us better than anyone else. In fact, all kinds of revelation are available to all believers. When the Holy Spirit speaks to our hearts, it says nothing about how spiritual we are, only about how loving and gracious He is.

I do not follow the procedure of the Tabernacle every time I come to pray. I always try to live my life in line with the requirements represented by each piece of furniture. But when

I have trouble hearing from the Lord, when my prayers seem to bounce off the ceiling and echo in the room, I come to the Tabernacle to find out why. I do this by seeing myself before each piece of furniture, and asking the Lord to speak to me through it. I usually find the reason for the communication breakdown by the time I enter the Holy of Holies. By this wonderful tool, I am able to tune my heart once again to hear what the Lord wants to say to me.

The Tabernacle is a means to help us see the condition of our hearts. We use it to accomplish our goal, which is to live in day-to-day, moment-by-moment fellowship with our Lord and Savior, Jesus Christ.

Let me encourage you to try the following journaling exercise as you finish this section. Using vision, present yourself before each piece of tabernacle furniture, and ask God to speak to you concerning the experience of it at this time in your life. Then record what He says.

1. *altar*—Am I a living sacrifice?

2. *laver*—Have I washed myself by applying the Word?

3. *shewbread*—Is my will ground fine before God? Am I walking in love and fellowship with the Body of Christ?

4. *lampstand*—Is God illuminating my mind and granting me revelation as I study the Word?

5. *incense*—Am I offering a continual sacrifice of praise and thanksgiving before my Lord?

6. *ark*—Do I stand quietly before His immediate presence and receive His words into my heart?

Be careful to quiet yourself in the Lord's presence before you begin journaling, so that you get His thoughts rather than your own. You will be able to tell the difference easily. Your thoughts will be very preachy—His will be very loving and gentle. Let His words come to you in the first person. Have a clear vision of yourself kneeling before each piece of furniture, and see Jesus standing there speaking to you. Write down the gentle spontaneous flow that bubbles up from within your heart. For confirmation and encouragement share it with a friend or two. Ask them if they feel it is from the Lord.

By the New and Living Way

Discovering the place of the Tabernacle experience in my prayer life enabled me to tune my heart to hear the Lord much more consistently and through it I could usually discover the reason for any inability I had to break through to dialogue with God.

Still, occasionally I presented myself before each piece of furniture, asking Jesus to reveal any failure to live according to the principle represented by it, and found myself going all the way into the Holy of Holies without being convicted, yet I was unable to enter into dialogue and fellowship with the Father. As I was pondering Hebrews 10:19-22, I saw how God has provided further fine-tuning to zero in on His voice. Since discovering and applying this passage to my prayer life, not a single day has gone by that I have been unable to make spirit-to-Spirit contact with my Lord.

Hebrews 10:19-22

We have confidence to enter the holy place by the blood of Jesus, by a new and living way which He inaugurated for us through the veil, that is, His flesh, and since we have a great priest over the house of God, let us draw near with a sincere heart in full assurance of faith, having our hearts sprinkled clean from an evil conscience and our bodies washed with pure water.

It is clear from the reference to going "through the veil" that the writer was referring to our entering the Holy of Holies.

This veil hung within the tent, separating the Holy Place from the Holy of Holies. The Greek text does not include the word "place" as used in the New American Standard Version in verse 19. The original simply reads "the holies." The writer of Hebrews was discussing the new and living way Jesus has provided for us to come into direct communion and relationship with our Father.

Full Assurance of Faith

The first phrase the Lord directed me to was, *"let us draw near...in full assurance of faith."* Lack of faith is the number one reason why I do not hear the Lord. Sometimes it is hard to believe that God is even present and I doubt that He cares enough about insignificant me to want to spend time talking with me. Or I am not convinced that it is really the Lord Who is speaking through my journal. Every time I come to Him in doubt, I receive nothing. "He who comes to God must believe that He is, and that He is a rewarder of those who seek Him" (Heb. 11:6). I must believe that the Lord loves me and desires to communicate with me even more than I want to speak to Him.

The remedy is to engage in activities that build your faith. You should choose those that are most effective for you. Singing and worshiping in the Spirit nearly always lift my faith level to where I am able to draw near to God. I wholeheartedly offer a sacrifice of praise until my entire being is convinced again of His goodness and mercy.

My level of faith rises when I use vision and see with the eyes of my heart the spiritual reality of Christ with me. The Bible is very clear that, through the working of the Holy Spirit, Christ is present with every believer. I may reread some Bible promises, especially those referring to God's love and desire to have fellowship with man.

Faith is also released when I go back through my journal and read again what the Lord has spoken. Especially when just starting to journal, another powerful tool in building faith is sharing your journal entries with someone you respect in the Lord, and asking him if he believes what you have received is from the Lord or not. It is much easier for someone removed from the situation to discern whether the entry is from God or from you. If you are a committed, Word-filled believer, you will nearly always find that this other person confirms that the journaling entry is from God. This will inspire your faith.

And finally, I sometimes simply take a leap of faith, abandoning myself to Him Who is faithful. I make a decision to believe with all of my heart all that God says. I pour out my heart fully and completely to Him. Then I begin writing down anything I receive, even if it is only one or two words. I remind myself that I can accept in faith whatever comes, because I will later be able to submit it to testing. And God is always there, waiting to meet with me, speak to me, and share His love with me.

A Clean Conscience

The next phrase the Lord spoke to me was *"let us draw near…having our hearts sprinkled clean from an evil conscience."* Sometimes as I quieted myself for prayer, my mind was filled with the guilt of an unconfessed sin. No matter how I tried to ignore it or go around it, the Lord's voice could not be heard above my conscience. My mind wandered about from subject to subject, trying to direct my attention to anything but my guilt.

It is impossible to approach God with unconfessed, covered-up sin in our lives. "Beloved, if our heart does not condemn us, we have confidence before God" (1 Jn. 3:21). But if our heart is condemning, we cannot draw near with confidence, except in confession and repentance. As we confess our sin, He is faithful to forgive us. The blood of Jesus Christ washes over us, cleansing us from all unrighteousness.

When I repent, I avoid making grand promises of greater obedience in the future. That is my desire, but I know my weakness and that there is no strength in myself to withstand satan's pressures. If I try to stand alone, my focus will be all wrong, looking to myself to perfect my salvation, when Jesus is the only One Who can sanctify me. I don't say, "I'm sorry and I promise never to do it again." Instead, I recognize that though I am weak, He is strong. So the closest thing to a promise that I can make is, "By your grace, I will seek to walk in holiness before You."

I must stop looking at myself and focus instead on Jesus. Mel Tari has said in his beautiful book *The Gentle Breeze of Jesus* that in order for us to have an ongoing intimate relationship with Jesus, we must stop focusing on our ugly shell and start focusing on our lovely Lord. If I keep looking at myself, I will never get to Christ. But if I look at Jesus, He draws me to Himself. By lifting up Christ in our thoughts, by recognizing that He is the Author and Perfecter of our faith, by knowing that only through His strength do we stand, we give Him freedom to do His will within and through us. His love draws us through the veil to where we can speak with Him face to face, as a man talks with his friend.

Washed by Obedience to *Rhema*

The third requirement I noted was, "*let us draw near...having our body washed with pure water.*" Ephesians 5:25,26 tells us that "Christ also loved the Church and gave Himself up for her; that He might sanctify her, having cleansed her by the washing of water with the word [*rhema*]." When God speaks to us in prayer, we must allow it to cleanse us by applying and observing the *rhema*. I have often found in my own life and those of my students that God has nothing more to say to us if we have not obeyed the last word He gave us. His grace may allow us to continue in communication for a time, but there comes a point when we must either obey or forfeit further communion.

I have gone to my journal, seeking a word from the Lord for the day, and only heard the Lord say, "I want you to do what I told you to do yesterday." Brought up short by this unexpected response, I could only ask forgiveness and leave my prayer time to obey. "To obey is better than sacrifice" (1 Sam. 15:22). God is not interested in how many hours we spend with Him if we only hear and do not obey.

A Sincere Heart

Finally, the Lord brought me back to the first part of verse 22, *"let us draw near with a sincere heart."* Our hearts must be true when we come to God. There can be no hypocrisy, no deceit, no lies. We cannot try to hide anything from ourselves or the Lord. This is not usually a big problem for me because I am a very straightforward, up-front person. I say exactly what is on my mind and tend to be quite blunt about it. But there was a time that the Lord showed me the deceptiveness of my heart.

The church I was pastoring felt called by the Lord to have a fund-raising campaign in an attempt to pay off their $60,000 mortgage. Everyone was asked to spend time in prayer to find out what they should do to help the campaign. I knew there wasn't anything I could do. My family was living on a very small pastor's salary. We had no savings account and our checking account registered $0.00 at the end of every week. Whatever came in immediately went back out to pay bills. I didn't even bother to pray about it because I knew we had nothing to give.

Then I had a fleeting (spontaneous?) thought that I should sell the duplex we owned and give the balance to the church. I thought that was a pretty stupid plan. It couldn't possibly be from God. I hadn't been in prayer when it came. It was just a dumb idea. So I didn't even ask the Lord if the thought was from Him for several days. You see, I didn't really want to know. I finally gave in and asked if He wanted me to sell the duplex and give the money to the church. When He said yes, I was really angry and frustrated. My first retort was, "I never did believe in journaling anyway!"

I didn't believe in having insurance, so the duplex had been my investment for the future. I had done much of the work in building it myself, so the mortgage was low and could be paid off while my wife and I were still young. After that it would continue to provide a monthly income to care for my family if anything happened to me, or to provide for me in my old age. And now Jesus was telling me to sell my security and give all the profit to the church!

I was so upset I didn't speak to the Lord for several days. The subject simply was not open for discussion. Finally I cooled off enough to bring up the question again. "Lord, do You really want me to sell the duplex?" Then He explained to me why: It had become an idol in my life. I was looking to it for security rather than to Him. My trust was in a pile of cement and wood rather than in the living God. I thought about that for a while and decided He had a good point. He always does! So, what did He want me to do about it? "Sell the duplex, pay off the mortgage, and give the balance to the church."

I considered that for a while longer and finally gave in. "All right," I said, "but You're going to have to be responsible for my family! And if I starve to death in old age, it'll be all Your fault!" He seemed more than willing to accept the responsibility.

The Lord told me how to advertise the duplex and what price to ask. Besides, I thought I still had an out, because I believe strongly in submitting major decisions of my life for counsel. I was sure that when I shared this hare-brained idea to my co-elders they would see the foolishness of it and counsel me not to sell the house. But when I asked them about it, they both believed it was God speaking to me. So much for spiritual advisors! With friends like that, who needs enemies?

We did as the Lord said and waited for the calls to start coming. And waited. And waited. After six or eight months on the market with no offers, the Lord said, "Take it off the market." I didn't really care if it were sold or not anymore. In my heart, it was no longer mine. Jesus said, "That's what I was after all along. Now your trust is in Me, not some building. The duplex is no longer an idol in your life. You have given it to Me, and now I am giving it back to you; be My steward over it."

Before acting on this new *rhema*, I again submitted it to my co-elders. Again they agreed that it was God Who had spoken. Maybe submission wasn't so bad after all!

I was reminded of Abraham, who was asked by God to give up the most important thing in his life, his son. Because he was willing to do so, trusting God to make it right in the end, Isaac was given back to him. The Lord was not interested in the sacrifice of a boy or a building. He is only concerned with purifying our hearts.

These four things—a sincere heart, fullness of faith, a heart sprinkled clean from an evil conscience and a body washed by water—were the final elements needed to make the way clear for me to have day-to-day, moment-by-moment intimate fellowship with my Lord.

Keeping Your Heart Pure

The Lord is not the only One Who seeks to inject His spontaneous thoughts into our minds. Just as the Holy One is known as the Comforter, the enemy is known as the Accuser.

Satan will try to project into your mind negative thoughts, bitterness, discouragement, and anger. He will accuse you and tell you what a rotten sinner you are, how unworthy you are to enter the presence of a holy God. He will remind you of your weakness and of sins already confessed. He will try to convince you that there is no forgiveness for one such as you, that the blood is not sufficient to cover your sins.

Then the Liar will begin accusing your family and brothers and sisters in the Body. He'll tell you that they are all hypocrites who just put on a good face to hide their evil hearts. He'll convince you that no one really loves you, that their kindnesses are only setting you up for the day that they will turn on you. He'll make you believe that only you are standing true before the Lord, that you are better than all the rest.

Finally, the Deceiver will attack the Lord with his lying words. He'll say that God is not love but anger, not mercy but judgment. He will tell you that God doesn't really care enough about you to want to meet with you. He will point to the injustices and tragedies of this world as proof that God is unconcerned with the affairs of men.

Does any of this sound familiar? Have any of these thoughts appeared uninvited in your mind? It was such a glorious day of deliverance and victory when I finally realized that the Accuser was the source of these thoughts and, therefore, I didn't have to put up with them! By the authority of Jesus Christ, I can reject the words of the Enemy and replace them with the peace of the Comforter. I keep watch over my heart, protecting it from the lies of satan.

I also keep watch so that no other person's negative, destructive spirit can be transferred to me. It is so easy to be drawn into bitterness, anger and despair by the conversation of those around me. If at all possible, I avoid people who constantly wallow in sin or hopelessness or criticism. Instead, I continue to assemble with other believers who are concerned with how to stimulate one another to love and good deeds (Heb. 10:24,25). If I must be with those whose spirits tend to bring me down, I pray for the Lord to be a shield for me, protecting my spirit from their snares and overwhelming them with the Spirit of Christ. I hold fast the confession of my hope without wavering, knowing that He Who promised is faithful (Heb. 10:23).

When the Lord Does Not Speak

I have said repeatedly that the Lord is always speaking and that we will hear Him if our hearts are right. There are at least four exceptions to this statement, four reasons why the Lord will not answer your questions or grant your requests.

As noted earlier, God will not speak if we have not obeyed His last word. King Saul found himself in that situation. He repeatedly disobeyed the Word of the Lord spoken to him through the prophet Samuel. Finally the Lord said, "That's enough. Your disobedience has cost you and your family the throne. You won't be hearing from Me anymore." The next time Saul had a problem and went to the Lord for wisdom, "the Lord did not answer him, either by dreams or by Urim or by prophets" (1 Sam. 28:6).

Occasionally I have watched in sorrow as students who have heard the Lord asking them to do a difficult thing refuse to do it. Gradually their hearts became cold as they turned against what they knew was the voice of the Lord because they were unwilling to obey. Thankfully such incidents are rare and almost everyone who hears from the Lord learns to draw strength from Him to obey even in very difficult tasks.

When It's None of Your Business!

The Lord will also not speak if you are asking a question He does not want to answer. God does not make Himself available to us as our own private fortune-teller. There are many things He does not choose to reveal to us, and if we insist on prying into those areas we will not only meet silence from the Lord, but we may open ourselves up to deception. Generally speaking, the Lord does not open the future for us to see. He will tell us all that is necessary for us to know, and only what is necessary.

This is illustrated in the story of the barren woman to whom an angel of the Lord appeared and told her she would bear a son. The angel told her to drink no wine or strong drink or eat any unclean food, because the boy would be a Nazarite to God from the womb and he would begin to deliver Israel from the Philistines.

When the woman told her husband Manoah about the angel's message, Manoah asked the Lord to send the angel back to instruct them in caring for this boy. The Lord allowed the angel to return and Manoah began to ply him with questions: "What shall be the boy's mode of life and his vocation?" The angel responded, "Pay attention to all that I said," and repeated again the same message he had given the woman the first time he came (Judg. 13:12-14). Manoah was prying where he had no business, seeking to know details about the future he did not need to know. So God simply ignored the questions and did not give him an answer.

Impure Motives

God will not answer if we are praying with wrong motives (Jas. 4:3). How often do we pray that our lives might be free from pain and pressure? How often do we ask for protection from the consequences of our sin? If an unhappy circumstance enters our life, we immediately pray that it might be removed, without looking for ways that we may grow through our suffering.

The Bible says that we "exult in tribulations; knowing that tribulation brings about perseverance; and perseverance, proven character; and proven character, hope" (Rom. 5:3,4). As the fire of the kiln is increased more impurities are burned off, and godly character is established. Therefore, when we encounter pressure, it is not usually wise to immediately pray for its removal. First we should seek God. Personally I have found my greatest growth has come during the times I have experienced the greatest pressure.

Consumed by the commercialism of our age, how many of us covet material blessings far above what we need to sustain our lives? Thinking only of our own comfort and pleasure, we plead for this and claim that. I believe that God wants to bless us materially and financially, but not so that our fleshly lusts are satisfied. He wants to bless us that we may be a blessing to others. He allows us to be stewards of much as long as we are wise and compassionate, giving to the needy, the widows, and the orphans, using His resources to extend His kingdom on earth.

God is concerned with eternal values, not temporary appeasements. He is concerned with proven, upright character, holiness and the healing of our souls and spirits far more than in the comfort of our flesh. When our prayers focus on the satisfaction of our flesh, we may not receive the answer we seek. Therefore, when facing pressure or an unhappy situation, we must first seek *rhema*, asking God to show us how to pray.

Then, when we pray according to God's will, we can be assured that He will answer.

The Need for Fasting

Fasting not only cleanses the body of poisonous wastes, it also cleanses the spirit so that it can more easily ascend to the presence of the Father. If I do not seem to be getting through to God, fasting helps me achieve greater spiritual receptivity. I have always found that God has come through for me, or I have gotten through to Him, when I have spent a period of time in fasting. Many of the most important steps of growth in my life have come through times of fasting.

Isaiah 58 is the greatest chapter of the Bible on fasting. It describes wrong reasons for fasting, the proper motives for it, and the results of fasting correctly. In verses 9 and 11, we are promised, "Then you will call, and the Lord will answer; you will cry, and He will say, 'Here I am!' And the Lord will continually guide you."

Fasting has been a normal part of the prayer life of the Church since its inception. Repeatedly in the book of Acts, Peter, Paul, or the whole Church together is shown fasting.

There are many kinds of fasts and partials fasts. A total fast involves abstinence from both food and drink. Such an absolute fast should be no more than three days. A normal fast would be the abstinence from everything but water. A variation of this is to drink fruit juices and other healthful liquids while abstaining from all solid foods. These types of fasts should not continue more than forty days. Partial fasts can also be effective. You can fast every day until a certain time. You can fast one meal a day. Or you can use Daniel's fast of vegetables and water.

The Lord will guide you into the right kind of fast. He may lead you into a regular weekly day of fasting. At certain times, He may call you to a special fast of up to forty days. We are not to come under a law of fasting, but to be responsive to the leading of the Spirit in this special area of prayer.

Before beginning to fast, I strongly recommend that you read a thorough book on the subject. I have found **God's Chosen Fast** by Arthur Wallis to be an excellent resource. Please note that individuals with chronic health problems that can be affected by diet, such as diabetes, should fast only under the supervision of a physician.

I Still Can't Hear!

When you have experimented with two-way prayer using the principles found in this book, most of you will find you can effectively dialogue with Almighty God. However, there may still be rare times when we seem to be blocked from hearing His voice. Sometimes we sit quietly with pen in hand and nothing flows. Frustration builds and we wonder what is wrong with us. Why can't we hear?

There are a number of things to check in a situation like this.

• First, see if you have actually written down a question to God. You might say, "Why, that's just a technicality. I've thought the question in my mind. That's good enough." No, sometimes it's not! Often it is important, especially when you are beginning, to actually write down the question you are thinking. That simple act will release you, and the response will begin to flow.

• Or maybe you think God is just not speaking. In this case you should pour out your heart fully and completely. Be earnest about the encounter you are having with God. Become fully committed to experiencing Him now, in this present moment. Then begin writing down any words you receive, even if there are only one or two. Remember the Holy Spirit's impressions are slight and easily overcome by bringing up your own thoughts.

A student from Finland named Pekka wrote to us about how important this act of faith is: "For me, the key to my 'hearing' was to write it down! Thank you for this insight from Habakkuk 2:1,2. Every time I start, I am hesitant and think, 'This cannot be anything.' Then God teaches me something new again. The threshold every time is to put my pen on paper and start writing out the first thought, however stupid or erratic it may feel. Only after having been obedient in jotting down this preliminary thought, there is flow."

There was one time when I felt I couldn't hear anything. I sat in frustration for several minutes, and the most I could get was the word "I." Now I wasn't going to write down the word "I." I was going to wait until I got more and then I would decide whether it was even worth writing down. Well, nothing more came, so in sheer desperation I simply wrote down the word "I." Then a second word came into my consciousness: "would." I wrote that down. Then came a third, a fourth, a fifth, "like to speak to you concerning..." —and we were off and running. You see, I was halting the flow, because I was unwilling to write down the simple word that was there. Therefore, write in faith whatever word appears, trusting it will lead to a stream of living water.

• Check to make sure that you are really asking a question. If not, make it into a question—a specific question. Often the more specific the question, the more focused you are, and thus the more apt you are to recognize the divine response in return. Obviously, as I have stated, you can get too specific and tend toward fortune-telling and other things that are none of your business. That is why we need to keep a balance.

• Sometimes all you seem to be getting back are your own answers. It isn't too hard to tell that they are simply your thoughts. It is you preaching a sermon at yourself. When this happens, start off by rejoicing that at least you have come to the point of being able to clearly discern when an answer is just your own thoughts rather than God's!

Then you must go deeper, quieting yourself still more, until you touch the depths of your heart and the divine flow is initiated. Go back to the chapter on stillness and learn to quiet yourself until God Almighty takes over. With some practice and experimentation you will be able to still yourself quickly and easily. As a matter of fact, you will begin to cultivate a lifestyle of inner stillness. You will learn how to stand still before God while you walk among men. This is abiding in Christ.

The Voice and the Fire

A final block I would like to deal with is the issue of fire. God's voice came with fire in Deuteronomy 5. Fire, in the Bible, stands for refining and purifying. A major block to hearing God's voice is the unwillingness of His children to stand in the fire and allow it to do its purifying work, freeing them from bondage to the flesh and releasing them to freedom in the Spirit. The story of the Israelites at the mountain illustrates this.

The omnipotent Yahweh had delivered His people! He told Moses what to do and Moses led the Israelites out of bondage, through the river on dry ground, giving them manna from heaven and water from the rock. Everything was going great! God had provided for all of their needs and had required very little in return.

Then they arrived at Mount Sinai, and Moses brought them some good news: God was going to come and talk to him and they were invited to listen in on the conversation. The next two days were full of preparations, everyone washing their garments and consecrating themselves so they would be ready to hear the voice of God.

The promised day finally arrived. The camp was buzzing with anticipation and speculation. "What will He be like? Will He whisper like a summer breeze or thunder like an autumn storm? Can we really hear His voice and live? Moses does, but he's special. Do you think Yahweh really wants to talk to us? Can we really have fellowship with God? What will this day bring?"

Suddenly the ground began to tremble. The mountain was burning with fire. Lightning flashed and a thick cloud of darkness hung in the air. Moses brought the people closer to meet with God, and they stood trembling at the foot of the mount. Suddenly they turned and ran in terror as the deafening sound of a trumpet gave way to a voice: "Moses! Moses! Come up to the top of the mountain!" Fearfully the crowd watched as Moses made his way up, half expecting him to perish at any moment before the awesomeness of Jehovah. Finally he disappeared into the darkness of the cloud, and they were left to wait.

As the day wore on, some kept watch near the base of the mountain. Others returned to their tents and their daily chores. The elders and heads of the tribes had a long committee meeting. Just as the skeptics' theory of Moses' death up in the gloom was beginning to gain a following, the cry went up, "Here he comes! Moses is coming down! He's alive! Hooray for Moses!" Moses was indeed returning and in his hands was a message from God. Almost before he had a chance to sit down and rest, the elders drew him aside and said, "Moses, we need to have a talk."

"Now, Moses," they said, "this has been a really nice day. It was a real treat to see God's glory and His greatness, and we even heard His voice. That was all well and good. But, enough is enough! Did you see that fire? If He talks to us anymore, that fire is going to get us! I mean, people just don't hear God speaking from the midst of a fire like we did and live to tell about it. So, here's what we want you to do. You go back and tell God that we don't want Him to talk to us anymore. He can tell you what He wants us to do, then you can tell us. We promise to do whatever He says. Then we won't have to go near that fire anymore. Got it, Moses? The voice just isn't worth the fire!"

Of course, God heard their words and said to Moses, "Everything these people have said is good. I wish that they had such a heart in them that they would do as they have said and obey me! Then I could bless them and their children as I long to. But go tell them that I will do as they have said. I won't come to them anymore. But know this, Moses, that because they have refused My voice, they must have commandments and statutes and judgments. If they won't live in communion, they must live in law" (Deut. 5:28-33, my paraphrase).

God has not changed in all the years since that fateful day at Sinai. With the voice of God still comes the fire of God, the fire that consumes the dross and purifies the gold. If you are longing for the life of communion with God, be prepared for the fire. Determine that for you, the voice is worth the fire! Choose to yield to His hand with whatever purging and cleansing of the flesh He requires.

An educated professional in his late twenties was learning to hear God's voice. When God expressed His love, he received it as truly from the Lord and basked in the pleasure of His acceptance. Then one day the Lord said, "Phil, remember the dishes and silver you and your wife pilfered from college for your first dinnerware? I want you to take them back!" Aauugghh! This couldn't be God! Why, he hadn't even been a Christian then! What kind of fool would they think he was? Everyone stole from the university. It was no big deal!

He brought this message from God to me, hoping that I would tell him to forget it, that it wasn't really from the Lord. But I couldn't. I knew from my own life that with the voice comes the fire. I encouraged him that what may not seem important to us can be very important to God. Until we are obedient to what He has spoken, He often has nothing more to say. Sadly, Phil chose to step away from the fire and the voice and live a life of "normal Christianity," a life of laws and rules and tradition.

Another young man who was on the pastoral staff of my church attended one of my classes on hearing God's voice. Afterwards he came to me in chagrin. He had been praying, asking the Lord for direction in his ministry. Suddenly the Lord brought to his remembrance a stereo system he had knowingly bought on the black market before he became a Christian. God told him to sell the stereo and give the money to His work. "Do you really think this could be God?" he asked. "I mean, I wasn't even talking to Him about this. I was asking about my future and all of a sudden this stereo comes into my mind from nowhere. Is that really God?" I reassured him and after a few months more of struggle, he obediently put the stereo up for sale.

The Purifying Fire in My Life

The fire had a big job to do in my life, and without the voice I could not have survived the flames. Patti had suffered a long time from depression and inferiority. I "knew" that her problems were her own fault. I even had biblical proof. Then, one day, the fire touched me. "You are responsible for a great many of Patti's problems. It is because of your failure to love and cherish her that she is in this condition." I slammed down my notebook, muttering, "I never did believe in journaling!" and stormed away.

I had cooled down by the next day, although I was still very skeptical. "Okay," I challenged God, "if I've done something wrong, show me where." Not expecting to receive any answer, I was more than a little surprised and chagrined when the response filled two complete pages!

He showed me how my early training concerning emotions had cut me off from the most important part of life. I had always believed that emotions were unpredictable, unreliable and part of my fallen nature. Therefore, I had trained myself to suppress all emotional responses, until finally they were completely gone from my life. My love for my wife was based on what I had learned in college about *agape* love, that it was a commitment, and a decision, not an emotion. My love for my congregation was a commitment to their growth and nurturing. My love for God was a commitment to service.

Is it any wonder that my wife's spirit began to wither and die? Because she was very shy and introverted and had no close friends, she depended largely on my love to sustain her. God was calling me to restore "care" to my life. This one commission changed not only my personality, but also my marriage and my ministry.

But I didn't even know where to begin. Every change I had ever made for God had been done by an act of my will. I willed to be an extrovert. I willed to be enthusiastic. I willed to be a leader. But how could I will to feel emotionally? I couldn't. All my tried-and-true methods of Christian growth were useless to me. So, I cried out for help, and God was there. He gave me four objectives to work on: study my journal and see how He had loved me; study the Gospels to see how Jesus expressed love for people; study the Psalms to learn how David expressed his love to God; and pray with faith for God to restore emotions to my life.

For a full year I concentrated on learning to care. I didn't even know what care was when I started. God gave me a definition: care is love expressed on an emotional level rather than an intellectual one. I studied the Gospels and Psalms again and again. And God began to work. The first emotions restored seemed to be all the negative ones: depression, fear and anger. For the first time in my adult life, I found myself crying. Night after night found me in my wife's arms, drawing comfort like a child as I wept at the hopelessness of my future. As I truly felt my weakness more layers of pride were peeled away and I was finally utterly broken.

Gradually the healing began. Joy and hope began to bubble within my soul. A new love and appreciation for the wife that God had chosen especially for me grew. As I learned to express it, death stopped working within her and, with the help of a counselor, she began to be healed as well.

My ministry had always been characterized by a prophetic nature. That's a nice way of saying that I hated sin and blasted the sinner! My church had tried to convince me that I was too harsh, but I wouldn't accept it. When God said the same thing, I couldn't deny it.

The Healing Voice

He directed me to Micah 6:8 (NKJV): "He has told you, O man, what is good; and what does the Lord require of you but to do justly, to love mercy, and to walk humbly with your God?" He showed me that He *loves* mercy and *does* justice. It brings Him joy to show mercy, but His holiness requires that He give justice.

All my life I had been just the opposite: I loved justice and did mercy. My approach to every person and situation was first to judge, and maybe, secondarily, to have mercy. He showed me the two aspects of His nature: light and love. God is both judgment and mercy, division and healing, conviction and comfort.

As I looked at Him, I saw how unbalanced I was in my whole approach to life. I had focused on the "light" aspects of His nature, living in challenge and requiring infinite precision in righteousness. Now I found Him calling me to focus on the "love" aspects: forgiveness, reconciliation and grace.

As I did so, a new spirit began to permeate my ministry. Where formerly I had reacted to differences of opinion with confrontation and separation, I was beginning to seek peace and reconciliation. Where righteousness according to the letter of the law had been my standard for fellowship, love was becoming the standard around which we gathered. Where judgment had always been required for every infraction of the law, I began to see mercy flowing from me.

My newly emerging balance between judgment and mercy was tested when a teenage girl under our care was discovered in a sexually compromising situation. Everything in my past screamed out for her chastisement. My mind composed endless sermons on the need for purity and the dangers of immorality.

But I was learning. Before I dealt with the situation, I brought it before the Lord. After laying before Him all of her sin and guilt and the need for action, He simply reminded me of His response to the woman taken in adultery, "Neither do I condemn you; go your way; from now on sin no more" (Jn. 8:11). The message was clear. She did not need judgment. God had already convinced her of her sin. Now she needed to experience His mercy and forgiveness from the hands of His servant.

My relationship with the Lord had also been affected by my emotional atrophy. Without real love for Him, there could be no fellowship, and, like the Israelites in the wilderness, I found myself living under law. I searched the Scriptures daily for principles of Christian living, and each week I stood behind my pulpit and issued yet another decree for successful Christianity.

Within four years I had accumulated fifty pages of rules by which I was trying to live. I distilled them into about thirty general principles, which I typed onto the front and back of a sheet of paper I then covered with plastic. Now I had Christianity down to a system. I had even improved on Moses, because I had thirty commandments carved in plastic!

The only problem was that when I was concentrating on obeying the fifteen on the front, I missed the fifteen on the back. When I turned it over to work on them, I failed to keep the ones on the front. Needless to say, my Christian life was more frustration than joy.

As the spirit of heaviness weighed upon my congregation, I began to recognize what the Bible had told me all along: the end of the law is death. My lack of personal communion with the Lord was bringing my wife, my church, and myself under the law, and death was becoming apparent wherever I turned. Worship was no longer exciting and spontaneous. Volunteers were scarce. Times of fellowship following the services became shorter and shorter. Home groups decreased in size and number. Finally, gossip, quarrelling and controversy divided the Body. Unfortunately I had not been walking in mercy long enough to undo the damage my years of teaching had done. The fruit of my leadership came upon me.

As I began to walk in communion with God and be aware of the spiritual world around me, I naturally tried enthusiastically to bring my congregation along with me in my new walk. But some of the concepts were too new, the principles too controversial. Perhaps I had not lived with them long enough to be able to communicate them to others. Some of my people could not accept this new emphasis and responded as I had taught them, with judgment and confrontation. We all tried to reconcile our differences, but there were too many hurts, too many resentments. Soon it became clear that I must resign.

During the months of unemployment which followed, it was daily hearing from God that sustained and guided me. Though our path leads through the fire, He goes with us every step of the way.

Summary

Jesus Christ has opened the way for us to enter the Holy of Holies by rending the veil and sprinkling us with His blood. He has given us the privilege of direct fellowship with the Father and Son through the Holy Spirit. The way is not burdensome or complicated. Jesus said, "I am the Way" (Jn. 14:6). It is Christ Who has done the work. He has shed His blood and applied it to our hearts. He has planted faith within us. He draws us to Himself. We simply need to be vessels, willing to receive the finished work of Christ. We need to set our love and attention solely upon Him.

In the last few chapters, I presented several concepts to help tune ourselves more precisely to the Lord's voice. Following is a list of summary questions you can use to discern any areas that may prevent you from hearing God speak. Remember, *we do not need* to go through this list every time we come to prayer. Normally we can simply sit down and say, "Good morning, Lord" and hear His response. But on those rare occasions when we cannot seem to make spiritual contact, this checklist can help us find the reason why and correct it.

The Tabernacle Experience

1. *The altar*: Have I presented myself as a living sacrifice? Am I denying the desires of my flesh and presenting myself to God as an instrument of righteousness?

2. *The laver*: Have I been regularly studying the Bible and obeying the clear commands I have found?

3. *The table of shewbread*: Have I been continuing in fellowship with the Body of Christ? Is my self-will being ground fine through close relationships with my brothers and sisters? Is the deepest desire of my heart to do only God's will?

4. *The lampstand*: Have I presented my mind to the Lord to be illumined by the Holy Spirit? Do I study Scripture with my heart tuned to hear His revelation through it? Are all of my thoughts and reasoning processes accomplished in a deliberate dependence upon the guidance of the Spirit?

5. *The altar of incense*: Am I continually offering a sacrifice of thanksgiving and praise to the Lord so that my emotions and reactions are under His control? Do I swing from high to low emotionally or is a continual attitude of worship and gratitude bringing me into balance?

6. *The ark of the covenant*: Have I learned to walk in His immediate presence and hear His words spoken into my heart?

Journaling

1. Have I found a quiet place, free from the distractions of the world?

2. Have I stilled my spirit? Have I taken care of the random thoughts that could distract me? Am I focusing on a vision of Jesus?

3. Am I ready to journal? Am I facilitating the flow of *rhema* by writing down our conversation?

Fine-tuning

1. Is my heart true and sincere? Am I free from all deception and hypocrisy? Am I being honest before the Lord? Am I harboring any reservations?

2. Am I coming in faith? Have I made a quality decision to believe all that God says with all of my heart?

3. Is my conscience clear? Have I confessed my sin and received the cleansing blood of Christ? Is my confidence in Him, that He will sanctify me and present me blameless before the Father?

4. Have I obeyed the *rhema* I have already received?

Removing Inner Blocks

1. Am I asking questions the Lord does not want to answer?

Am I trying to get information I don't need to know? Am I trying to manipulate my journal like a crystal ball?

2. Are my motives right? Have I asked the Lord how He wants me to pray?

3. Is the Lord calling me to fast to release the answer?

Once again I want to emphasize that these questions are not the prelude to my every prayer time. They are the exception rather than the rule. Even when I am unable to achieve spiritual encounter, very rarely do I need to go through the entire list of questions. Being aware of potential areas of difficulty, it is usually quite easy to zero in on the problem. However, a knowledge of each of the questions has made it possible for me to have intimate two-way dialogue with the Lord every day, every time I turn to Him.

7

How Can I Know for Sure It Is God's Voice?

Most Westerners have been taught to live rationally, according to the dictates of our minds; I have tried to dethrone the mind by recognizing that it is not the organ that receives revelation from God. The heart is the place of Spirit-to-spirit encounter. However, we must never get the idea that as Christians we should throw our minds away. The mind has a very necessary place in the spiritual walk—it is the organ used for testing.

As we try to live out our spiritual dimension, we will make mistakes. The Bible recognizes that fact and accepts it. First Thessalonians 5:21 tells us to "examine everything carefully; hold fast to that which is good." We shouldn't jump on what is not good, and berate ourselves for our mistakes. Instead we should simply test everything we receive, ignore whatever is not of God, and move on with what is good. To make mistakes is human. The important thing is to learn from those mistakes.

Our goal, as always, is to come to a balance. Most of us tend to operate in extremes. We may look down on those who claim to have mystical experiences. Or, especially if we tend to be somewhat mystical by nature, we may scorn those "intellectual snobs whose religion is all in their head." Neither attitude is proper. God created both the head and the heart. He ordained the functions of each to complement the other. If we try to live our Christian lives depending on either one alone, we will find ourselves going in circles. We need both the head and the heart, the rational and the spiritual aspects of our communion with the Lord.

The number one question people ask in my seminars is, "How can I know for sure it is God speaking to me?" And my number one answer is, "Submit it to your spiritual counselors for their evaluation and testing." I'd like to share two examples that firmly planted within my heart a conviction of the need for testing and a deep desire to always do so in my life. First, there was a man in a church I pastored whose ability to hear from the Lord and whose gift of prophecy were highly regarded by the fellowship. One day we heard that he had received a "revelation" that his marriage was not of God because neither he nor his wife had been Christians at the time of their marriage. Therefore, he had been told "by the Lord" that he should put away his wife in divorce.

As soon as I heard this rumor, I went to his home to see if it was true. He confirmed his "revelation" and his intentions. I shared with him from Scripture that God hated divorce and that his "leading" violated both the letter and the spirit of the Word. Therefore, I felt that he was being deceived. He rejected my words, insisting that he knew the Lord's voice and that was that.

As directed in the Bible, I returned to him a few days later with the other two elders, who confirmed my position and shared more Scripture contrary to his "leading." He responded by showing us biblical examples and verses (all out of context) that supported his "revelation." We met with him many times during the next two or three months, seeking to draw him out of his deception. However, he grew increasingly arrogant and self-righteous.

Finally we had no choice but to bring the issue before the entire Body. He presented his "revelation" to them and they unanimously assured him that he was in error. But he responded, "I don't care. I'm going to do it anyway." He walked out in his pride, bringing destruction into not only his own life, but also the lives of his wife and children and the young woman who believed his "revelation" that she was to be his wife "in the Lord."

Another time, I was in prayer when I received a "revelation" that a certain man in my congregation was having an affair with his secretary. I wasn't too thrilled with the prospect of confronting him with this word. If it were not true, it could cause a lot of problems. In fact, even if it were true, it could cause a lot of problems! But if the Lord had given me this information so that I could help lead him out of his sin, I was willing to risk it.

First, however, I shared my "revelation" with my co-elder Charles, whose ability to hear from the Lord I highly respected. After listening carefully to what I had to say, he went home to pray about it. Later he returned to me with the two words he had sensed from the Lord, "Lying spirit." He believed that a lying spirit was seeking to deceive me and cause great destruction of relationships within the fellowship.

I returned to my journal and asked the Lord to take away the leading I felt if Charles were correct and my "revelation" was a lie. Within days the feeling, which had remained very strong for three weeks, began to wane and soon disappeared. I blessed God for giving me wise spiritual counselors before I made such a big mistake.

Factors Affecting the Spirit

One of the primary reasons why we need to test all revelation we receive is that our spirits can be affected by factors other than God. According to 1 Corinthians 6:17, the spirit of a Christian is joined together with the Holy Spirit. However, this does not preclude other factors from moving upon our spirits and tainting the revelation we receive.

When we are overcome with a great sorrow, our spirits can be affected and the messages received through them can be incorrect. There is an example of this in 1 Samuel 1:1-15. Hannah was "oppressed in spirit" because she had no son.

Our physical, bodily condition can also influence our spirits. In 1 Samuel 30, David's men came upon a man who had been left for dead by a retreating army. He was very ill and had had neither food nor drink for three days. They gave him bread and fruit and water to drink, and "his spirit revived" (v. 12). We have all experienced the effects of sickness upon our spirits. Doubt and discouragement easily find their way into our hearts when our bodies are weak or filled with pain. We must be particularly cautious about acting upon revelation received when we are physically weak or in pain, until it has been confirmed by another, or tested when we are physically stronger. This does not, of course, always apply to weakness during a fast.

Satan is also able to affect our hearts. John 13:2 shows that satan put the idea into Judas' heart to betray Jesus. The man who sought to divorce his wife and I were both deceived by lying spirits. Often it is difficult for us alone to recognize that we are being led into deception. We need the help of a brother who loves us to show us the truth.

Finally, I myself can influence my spirit. Proverbs 16:32 tells us that "he who rules his spirit, [is better] than he who captures a city." Our motives must be pure and our wills aligned with Christ's or the "revelation" we receive will be a dream of our own making.

Testing Revelation

Since so many factors other than the Holy Spirit can influence our spirits and cause impurities in how we hear God, the first thing we must look for in testing any kind of revelation is evidence of these other influences. In the chapter on vision, I laid out three specific aspects of revelation that can be tested: the origin, the content and the fruit. Vision and revelation from myself, satan, or God will each have distinctive characteristics.

Thoughts from my own spirit are born in contemplation. They are the result of a progressive building of ideas, based on what I have learned. If I have been feeding on what is worldly or evil, that is what will come out of my heart. If I have been guarding my spirit, allowing only what is good and pure and holy to enter, then the meditations of my spirit will be a reflection of that.

Satan's injected thoughts come as flashing ideas or images into my mind. They do not fit my train of thought and seem like an intrusion. They are destructive and evil. They bring me into fear or bondage. I may feel pressured or compelled to obey their promptings. They are contrary to both the nature and Spirit of God. They will resist being submitted to the Word or even shared with the Church, often by appealing to my ego.

Revelation from the Holy Spirit is encouraging and comforting. If it involves a conviction of sin, it is specific and instructive, not general or condemning. It has no fear of testing and even encourages it. It is completely in harmony with the nature and the Word of God. *Rhema* quickens my faith and brings peace to my inner man. It is wise. It encourages the development of the fruit of the Spirit in my life.

Every *rhema* and vision we receive should be tested to determine its source. Every revelation should also be compared to the *Logos*, the written Word of God. It is absolutely essential that you have a good working knowledge of the Bible if you are going to investigate the spiritual dimension. The Bible is our absolute standard of truth! Any revelation from God will be in perfect agreement with the letter and the spirit of the Word. It will be in keeping with the whole counsel of God on that subject, as revealed throughout the entire Bible. A single verse is insufficient grounds for doctrine or belief.

The first commission of the Lord to me was to become a biblical man. I devoted ten years of my life solely to the study of the Word of God. During that time I read and reread the complete Bible, outlining and diagramming every chapter. And as I studied, I sought by the grace of God to bring myself into obedience to its commands. Only after I had a good knowledge of the *Logos* did God call me to become a spiritual man. My Bible knowledge provided a solid foundation for my spiritual growth.

The Safety of Relationships

Another vitally important tool for testing revelation is the Body of Christ, the Church. When we become Christians we become members one of another, united as the visible expression of Christ on the earth. There is safety in our relationship to a Bible-believing fellowship. And the power and ability to grow are dynamically increased when we are covenanted together with others of like goals.

It is especially helpful to be in an accountability relationship when we are trying to change deeply ingrained habits. If you've tried to shed some extra pounds alone, you probably have experienced discouragement and failure. But when we join with others who are experiencing the same difficulties in achieving the same goals, and especially others who have successfully achieved those goals, the chances of success are greater. It is even more effective when those others know your goals and will hold you accountable for progress toward them on a regular basis. An alcoholic rarely is able to remain dry alone, but with the help of relationships found in Alcoholics Anonymous many are able to succeed.

How often have you read self-help books that promised to reshape your personality and make you a success? You probably tried on your own to apply the teachings, but rarely had long-term success. But, if you have studied the same kind of book with a group of others, meeting regularly to share how you've applied it, the results, and your goals for the next week, you likely have experienced a change in your life for the long term.

This book is no exception. I believe that you may become very excited about what you read here. You might apply all of the principles and suggestions and have wonderful experiences of spiritual encounter. But unless you find another to walk with you on this journey, the excitement will soon disappear, especially when obstacles block the path. This book will then join the host of others collecting dust on your shelves. Growth and change rarely come to those who try to make it on their own. Growth and change happen within relationships.

Submit Yourselves

God has ordained that everyone is to have a particular type of relationship with at least one other human being. Ephesians 5:21 tells us to submit ourselves one to another. Protestant Americans seem to have a particularly hard time with this type of relationship. One of the things that Protestants reacted against at the time of the Reformation was the excessive authority exercised by the Roman Church. In this reaction, however, the truth of submission was thrown out by many as well. There is a God-ordained need for submission among believers.

The American ideal of rugged individualism also prevents us from embracing the concept of submission. Our American heroes tend to be rebels, non-conformists who fight the system.

We admire the Lone Ranger, John Wayne, Butch and Sundance, and criminals who outsmart the law. We laugh and applaud when the police or other authorities are depicted as bumbling fools. We are the culture of the anti-hero. We don't want to hear about authority or submission or accountability.

God did not give us authorities to make our lives more difficult. Authority is a precious gift from the Lord, given for our protection and benefit. Proverbs 11:14 declares, "In abundance of counselors there is victory." It is so easy to make a mistake or be deceived, and God has blessed us with the counsel of our brothers and sisters to minimize this potential. Romans 13:4 reminds us that authority "is a minister of God to you for good." In an age of lawlessness, lawfulness and order should characterize God's people.

Especially for those of us who desire spiritual encounters, there is a need for accountability relationships. I wouldn't walk this way alone. There is too much possibility for error and deception, too much temptation to pride and self-righteousness. I need a brother or sister who is also walking in the Spirit to help me stay on the right track. When I receive what I believe to be a word from the Lord, I want the confirmation of another who also knows God's voice. I do not make any major commitment of my time or my money, or make any major change in the direction of my life without first sharing it with my brother and receiving his input.

I am not talking about a life of bondage in which I can do nothing without another's permission. I don't run to my brother every day with what I have received in my journal. I am free to grow and make mistakes on my own. But before I make a most important move, one that could have a long-term effect on my life and my family, I want the Lord's counsel and confirmation through another.

166

I have heard people say, "Why should I submit to anyone else? The Lord talks to me as much as He does to them. Why should I have to listen to somebody else?" That is exactly what Miriam and Aaron said about Moses (Num. 12:1-15). It was true! The Lord did speak to them and through them. But God became very angry when they used that as an excuse for a rebellious attitude. As a result of her words, Miriam became leprous and only Moses' prayers brought her healing.

Finding a Counselor

People often ask me how they can find a spiritual counselor, someone with whom they can share their *rhema* and their major decisions. The greatest thing you can do is pray for God to bring you together. He wants you to walk with another. He is the One Who said, "It is not good for the man to be alone" (Gen. 2:18). He will help you.

There are certain characteristics you should look for in a counselor. First and foremost, he or she must be a friend. This relationship is built on love and friendship. He will be someone who is willing to spend much time with you. This is especially important at first, when you will have lots of questions that need discussing. Your friend should take this relationship seriously, being willing to really seek the Lord with you, not just offer his own advice.

Your counselor should be a "biblical" man (or woman). He should have a good knowledge of the Word and should base his life upon it. He should also be a spiritual man, able to discern the purposes of God. And he should be someone who is himself in relationship with spiritual peers. Anyone who is standing alone is susceptible to deception. You do not want to be led astray by the rebellion of another.

Finally, your friend does not need to be an ordained minister. In a practical sense, not many pastors are able to have the kind of close relationship we are talking about with everyone in his congregation. But more importantly, it is not necessary to be ordained to be able to walk in the Spirit.

There is often no need to look far to find a spiritual counselor. Your spouse is a good place to start. I don't make any major decisions unless Patti and I are in agreement. However, sometimes we are both too close to a situation to completely trust our own discernment. Then we agree to look to another for confirmation. A cell or home Bible study leader may be the right person for you.

As a young youth pastor fresh out of college, I watched as a mature pastor stood alone and unsubmitted and brought a major division in his church. Therefore, when I found myself in the position of senior pastor at the very young age of twenty-four, I knew I could not adequately fulfill the role alone. As a result of our study of New Testament Church structures, our fledgling fellowship wrote the concept of submission among the elders of the Body into its constitution. I voluntarily brought my life under the authority of two of my brothers. I began to submit myself to them not only in matters of the church but in all major decisions of my personal life as well.

Since that time I have remained in submission to two or three men at all times. I do not make any major commitment of my time or money, or any change in the direction of my life, without first sharing the decision with the appropriate people for their input. I cannot express how highly I value these relationships. I honor these men who willingly give of themselves to care for us in such a close personal way. I am so thankful to the Lord for His protection of me through these authorities. They have guided me in troubled times and prevented me from making mistakes that could have cost me my family, my resources and my ministry.

Understanding the Principle of Authority

I am grateful to Bill Gothard for the teaching on authority he gives in his seminar, *Basic Youth Conflicts*. Many of the ideas expressed below are based on what I have learned from him.

In order to properly relate to and respect authority, there are several things we must realize. First and foremost, we must accept the fact that God is responsible for placing all authority over us. Romans 13:1 declares, "There is no authority except from God, and those which exist are established by God." The psalmist tells us that, "Not from the east nor from the west, nor from the desert comes exaltation; but God is the judge; He puts down one and exalts another" (Ps. 75:6,7). No one can usurp any authority without God's permission. No one has authority over us except the people God allows to have authority over us.

A question that often arises is, what about evil authority? What about people like Hitler? Surely he wasn't God's minister! Surely he was a man out of control. The Israelites had their own version of Hitler—Nebuchadnezzar. He swept down upon Judah, bringing death, destruction and terror upon all the land. The people cried out for deliverance from his hand, but a prophet of God named Jeremiah rose up and said, "Don't resist him. Nebuchadnezzar is God's servant, sent to repay us for our evil ways. He is but God's war-club, a weapon of war in God's hand." (See Jeremiah 25:8-12 and 51:20-23.)

But do we really have to obey such evil authorities? The Roman government Paul lived under when he wrote the epistle to the Romans was perverted, sadistic and wicked. Christians were used as torches to light the streets, as bait for hungry lions, and were tormented by the gladiators for the amusement of the people. Yet, to believers living in the very seat of that cruel government, Paul wrote that they were to subject themselves to the governing authorities. "He who resists authority has opposed the ordinance of God; and they who have opposed will receive condemnation upon themselves…wherefore it is necessary to be in subjection, not only because of wrath, but also for conscience' sake" (Rom. 13:2,5). Jesus told His disciples to render to Caesar the things that were Caesar's.

Peter exhorted us to submit ourselves "…for the Lord's sake to every human institution…For such is the will of God that by doing right you may silence the ignorance of foolish men…Servants, be submissive to your masters with all respect, not only to those who are good and gentle, but also to those who are unreasonable. For this finds favor, if for the sake of conscience toward God a man bears up under sorrows when suffering unjustly. For what credit is there if, when you sin and are harshly treated you endure it with patience? But if when you do what is right and suffer for it you patiently endure it, this finds favor with God. For you have been called for this purpose, since Christ also suffered for you, leaving you an example to follow in His steps" (1 Pet. 2:13-21).

The second important principle to remember is that God is bigger than any authority. My confidence is not in a man, but in God's ability to work through the man. Sometimes we are tempted to protest against submitting to another imperfect human. It's easy to say we are submitted to Christ because He is perfect. But why should we open ourselves up to the influence of another person who could be wrong?

The simple answer is that my assurance is in God, that He will work through the authorities He has ordained in my life. Proverbs 21:1 says, "The king's heart is like channels of water in the hand of the Lord; He turns it wherever He wishes." As we confidently place ourselves in the hands of those He has placed over us, He will cause their hearts to be turned according to His will. And even if they try to arrogantly resist the Lord's influence upon their hearts, He can cause them to say the opposite of what they planned, so that His will is still accomplished! (See Proverbs 16:1.)

All authority is from God. Anyone who has authority over me does so only because the Lord has allowed him to exercise it. The authorities in our lives cannot exist except through the power God has given them. Jesus didn't answer Pilate when He was being questioned. Finally, in fear and frustration, Pilate cried, "Why won't You answer me? Don't You know that I have the authority to either release You or have You executed?" But Jesus replied, "You would have no authority over Me, unless it had been given you from above" (Jn. 19:8-11). There are not two or three or four authorities in your life. There is but one authority, who is God, exercising His will through men.

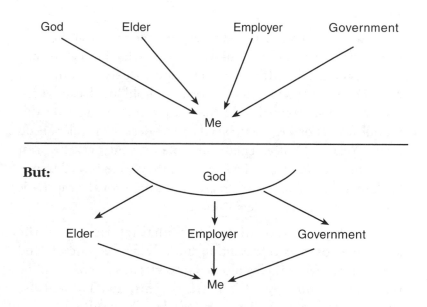

Not:

God   Elder   Employer   Government

Me

But:

God

Elder   Employer   Government

Me

When God used nations such as Assyria to chastise His people in the Old Testament, they were allowed to have a certain amount of authority over Israel. But those nations grew arrogant, and soon thought that it was by their own greatness that they had taken Israel captive. So when they had accomplished the purpose for which they had been ordained, God withdrew their power and punished them. He said, "Is the axe to boast itself over the one who chops with it?" (Is. 10:15). All authority comes from God, and He has authority over all authority. Authorities over us can do only what He allows them to do.

Since God is over all of our authorities, Timothy urged us to make entreaties and prayers, petitions and thanksgivings on behalf of all who are in authority (1 Tim. 2:1,2). Through our prayers we are able to lead a quiet and tranquil life in all dignity and godliness.

If we do believe that God is responsible for the authorities in our lives, we can certainly ask Him why He has placed them over us. He does not act capriciously or unjustly. Nebuchadnezzar was given authority to hold Judah captive for seventy years. Jeremiah told the people the reason why this was allowed. For 490 years, Israel had neglected the celebration of the Year of Jubilee. They had stolen seventy years of rest from the land and from the Lord. So, they were forced to pay back that time. There was a reason, not only for the captivity, but also for the precise length of it.

The hard-to-get-along-with characteristics of the authorities over us represent an underlying purpose of God for our lives. We are being molded into His image; and molding requires pressures. God is perfecting us, and He will use authorities to do so. As Peter reminded us, if we suffer injustice patiently, we are following in the steps of our Lord.

Disagreeing with Authority

There are times when we will be in disagreement with our authorities and counselors. Perhaps it is simply a difference of opinion, in which there is no clear biblical command to determine the issue. Perhaps we believe the Lord has told us to do something, but our spiritual friend disagrees. What do we do then?

We have a few choices. We can reassert our independence and break away from the relationship, confident that we know God's voice and what is best for us. Or, since we are convinced God works through submission, we can lay down and become a non-person. We can shut off our own minds and lines of communication with the Lord and respond like robots. So often we seem to think that these are our only two choices in an accountability relationship. Personally I don't like either one.

God, as always, has a better idea! If we do it His way, we can have disagreement without destruction. We can be submitted, meek persons without becoming mindless, spiritless doormats. In Daniel 1 we find a clear description of the way God guides us in providing creative alternatives which can satisfy both our counselors and ourselves. Daniel was a young man who was taken into captivity by Nebuchadnezzar. He was chosen for training at the palace for service in the king's court. As such, he was given rich, unclean foods and wine as his daily ration. Daniel had never eaten such things and didn't intend to. There was a great potential for trouble in that situation: government versus religion. But Daniel was able to resolve the issue with no exchange of hostilities.

The first thing he did was make sure his own heart was purified with tender love. He made certain his conscience was clear, that there were no critical, resistant or condemning attitudes in him. He knew that if he approached the commander with those kinds of feelings the commander would sense them, which would destroy any possibility of relationship. But because Daniel's heart was right, the commander responded with favor and compassion (Dan. 1:9). Though there was disagreement, there was love and honor between them.

If we find that our attitudes have been wrong, if we have felt anger and condemnation toward the authority God has placed over us, we must ask forgiveness of both God and that person. There is no place for "I think I might have had a bad attitude toward you." There can be no passing the buck: "I have been angry because you did such and such." Nor will generalizations do: "If I did anything to hurt you, I'm sorry." We are responsible for our own actions and reactions. Therefore, we need to repent deeply for our wrong thoughts, attitudes or words. We can either rationalize or repent. If we want to be open to the movement of God, repentance is the only choice. A pure heart opens us up for good things to happen.

When Daniel was sure that he had done his part to maintain a good relationship, he sought to discern the basic intention of the one over him. The commander's intention was simple—he wanted to live! If he disobeyed the king's command and the young men suffered as a result, the king would have him executed. But why did the king want the boys to eat such rich foods? Was he trying to defile their religion? Was he deliberately forcing them to choose between obedience to God and man? No! Nebuchadnezzar wanted the boys to be strong and healthy and intelligent. He was giving them the best he had to offer, food from his own table. His basic intention was their well-being.

Many times when we disagree with someone we can only see our own point of view. We are blinded by our own wrong attitudes. But when our hearts are pure, we are able to recognize the motives behind their requests. Often we are then able to see that they are really looking out for our best interests.

Daniel was faced with an authority who told him to act in disobedience to God's law. He could have risen up in rebellion and simply said, "No! I will not obey!" And he would no doubt have lost his head on the spot. But by keeping his heart full of love, he was able to come up with an alternative that allowed him to obey his God without offending his king. As a result, he rose to a position of authority, where he was able to exercise godly influence in an ungodly land.

The solution Daniel suggested was that he and his friends take a ten-day test. During that time they would abstain from the king's food and eat only vegetables and drink only water. At the end of the trial period, the commander could compare them to the other youths who continued to eat the king's delicacies. Based on what he observed at that time, he could then make his decision.

The commander could accept that. The boys would be in his care for three years. Any damage done in ten days could easily be repaired in three years. So he agreed to the test, and, of course, Daniel and his friends were in better physical condition than the rest of the young men at the end of the trial period.

In order to come up with such a creative alternative, we must be in touch with the Creator. We must have moved beyond anger to love, so that God's voice is able to clearly be heard in our hearts. When we are faced with a disagreement with our counselor or other authority, we need to prayerfully ask the Lord for an idea that will bring a mutually satisfactory resolution to the problem.

A Creative Alternative

Several years ago, I was asked to leave a community church in which I was serving as associate pastor because of a theological difference. A large group of faithful attenders were also asked to leave for the same reason. There was no other church in the area that would welcome us into their fellowship, so I was asked to pastor a brand-new church.

Laying out the foundation of a new ministry was quite an experience. There were many joys and many heartaches, but mostly a lot of hard work. After five years, we had our own building and had established policies and traditions we expected to last a long time. I planned to live in the parsonage and pastor those people the rest of my life.

Unfortunately such peace and satisfaction didn't last forever. Theological issues again threatened to bring division. Finally a group of six men presented me with a formal request for my resignation. I was shocked and, of course, very hurt. How could they ask me to leave the fellowship for which I had labored so hard? At the same time, I knew that I could not pastor anyone who didn't want me as their shepherd. If it were a consensus of the people, then I would leave.

I needed wisdom, so I went to the Lord. He told me in my journal that I was not to resign. He had placed me as pastor over that flock and I was responsible for it until He told me otherwise. I was there not by the will of man, but by the ordination of God. The men had made no provision for someone to take my place so, if I resigned, I would be guilty of leaving the flock of God unprotected without a shepherd. I couldn't do that!

That still left me with a problem. An outright refusal of the request of those men could have caused such damage that the church might not have recovered. But I couldn't disobey God's commission either. I asked the Lord to show me the underlying reason for the men's request. He showed me that the men were unhappy with some of my beliefs and teachings. They really wanted the problems worked out. They didn't want the church split any more than I did. But as long as I was in the forefront of the church activities, teaching in all the services and fulfilling my other pastoral duties, the problems also remained in the forefront. What the men really wanted was a "time out," a chance for tempers to cool and attitudes to be cleansed. Then we could discuss our problems and our differences could be worked out.

The Lord gave me a creative alternative. I would not resign as pastor, but I would step into the background for a period of six weeks. I would maintain my God-given responsibility for the flock, but all of my pastoral duties would be assumed by those men and the other elders. I submitted this idea to Roger, my co-elder, and he agreed that it was the right action to take. When I presented this alternative to the six men, they accepted it and immediately put it into effect.

I had a wonderful six weeks. Essentially I had been given a paid sabbatical in which I could do the thing I loved most—study the Word. During that period, I did an intensive examination of the heart and spirit of man, exploring every verse in the Bible on the subject. I organized what I found and, as a result of that time away, wrote two books!

During those six weeks, our congregation also spent time talking about our problems and differences. We brought in a well-known pastor respected by everyone to help arbitrate. Understanding was restored. Compromises were made and a major division was averted.

Over the next six months, the Lord began working in my heart. He showed me that the deepest gift and calling in my life was teaching rather than pastoring. The desire grew in me to devote myself to full-time study and teaching. Eventually I felt that the Lord had released me from my pastoral responsibilities, freeing me to seek other employment. I again submitted this leading to Roger, who confirmed that the time was right. I announced my resignation, giving thirty days notice, and we separated on friendly terms, because God had given me a creative alternative to division.

When Daniel presented his alternative to the commander, he did so respectfully, emphasizing how it would meet the king's goals (Dan. 1:12,13). He made it clear that the decision would still be the commander's at the end of the test period. We must also be careful to present our appeals with respect, maintaining our meek spirit and allowing no hint of condemnation to contaminate our hearts or our words.

Once we have presented our alternative, we must then step back and give God time to change the authority's mind. We should be aware that, since God is putting pressure on him, he is likely to put pressure on us also. When God is trying to change our mind, there is often an inner warfare that spills over onto those around us. When this happens, we should allow God to use the pressure being put on us to build godly character into our lives. We must continue to respond in love and righteousness.

In rare situations, an authority may force us into the position of Peter and John, who found that they must choose between obeying God and man. Occasionally it is impossible to work out a creative alternative that can satisfy the authority's goals without violating our own conscience. If an authority commands us to do something which is directly contrary to the Word or *rhema* of God to us, if no alternative can satisfy, we must obey God, not man. In such a case we may have to suffer, even though we have done nothing wrong. Better to suffer at the hands of unjust men than to stand at the judgment seat of God to give an account of ourselves with no better excuse than, "I was just following orders."

Daniel faced that situation when he was in a position of high authority in the Babylonian government. King Darius was tricked into signing a decree that allowed no prayers to be made to anyone other than the king for a period of thirty days. This time there was no room for compromise, and Daniel went to the lion's den. But God was his strength, and through supernatural deliverance the name of the Lord was glorified (Dan. 6).

It is important, however, that we first make very sure that there is no way to obey both God and His ordained authorities before we resist that authority. Our disobedience must be based on a clear command of Scripture, not our fuzzy personal interpretation. We must remember that if we resist our authority when they are not asking us to disobey God's Word, then we are resisting God Himself (Rom. 13:2).

Changing Authorities

There are times throughout our lives when we make changes that disrupt existing authority relationships. When we marry, get a new job, move to a new location, or change churches, our relationships will change. Whenever such a change must occur, we should do our best to make it a smooth and harmonious transition. "If possible, so far as it depends on you, be at peace with all men" (Rom. 12:18). If there has been tension, seek forgiveness. Be sure your heart is filled with only love and acceptance. Ideally, there should be agreement between you and your counselors concerning the upcoming change. Regrettably, however, this is not always possible.

The important thing is that as we leave one relationship we should enter another. We should always be part of a local expression of the Body of Christ. God's truth and knowledge and wisdom are too big to be contained in just one person, no matter how great you are! Truth lives in the whole Body of Christ, and we need one another.

Conclusion

The principle of authority should never become a source of bondage in a believer's life. It is a principle that must be applied through the revelation of the Spirit. Authority and submission can be a great blessing, or a great source of pain. My goal is not to bring anyone under a new law, but to illustrate how great the value of submission has been to me. If this teaching seems foreign or burdensome, if it would be a great struggle for you to put it into practice, know that you are not alone. Although I have a great love for submission, there are times when I, too, struggle and resist it. But when I give in, it has always been a blessing in my life.

Permit me to share one more story. From the time we were in college, Patti and I had a strong interest in Christian communities. We believed that by pooling our resources and sharing expenses with other families, we would be able to give much more financially to the work of the Lord. We even designed a house in which we planned to live with our best friends.

Our college plans didn't work out, but several years later the desire for community again rose within us. We had grown very close to two other couples in our fellowship and began making plans to live together. We were looking for houses that could accommodate three families when I suddenly realized that I was planning to make a major decision without having shared it with my brothers. Not expecting any problem, I submitted the idea to Roger. I was shocked when he replied, "I think you had better wait."

I had journaled about this plan and I believed the Lord was calling us to the communal lifestyle. But I also respected Roger and the Lord's ability to speak through him. So instead of growing angry and rebellious, I looked for Roger's basic intention. It was easy to find. He loved us and wanted our well-being, not our hurt. And the Lord gave me a creative alternative that met with Roger's desire for us to wait, and my desire for community living. With Roger's blessing, we began visiting communities throughout the northeastern United States and Canada. We lived with various communities for two or three days, working with them, eating with them, and worshiping with them. They represented many theological convictions and many different ways of implementing community life.

When we returned home, I wrote a summary paper of all that we had observed and learned. (I haven't really learned something until I write it down!) One of the biggest things we discovered was the concept of a "ministering household." Rather than complete families coming together in one house, a family unit took in individuals and broken families. Singles, divorced people, single-parent families, and runaways could all find the love and acceptance of family in a ministering household.

We felt drawn to this and asked Roger if he could confirm our moving in that direction. He did, and over the next three years we had thirteen different individuals staying in our home. They ranged from pre-teen runaways to sick elderly men, from seminary students to single mothers. Their stays with us lasted from one night to two years.

Eventually the Lord led us out of that ministry and into others, but the important thing here is that we have never regretted receiving Roger's counsel. We now realize that for us, at that time, community would have been a disastrous mistake. We will always be grateful to the Lord and to Roger for protecting us from going our own way. Our journaling had been mostly correct. God was calling us to share our home, our money, our love. But the words that described His call to us are "ministering household," and those words were not in our vocabulary at the time. I thought God was saying "community house." Our misunderstanding could have resulted in a costly mistake had we not listened to our spiritual advisors.

If you don't feel you can accept all that I have said here about authority, just "put it on the back burner and let it simmer awhile." You don't have to wrestle with it. Let the Lord work out the truth of it for you. Let Him teach you how He wants you to apply it in your life. But please, at least find a friend with whom you can share. Don't try to explore the spiritual dimension of Christianity alone.

Two are better than one because they have a good return for their labor. For if either of them falls, the one will lift up his companion. But woe to the one who falls when there is not another to lift him up...And if one can overpower him who is alone, two can resist him (Eccl. 4:9-12).

8

More Thoughts on Prayer

Although in Jesus and through the Holy Spirit we have returned to the fellowship with God for which we were created, we have not yet learned all that the Bible has to teach us about prayer. My investigation of the Scriptures about prayer revealed to me other insights and principles applicable to our fellowship with the Lord. Many excellent books have been written that cover these various aspects of our prayer life; however, there are six important principles I feel strongly should be covered here.

It is important that we remember the proper place of these principles as we explore them. They are not laws to again bring us into bondage. We should not focus our lives on principles, striving to bring our lives into obedience to them. I made that mistake for many years. As a result of my preoccupation with finding, teaching and obeying the principles for successful living, I brought myself and my congregation under law. Our focus should be on Christ, not principles. It is important to thoroughly learn and understand these principles of prayer, but then we must turn our attention to Jesus, trusting Him to draw forth whatever we need to know in any situation.

When You Pray, Forgive

The most important key to answered prayer is forgiveness. Jesus taught His disciples about the power released through prayer (Mk. 11). After telling them that they could even move mountains by prayer, Jesus added, "And whenever you stand praying, forgive, if you have anything against anyone" (v. 25). This command is amazing in its inclusiveness—there are no exceptions allowed. If we want mountain-moving results to our prayers, we must forgive everything we are holding against anyone.

When we are living in unforgiveness, we become constricted and closed. Our muscles contract and our jaws tighten. All the functions of our body lose the fluidity and balance needed to operate smoothly. The same thing happens within our spirits. We contract and stiffen, raising our fists in a defensive posture. We effectively prevent the love of God from flowing through us and out to others.

Jesus called His disciples to abide in Him, explaining that if we abide in Jesus, we abide in His love (Jn. 15:4,9). No anger, no bitterness, no critical spirit can be within us if we are abiding in the love of Christ. It is impossible to love more than Christ has loved, for He laid down His life for us. Yet, this is the love we are called to show, a love in which we are willing to lay down our lives, our rights, our all, for our family and friends (Jn. 15:12,13). This is the love that returns forgiveness for injustice, blessing for cursing, acceptance for rejection.

This love is impossible for man. There is only One Who has the power to love in the face of any pain. I cannot grit my teeth and force myself to love. I am weak. But the One Who is strong, the One Who is supremely able to love immeasurably, the One Whose name is Love, lives inside of me. It is clear in 1 John 4:12 that if we love one another, no matter what, we have clear proof that God abides in us and that His love is perfected in us, because it is only by His living through us that we will express such love.

If I find myself unable to love another, I don't struggle and strain, promising God, "I'm trying to love him. I'll do it! Just let me try a little harder." Rather, I come honestly before Him, with no pretense or claim to any strength within myself: "I can't love him, Lord. But thank You that You live inside of me. Thank You that the love of Christ is spread abroad in my heart. Thank You that, though I am weak, You are strong. Thank You that You love this person dearly, and that by Your grace, You exchange my lack for Your abundant supply. Thank You for being all that I need." As I turn my eyes to the reality of Christ within me, love and forgiveness are released and "I" am able to love.

Jesus promised that His yoke is easy and His burden is light. The Lord gave us a beautiful picture of our covenant relationship with Him in the Psalms. Our Father tells us, "Open your mouth wide and I will fill it" (Ps. 81:10). Can you see the picture? Imagine a nest of little baby birds. As you peek into the nest all you see are mouths, wide open and waiting to be filled. When they are hungry, mama bird doesn't allow them to try to get food themselves, because they would just fall from the nest and be badly hurt. Instead, she says, "Just open wide. I'll do the work. I will fly about and catch your breakfast. You just rest and open wide to receive all I have to give you."

That is our relationship with God. We don't have to flutter about trying to supply our own needs. He is the strong one. He is the provider. Our part is to simply open up and receive all He has to give us. Forgiveness is only possible by the grace of God. But if we will receive His grace, His ability, love and forgiveness will flow from us.

First John 4:18-21 declares that there is no fear in love because perfect love casts out fear. I use this verse as a barometer to gauge how completely I am abiding in Christ's love. If I enter a room with fear or judgment, it indicates that my life is out of focus. If I face a situation with fear, I am not abiding in love. Love lifts me out of myself, out of my own concerns and needs. Love focuses me on Jesus and others, so that my greatest desire is to minister His love to them.

Anger binds; forgiveness releases. Forgiveness frees both the one who forgives and the one forgiven. And it releases the power of God to work in each one and in situations to bring glory to Him. I discovered the power of love and forgiveness several years ago when I forgave my father.

For some time I had been having a lot of trouble bringing up my parents in the nurture and admonition of the Lord! There was so much truth that I had to teach them, but my father especially was very resistant to my instructions. One summer the situation finally came to a head. Patti and I were visiting my parents at their camp in the Adirondacks. There was so much wisdom I wanted to impart to them but they just wouldn't accept it! Angry words were exchanged and the remainder of the visit resembled the Cold War.

As I drove home, I thought about all that had happened. Gradually I realized that my attempts to teach my parents had represented a role reversal. I was not called to shepherd my parents. They lived in Florida and had a very capable pastor who was ordained to be their teacher. My ministry was to my congregation in New York. I was very careful not to harbor any anger toward Dad. I was just glad that there was 1500 miles between us and that we would not need to meet again for a long time! I have a feeling he felt the same way. For four months there was no communication between us.

That fall I was at a home Bible study. After a time of worship, we sat quietly, allowing the Holy Spirit to speak to us individually. I suddenly heard the Lord say, "You don't love your father." Quickly, I shot back, "Well, I don't hate him!" "But you don't love him either. Love is active, aggressive, reaching out. You are simply neutral, and that is not love."

I realized the truth of His words and repented of not loving and honoring my parents as I should. I shared with the Bible study group what was happening within me and they joined me in prayer that the relationship might be restored.

I did not immediately contact Mom and Dad, but two days later I received my first letter from them in over four months. If this were not surprising enough, the content of the letter nearly overwhelmed me. My parents held part of the mortgage on the duplex I owned. The interest rate was reasonable at the time we made the agreement and as rates rose over the next few years, the rate paid to them became even more of a blessing. However, Dad wrote the letter to say that the Lord had convicted him about charging interest to a Christian brother. Therefore, he was no longer going to charge us interest, and he applied all the interest we had paid up to that point toward the principal.

I could hardly believe it! The power of forgiveness had reached out across 1500 miles to touch my parents without my ever speaking a word. It released them to reaffirm their love for their son. I am glad to say that our family has been restored and that we have a wonderful relationship today.

I don't believe the power of forgiveness can be overemphasized. A pure heart, free from anger and bitterness, provides a vessel through which the power of God can be released through prayer.

Wholehearted Prayer

I would be greatly amiss if I left anyone believing that sitting quietly at a desk writing is the only way to pray. Sharing love with Jesus is absolutely vital, but it is not the totality of our relationship with Him. There are times when intense, fervent prayer is called for.

Elijah was a man with a nature like ours, but when he prayed *earnestly* it did not rain for three years (Jas. 5:17). At the end of those three years, he prayed that it would begin to rain again. He crouched down with his face between his knees, seeking God fervently. Six times he sent his servant to look for a cloud, and six times the skies remained clear. So he continued his earnest petition and the seventh time he looked, there was a small cloud. Elijah knew his prayers had been answered and the two men ran for cover before the storm hit (1 Kgs. 18:42-45).

The psalmist entreated the Lord's favor with all his heart (Ps. 119:58). All of Judah swore with their whole heart to obey the Lord and sought Him earnestly with their whole desire (2 Chron. 15:15). Because of their fervency, the Lord drew back the veil and let them find Him.

There is a place for agony in prayer, for compassion, burdens, tears, groanings, and travail. Jesus was moved with compassion to heal (Matt. 20:34). He offered up prayers and supplications with loud crying and tears (Heb. 5:7). In agony in the Garden of Gethsemane, He prayed *very fervently* and sweat drops of blood (Lk. 22:44).

The psalmist called us to pour out our hearts before God, for He is a refuge for us (Ps. 62:8). Can you see what he means? Can you visualize the intensity of feeling in one whose heart is poured out before God? The Lord is near to the broken-hearted and saves those who are crushed in spirit (Ps. 34:18). The Holy Spirit Himself makes intercession for us with groanings too deep for words (Rom. 8:26).

Years ago I attended "Washington for Jesus," a rally designed to call our nation to repentance and to intercede for her sins. I went with the intention of spending time in travail before the Lord. I felt the burden of the Lord for our nation and expected to join thousands of others who carried the same burden.

As we gathered for the program the first night, I anticipated a time of corporate prayer for our government and our people. Instead, we listened to speaker after speaker and were entertained by singer after singer. The atmosphere was more like a festival than like a time of mourning and repentance.

Finally the late Keith Green came to the microphone. He obviously felt the way I did, for his message was short and pointed, "Where are your tears?" he asked. "Where is your mourning? Why aren't you crying out to God for mercy instead of clapping your hands and having fun? Now is the time for sorrow, not rejoicing, the time for tears, not laughter. Let's get on our knees and pray that God might spare our nation and cleanse her from her sin!"

There are times when I must fall on my face before the Lord. There are times when I must pace my study, literally crying out to God, times when, if He doesn't come through, I am not going to make it. God wants us to come honestly and wholeheartedly to Him.

Speak to the Mountain

When Jesus cursed the fig tree, His disciples were amazed to see it die within just one day. Seeing their surprise, Jesus told them of the power of prayer, that if they spoke to a mountain in faith, commanding it to be moved into the sea, it would be accomplished (Mk. 11:23).

There are times when our prayers should not be addressed to God as petitions, but to circumstances as commands. When Jesus faced the stormy winds and the crashing waves, He did not say, "Oh, Lord, please make this storm stop. Please don't let the wind blow so hard." No! He spoke directly to the problems and said, "Be still!" And they obeyed.

After Moses led the people out of Egypt they were soon in big trouble. In front of them was the Red Sea. To the left and right were mountains. And behind them was an angry army of Egyptians. The people were whining and Moses was praying. Finally God said, "Why are you crying out to Me? Tell the sons of Israel to go forward. And as for you, lift up your staff and stretch out your hand over the sea and divide it" (Ex. 14:15,16). They didn't need to wait for God to act—He was waiting for them.

We have been given authority to rule and reign in this life. We don't always need to ask God to accomplish His will on earth as it is in heaven. That phrase in the Lord's Prayer is not a supplication but a command; not a command to God, but rather to situations to align themselves with the will of God. We have taken our misunderstanding of this phrase and made it the suffix to all our prayers. Because we don't know God's voice, we don't know His will before we pray. Therefore, after presenting our ideas of what He should do in a situation, we tack on the words, "If it be Thy will."

But that is not at all how Jesus was teaching us to pray. The phrase is actually, "Come, Thy kingdom! Be done, Thy will!" We are those who hear God's voice and see His vision. We do nothing out of our own initiative but only what we see the Father doing. We speak only what we have already heard the Father saying. We have seen God's will and God's plan for the situation and we speak it into existence. Like the dynamic power that brought the worlds into being when there was nothing, the Spirit goes forth with the command and God's will is done!

For example, if I am praying for the healing of a broken leg, I do not focus on the limb in a cast and the limitation that brings. Instead, I look as Jesus did, beyond the sickness to the deeper reality of divine health. I see the patient running and leaping, praising God. Then I speak forth, as Jesus did, the kingdom of God, and command the bone to be made whole, just as it was created.

Because of the authority we have received as children of the King, sometimes we must speak to the mountain and see it moved. Then we must hold fast the confession of our hope without wavering, knowing that He Who promised is faithful. God lives in timelessness and sometimes we must wait to see the fulfillment of our declaration. During that time, we must be careful not to give in to doubt but to continue steadfast in our confession.

Pray Until You Praise

A need has not really been prayed for until it has been overcome by the power and promises of God, and until you have entered into peace. Philippians 4:6,7 exhorts us to "be anxious for nothing, but in everything by prayer and supplication with thanksgiving let your requests be made known to God. And the peace of God, which surpasses all comprehension, shall guard your hearts and your minds in Christ Jesus."

Notice the progression. We begin with prayer, presenting our requests to the Lord. We then move into supplication, a more intense form of prayer. But how do we move from asking to thanking? How do we move from begging to receiving? Only by taking the time to be still and feel the movement of God. He may show us by vision or tell us by *rhema* how He wants us to pray. He may show us or tell us that the request has been granted. There may be a lifting of the burden or simply a sense of peace in which we relax in the knowledge that He is in control and all will be well. When we know that He has heard and answered, we worship and thank Him for His goodness to us.

There have been times when peace did not come the first day that I prayed for a matter—only after several days of earnest supplication did I feel the release in my spirit that told me my prayer was answered. Other times I have only needed to pray once and the assurance has come which moved me into thanksgiving and peace. We must let the peace of God rule in our hearts, determining when the matter is settled and praise can break forth.

Pray When You Need God's Strength

In Psalm 50:15, the Lord encourages us to call upon Him in the day of trouble and tells us He will rescue us. The writer of Hebrews called us to draw near God's throne with confidence that we might receive mercy and help in the time of need (Heb. 4:16).

So often we are tempted to do just the opposite. In our time of need, when we have sinned and feel so dirty and so unworthy, we are tempted to run and hide from the face of God. We want to scrub off the dirt and clean ourselves up before we come before the throne. But if we try to do that, we are rejecting the grace of God and relying again upon our own self-righteousness. Only God can make us pure and clean; and He longs to do so. He longs to clothe us in His power and righteousness, but He can only do so if we come to Him in our time of need.

When temptation is strong and we feel that we have no strength to resist, we can call upon God. We do not need to fight satan with our own power. In fact, we cannot. But the One Who lives within us has already defeated him! When we call upon the Lord, He will deliver us from temptation.

The Bible repeatedly reminds us not to try to fight the enemy with our own strength, but rather to put our trust in the Lord. James told us to submit ourselves to God, resisting the devil (Jas. 4:7). We can be assured that he will flee from us. In 2 Corinthians we are reminded that the weapons of our warfare

are not of the flesh, but of divine power (2 Cor. 10:4,5). With them we are able to destroy anything raised up against the knowledge of God. We are strong in the Lord and in the power of His might. By putting on the whole armor of God, we are able to stand firm against all the schemes of the devil (Eph. 6:10,11).

The Movement of God in Prayer

There is a tendency to think of prayer as an activity of the believer. We decide what to pray for, how to pray, and what answer we want. We come to God and present our requests. But such a view represents only part of the true picture of prayer.

In Romans 8:26, the Lord reminds us that we do not know how to pray as we should. Our understanding is limited. We tend to see only from our own perspective. Our minds don't always perceive divine purposes. Yet so often we forget our limitations and think we know enough to tell God what to do and how to do it. And if arrogance doesn't motivate us, ignorance does. It takes a revelation from the Lord to make us recognize that our weakness in prayer is perpetual, so that we might learn to be perpetually dependent on the Holy Spirit.

Because we do not know how to pray as we should, the Holy Spirit works through us in our weakness. We do not need to hide in our weakness, or strive in our weakness. We must learn to rest in dependence upon the Lord to work through our frailty. Because we do not know how to pray, God Himself takes over the whole process of prayer. His strength is perfected in our weakness. If we entrust ourselves to Him, the entire Godhead will become involved in our prayer life.

God Himself will be the initiator of our prayers. When a need is presented to us, if we will wait quietly before Him, the Holy Spirit will form the proper words for us. "Guard your steps as you go to the house of God, and draw near to listen...Do not be hasty in word or impulsive in thought to bring up a matter in the presence of God. For God is in heaven and you are on earth; therefore let your words be few" (Eccl. 5:1,2). If we will still our hearts through worship and contact the Holy Spirit Who dwells within us, He will reveal to us the way we should pray. He may speak a word, give a vision, or allow us to feel His emotions.

Not: **But:**

Prayer is being caught up in the flow of God.

When the Holy Spirit has taken hold of us, giving us wisdom concerning how to pray, we can then speak what He has revealed. If we pray at all times in the Spirit, our prayers will be inspired, guided, energized and sustained by the Holy Spirit. "And this is the confidence which we have before Him, that, if we ask anything according to His will, He hears us. And if we know that He hears us in whatever we ask, we know that we have the requests which we have asked from Him" (1 Jn. 5:14,15). If we pray out of the promptings of the Holy Spirit within us, we know that we are praying according to His will.

Sometimes we feel pressured to pray without first becoming still and tuning in to the voice of the Holy Spirit. This is especially true for me when I am called upon to pray in groups. I feel that I should immediately say something, anything, even if it is not exactly what the Spirit wants said. It takes courage to wait in silence until I sense the movement of God. I admit that sometimes I give in to the pressure and speak out of my own heart. But what is the use of praying if it is only to fill an uncomfortable silence? Surely it is worth the momentary embarrassment to know that God has heard and that He will answer.

The Holy Spirit is not the only person of the Trinity involved in our prayers. Jesus Himself is seated at the right hand of the Father, presenting our prayers to Him and interceding on our behalf. Prayer is an activity of the Godhead, and I am caught in the flow of Father, Son and Holy Spirit.

9

The Lord Speaks Back

I want so much to encourage you to begin journaling every day. To help you see what wonderful things the Lord has in store for you, I would like to share some of the healing, wise and delightful things the Lord has said to other people just like you. These are examples of normal journaling, the kind I hear in every seminar and every day in my mailbox. They come from men and women, young Christians and mature ones, pastors and parishioners from all across the world. I wish to thank the many people who have opened their lives and hearts to us by sharing these journaling excerpts.

I hope these entries will give you confidence as you start out in journaling yourself. In a way, they can be a sounding board against which you can bounce your own initial experiences. Of course, they do not take the place of testing against Scripture and sharing your journaling with your spiritual advisors.

These examples demonstrate several amazing truths. First, they have come from many people of different ages from various cultures, confirming that anyone can hear God's voice. It is not reserved for a select few. Second, they prove that the techniques presented in this book actually are effective in bringing people into two-way dialogue with Almighty God. Finally, I find it remarkable how much like my own journaling all of these individuals' journals sound. This is one powerful proof that we are all contacting the same God, the LORD, the great I AM.

(For clarity, all pronouns referring to God have been capitalized, although they were not always written this way in the journals. We have also italicized the words of the Lord. This does not in any way indicate that we believe these words are equal to or should be added to Scripture. It is simply done to clarify the flow of the conversations.)

Fear Not the Storm

"What would You say to me?"

"You are a beautiful child with innocent eyes. See the clouds forming on the horizon? My arms will keep you safe. Storms are exciting times. Thunder and lightening—not to be feared, for My arms are around you and I'll not let you go.

"We can dance to the music of the storms—your feet on Mine; My hands holding yours.

"We dance with abandonment. The pounding of your heart is not from fear but pleasure and anticipation. The wind wraps My robes around you. Watch and be amazed at what I do. You will find peace in the midst of chaos."

Carole

I Will Not Make a Mistake

"Little one, I understand you very well. I do not condemn you for these doubts. I know your heart's desire, and it is good and pure, and these doubts will fade as you step out in faith. Because you are yet human, you will make mistakes, but I am even in charge of these. I will not let disaster strike, simply because in

the period of growth you may wrongly perceive what I say to you. Trust Me to make no mistake in My growing you. What you are asking for I am in the process of giving. Do not be afraid to make a mistake.

"Just keep pressing inward to Me. I am always faithful. I love you. A father does not always spare his children from mistakes, because this is the way they must learn. But he will not knowingly allow them to make a mistake which will bring disaster, great harm or hurt, to themselves or others. Do you not trust Me, who knows the future, to keep you from harmful, unproductive mistakes? I love your heart. Trust Me."

Anonymous

Healed of Inferiority

"As I looked for vision, I saw Jesus and myself walking together, and I asked the Holy Spirit to take over the vision. Instantly, I saw myself starting to shrink until I totally disappeared. As I looked at the vision, I thought, 'Where did I go?'

"All of a sudden, the picture changed, and I saw the face of the Father from the left profile gazing upward. I knew instantly that He was thinking of me, but it was billions of years ago, before the foundation of the earth. He was planning me in His thoughts.

"The picture suddenly changed again; just as before, I saw Him at a left profile, but this time He was looking down at something. I looked over His left shoulder and I saw the sperm and the egg coming together. The Father had such an excitement on His face as He was watching over my creation. I heard Him say to Himself, *'Here comes Buck!'*

"Again, the picture changed, but this time He was looking upward at an unformed embryo in my mother's womb. He was looking at me and He was speaking His love for me and

His plans and purposes for my life. The vision ended there and for the first time in my life I knew the Father was my true father. He was my Daddy. My earthly parents did not even know I was there yet.

"He had planned me billions of years earlier and was excited about my conception as it occurred. He then spoke life into me before my mother was aware I was even there yet.

"This vision gave me a sense of value to God that I had never known before. I grew up with self-image problems and this totally changed when my Father showed me how He saw me before I ever took a breath on the earth, before I ever experienced any rejection. He had planned, watched over, approved and spoken life into me. He was my true Father that knew me before any person knew I even existed."

Buck

Hearing God's Voice
Transforms Lives Behind Prison Walls

"I never knew if the Lord heard my prayers and certainly would not have even thought that He would want to talk with me in the way that I have experienced in the past few months. Because of this new relationship that I have, as well as the wisdom provided me by the Spirit, my life has changed a great deal and every day is now a pleasure to walk through, instead of the dark, empty hours I became so accustomed to here in this cold, lonely place. Today, whenever I walk in the compound, I have Jesus at my side talking and enjoying His company. I no longer feel alone. I have a sense of peace that I have never known in the past and even in this place, one of the darkest on this earth, He lights my way and guides me through as I put my complete trust in His mighty power."

Steven

Journaling Releases Anointing for Business

"My husband Leo had been put on a team assignment at work that was very challenging. For weeks everyone had been trying to complete a specific project, but no progress was being made at all. Hours were spent in meetings, idea after idea was examined and rejected, and nothing seemed to be quite what they were looking for.

"Leo started in on another weekend of brainstorming at home and he asked me for my thoughts on the project. I told him he should journal about it. (Actually, I told him he should have journaled about it a long time ago!) So, he asked God for His ideas on what should be done and wrote them down. They were brilliant, of course!

"Leo organized the revelations and made sure the presentation was just right. He took it in to work on Monday and waited for his turn to share. The meeting started as usual, with a few other associates giving their suggestions on the project, all of which were determined to be unacceptable.

"Then my husband shared the ideas that God had given him—and everyone loved it!! It was unanimously decided that this was the best presentation that anyone had come up with and it was just what they wanted! Finally, a breakthrough idea that everyone agreed on—a miracle!!

"The thing is, God's got the best perspective on everything, so instead of waiting until all else fails, maybe we should start by asking Him what He thinks. Tap into the divine creativity that is resident on the inside of us and release the anointing of God into our workplace. After all, isn't that why He put us there?"

Charity

Math in a Dream?

"It was in 1995 that my husband Roger was working on his Ph.D. thesis in aerospace engineering. He was working on robotics and the title of his thesis was 'Kinematics and Design of a Class of Parallel Manipulators.' Obviously a lot of math is needed for the control of the parallel manipulators; the only trouble was the math was not working as well as Roger needed it to be.

"It was during a dream one night that Roger got the equation he needed to control his robot. He got up and began writing down what he was getting. This math he received in his dream led to a 33-page equation at the end of his thesis. At the front of his thesis, Roger stated, 'I would like to thank God for giving me constant wisdom, guidance and strength.' He got a lot of flak for this statement, especially from his supervisor, but he never wavered."

Susan

More Business Solutions

"I have been journaling since 1992 using your material. I have often journaled about business issues and problems and God has given me wisdom to solve business problems as well as give direction in relationships, sales campaigns, and solution approaches.

"There were two examples I felt that you might be interested in. The first occurred in a marketing meeting where we were trying to develop a new marketing tag line that captured the value of a new solution we were bringing to market. The team was stumped, so I journaled and the Lord gave me a marketing tag line. I told the team, they were amazed and said that was great, and it opened an entirely new approach for the team to work on.

"On another occasion I was really stumped trying to write a marketing brochure for a seminar my wife and I are doing, I tried to write it but I was really stuck. I journaled and the Lord gave me the entire copy. I simply wrote it down."

Bill (Business Solution Manager for an international company, Canada)

Encouragement Through a Dream

"One night I dreamed that I was part of a highly successful baseball team. I was a well-respected member of the team and did not want to let the team down in any way. It was my turn to step up to the plate. The pitcher gave me his best ball and I hit the ball out of the park! I did not run for the home run. I waited for another pitch. He tried every ball in his repertoire. I thought that this was just too easy. Every ball he pitched at me ended up out of the park. Even the dreaded curve ball I knew I could not hit. Then the setting of the dream changed and I was the pitcher and the opposition fielded their best hitters. I pitched at the best of my ability and no one could hit any of my pitches. They all struck out!

"I was very excited about this dream. Being a native South African, I did not grow up with baseball. I have a working knowledge of the game, but I would not be comfortable playing on any competitive level. When the Lord called us to become missionaries to America we left the familiarity of ministry in South Africa and joined the 'foreign flavor' of ministry in the U.S. The people are different. The way they do things are different. I was like a cricket player (a game we play in South Africa) on a baseball court. I knew we were part of the Lord's team because He called us here. Still I was nervous about my abilities. I could hold my own in ministry in South Africa, but what would happen in America?

"The Lord assured me that I would be able to handle every ball! No matter what the challenge, circumstance or attack, I would hit it out of the park! Even the situations (curve balls) I normally had difficulties with. The Lord also assured me that all my efforts (pitches) would hit the mark. They would not be hit away. They will penetrate and accomplish what they were designed to do.

"This has been a tremendous confidence-building dream to me personally. I was surprised that the Lord would put me in a setting of a game that I really had no or little interest in, but it made so much sense. All apprehension is gone and I'm swinging at every ball the ministry, circumstances or the enemy throws at me. I am highly confident in the abilities the Lord has given me, purely because of the reassurance He gave me in the form of a dream."

Rudolf (Senior Pastor of a church in Ohio)

Together We Are a Unique Treat!

"Lord, what would You like to say to me?"

"You are too hard on yourself. I don't expect you to be perfect. I called you out so that I could live in you and so that we could both experience what the combination of the two of us looks like when we are expressing our personalities through this 'one' body. When we are separate—I am like chocolate and you are like peanut butter. Blend us together and the result is a tasty treat. Except that there is only one like us in the whole world. Together we are a RARE tasty treat.

"I want you to enjoy that about yourself—in Me—and stop lamenting what you are not. I will complete you in your weak areas. Take captive and put away thoughts of inadequacy in your area of gifting. Remember to look to Me and rely on Me

and depend on Me, and I will supply everything you need to serve the Kingdom."

Anonymous

Love As I Love You

"Father, I know I need to concentrate on being more loving and romantic with Jeanie, to show her love daily in practical ways. I fear so much being taken advantage of. What do You want to speak to me concerning this?"

"To close your heart in fear of being hurt or taken advantage of robs you and Jeanie of the joy and fulfillment of love. Love gives. Love opens up and gives away. Selfishness holds back. I know this is not what you want. You heard that what you sow, that you will reap. And when you sow, you always get back much more than what you sowed. Always. To love Jeanie, to be sensitive to her and her needs is sowing in good fertile soil in which there will be a great reaping and harvest.

"As I have loved you, so love one another! Forget how you have been taken advantage of and even your perception of being taken advantage of by Jeanie and others. Showing love should never be based on what others have or have not done. It should be based solely on what I have done. As I have loved you...is where your focus should be and out of that realization and acceptance of My love will flow love to others. Do not allow your vision and focus to go on man, but keep it on GOD SO LOVED, THAT HE GAVE!

"Again, see Jeanie as a tender flower. When showered upon and treated with tender care, it will blossom and bring forth a rare and beautiful smell and aroma. When you give to her, you are watering this flower, and when you put her first and give out of My love and resources, it is like the sun beaming down upon that flower and giving it strength to be beautiful and bright.

"Your fear of being taken advantage of with Jeanie is unfounded. She loves you and is committed to you. Invest in her. There are great dividends ahead. She is the best investment you could ever have. She is well worth selling all and to invest in and pour into. Be sensitive to her today, serve her. Help her with the children. Be on the lookout to where you can bless her.

"You will not regret it. I never once have regretted giving My all. Pouring out My entire life for you and all the world. You are well worth it. I would do it all over again if it was necessary. Greater love has no man than this, that he give his life for another. Give your life for Jeanie. There is no greater love. See and receive My love for you and then give it away. This is My commandment that you love one another. In doing this your joy will be full. I love you, Mike, with tender love and with an everlasting love!"

Mike (Canada)

What I Put in Your Hand…

"I saw the Lord next to the sea; I joined Him and began to skim stones on the water. I got 3 skips. The Lord did the same and it skipped to the horizon. He grinned. I did it again and this time did better—5 skips. Again the Lord did it and it went to the horizon. As I bent to get another stone He stopped me and gave me a stone. It didn't look like a good skimming stone, but I took it. I threw it and it skimmed TO THE HORIZON. The Lord looked at me with a smile and said, *'Paul, what I put in your hand goes further than the things you pick up.'* WOW…it has caused me to ask the question when things are offered me and invitations come, is this what the Lord is putting in my hand or is it something I am picking up!"

Paul (England)

You Are My Joy

"Lord, I have drifted away and so easily for the last two weeks. You know the why's. I need You. I must have intimacy with You above all else. My life depends on it. Speak to me this morning."

"It's hard for you to see Me or to understand when I dance over you with joy. I do not see you as you see yourself. I am not bogged down by the past and the failures. You are My joy. You are a joy to Me."

"But what about all my failures, even my most recent ones?"

"They are gone. Washed away. Forgotten. You have confessed them. I see your heart, My heart in you. There are two choices before you today. To dwell in Me or to dwell in you, on your sins, your failures or your struggles. Choose the better. Sit at My feet and learn of Me. You will find rest for your troubled soul. Come and sit. Dwell. Rest. Relax in My presence."

Anonymous

I Want You to Succeed!

"I was going out to jog (after about a three-month break) and was trying to determine how much to run...against my feeling of compulsion I listened to what was coming from within. I was able to run this amount, realizing that if I had followed my compulsion, I would have failed to succeed in the goal. As I thought on this (nearing the end of my jog) I felt God saying to me *'Lynda, I want you to succeed!'*"

Lynda

Surrender Into Your Destiny

"Tell me again why I should surrender?"

"You don't have enough disk space to hold the answer, nor the ink to print it out! But yes, I understand that you need a reason. Surrender to Me because doing so allows you to be what you were made to be: a child of your Father. Some people never realize their destiny because they don't want to give up their grown-up power and position. Don't be one of those people, Jess!"

Jessie

I Am the One Who Brought You Here

"The Lord taught me a very valuable lesson yesterday between living out of the law and living out of the flow of His Spirit.

"I am a missionary sent out through my church. I was in the Philippines, but because of a rather serious motorcycle accident, I had to return to Canada for medical treatment. I was told that once I was ready, I would be going back to the Philippines. Then, I was asked to pray about going to Taiwan. My heart didn't want to go. I loved the Philippines and wanted to return. The next day, our missions' director called me in and told me that I was being sent to Taiwan. I completely believe in the principle of submission to authority, so I went to Taiwan.

"That was a year and a half ago and it has been what I would call a desert. All I could think of was the Philippines and the people I loved there. I felt very frustrated. Then a thought came into my mind: Why not put the principles of the Communion With God course to work and see what the Lord had to say.

"So, after getting rid of the idol in my heart and focusing my eyes on Jesus instead of the Philippines, I asked the Lord what He wanted to say about the situation. I didn't even have to set the scene. As soon as I asked the question, the Lord brought into my mind the scene of the disciples out in the boat in the storm and Jesus walking to them on the water.

"As I looked more into the vision, I was the one in the boat struggling and straining to row to bring the boat safely to shore. Then I saw Jesus getting into the boat and not only calming the waters, but taking the oars and rowing the boat Himself. The boat came safely to rest in a harbor and as I looked, I knew it was Taichung Harbor, the city where I live now.

"Then the Lord spoke to me and said, *'I have been with you guiding and directing everything that happened in your life. I am the One Who brought you here and it wasn't a mistake.'* That vision and word have brought such a release and freedom to my spirit. It has brought life.

"I could have spent the next two and a half years very miserably by just living out of the law of obedience. It is the Scriptural principle and the right thing to do. In the past I would have just lived out of that principle knowing it is right. But, I would have missed the abundant life that the vision and the flow of the Spirit have released me into in this situation. I want that life to flow continually."

Cindy (Taiwan)

I Know You By Name

"I have worked hard in life not to defile myself with women and now I am ready to seek my own future partner, to settle down and to enjoy the rest of my life in the love of God.

"Dear Lord, how exactly do I know who to really go out with, and from which tribe and background she should be from? What will be the color and the trait that I will see in order to be sure it is the right person?"

"The Lord said to me, *'Before you were born I know thee and I form thee in your mother's womb. Don't you think I had a plan for your life? I have kept you since you were born into this world and without doubt I have led you on the right course of life. All you've seen and gone through is not by accident. Your ability is my ability. I have given you the grace and privilege that has sustained you throughout all your life.*

"'And now that you're set to go into a new phase of your life by choosing your life partner, don't you think I am still with you? Or have you forgotten I said in My Word that I would never leave you nor forsake you in life? Take note of Isaac My servant. At the right time for him I made a provision for his partner, and I am still the God of Abraham, Isaac, Jacob. I change not. Put your trust and hope in Me and believe My words. Cast all your cares upon me for I care so much for you. Though the world may have become corrupt, there is still a way for My children. I know how to program your life for success. Don't bother yourself much on this issue, for you are Mine and I will always be there for you. Be focused on all I call you to do and work in the ways I set before you.

"'I will give you the bone of your bone and make life to be so interesting for you. Akintayo Ebenezer, I know you by name and I have predestined you for great success in life. Look and focus on Me, the Author and Finisher of your faith.'"

"Oh Dear Lord, I bless Your name for opening my eyes to know You and to be called Your son. I will forever trust in You and I will not allow this partner stuff to delay my progress in life. Lord, I count on You and I will be forever grateful for that which You've done for me. Lord, I will not complain or be dismayed because I am sure You're by my side. Thank You, Lord Jesus, for Your words to me today and I know You will always be there for me. I count on You, dear Lord."

Pastor Akintayo (Nigeria)

Protected by His Voice

"I have found God's voice to be very gentle and yet very distinct from my thoughts. The text teaches that we all have spontaneous thoughts, ideas, feelings or impressions at times and if we pay attention, we will find that God is speaking to us. For instance, my sister and I were on the freeway going to a movie. On our way there, the thought kept coming to me to get off at the next off ramp. I ignored it for a while but it would not go away.

"Finally, I told my sister that we were going to take a different route to the show and got off the freeway. When we got home, my mom rushed to the door and said, 'You guys are all right!' We told her, 'yes,' and then asked what was wrong. She said that when we left, she saw us in a terrible car accident. So she started to pray and pray and did not stop until she felt that we were safe. I told her about the impression I had to get off the freeway and when I told her what time it was that we got off the freeway, we learned that it was the exact time she had stopped praying. Coincidence? I don't think so."

Anonymous

I Rejoiced at Your Birth!

"Happy Birthday, son! I rejoiced at the day of your birth. I blessed the hands that brought you forth and I was watching over them with tender jealousy and have watched over you all the days of your life. I blessed you and welcomed you into this world and as you heard [from My prophet], I will show you off. You are a trophy of My grace."

Michael

Trust in My Love for You

Notice: In the next journaling entry God was helping this person face some serious personal problems stemming from earlier hurts and rejection. She shunned close relationships for fear of being hurt again.

She began journaling by speaking to God—then God began to speak to her. In Psalm 95:7-9 we see that the psalmist began the sentence as if it were himself speaking, and then in mid-sentence, realized that it was actually God speaking, and he changed to the first person, and continued on as if it indeed were God speaking, which, of course, it is. The first line of this next journaling entry was very likely God speaking, and could have been written, "You are a new creation in Christ."

"I am a new creation in Christ. Old things have passed away; behold I make all things new! My love for you is greater and stronger than your fears. My love will overcome your weaknesses. My love will renew your heart and soul and I will make you whole in Me. Have faith, believe, trust in My love for you. Do not doubt it, for I died for you in order to possess you as My very own.

"I have great things in store for you. Do not doubt, only believe. Together we will conquer the world; for you are My right hand and My sweet savor to this earth. Through you they will come to see Me.

"Peace be with you, for My peace I have given you. Not as the world gives, but as My Spirit abides in you, you will know My peace."

Anonymous

In the Throne Room

"During the early morning worship time that begins each day at the Leader's School...I told the Lord that I wanted to come into the Throne Room and sing to Him. I am not a singer, but I knew the Lord inhabits my praise, so I knew He could handle it.

"I asked the Holy Spirit to take me to the Throne Room. I looked for vision again, and instantly I saw an open door. I walked in and could see the Throne, but there was a haziness covering my Father and I could only make out the outline of His legs. But, I saw Jesus standing up next to the Throne leaning very casually against it with His left elbow resting on the right armrest of the Throne itself.

"Jesus' ankles were crossed as He stood there completely relaxed against His Father's chair. As I looked at the scene, I noticed Jesus had the coloring of a person. I tried to look through the Glory to see my Father as I had in the previous vision, but could not see Him. So, I focused my eyes on the eyes of Jesus and began to sing to Him. My total focus and attention was upon Him. I did not look away to break eye contact with Jesus.

"After a couple of moments, all of a sudden, our Father jumped off the Throne and landed on both feet with His arms outstretched and said, *'I want to be a part of this!'* This was a big surprise to me. I was stunned for a moment, but I collected my thoughts and said, 'Okay, I will sing to both of You.'

"Jesus and our Father stood side by side as I started singing praise and worship to Them. I noticed that the Father did not have the same coloring as Jesus did, Who looked like a man. He was completely brilliant, 'white as the light,' as Matthew 17:2 describes the transfiguration of Jesus. The only comparison I can think of that somewhat resembles what I saw, is a bolt of lightening. Also, in this vision, They were exactly the same height.

"After a few moments of singing to Them both, Jesus reached out with His right hand to my upper left arm and brought me into an embrace with my Father. As we embraced each other, I could feel His love pouring over me and through me. I thought to myself that I would never leave this place. I am in the bosom of the Father. Can there be any better place in all existence? But, after a little while, Jesus reached out again to me and pulled me back, pointed me back to the door and said, *'Now take this love and share it with My people.'*

"As I stepped back and heard Jesus say these words, I noticed that every part of me that had been in contact with the Father, from my waist up to my face, had become the same 'white as the light' that consumed our Father.

"I said to myself, 'This is going to be easy,'—referring to the words Jesus had commanded me to do. I had always been nervous and fearful about doing the work of the ministry. But this had completely delivered me of that fear. With my Father's touch upon me, I knew He had made me capable of following His calling and the fear instantly left. I could walk out His plans for my life without any fear whatsoever. Thank You, Jesus!!"

Buck

Promotion Comes from Me

This man had just received low scores on some aptitude tests he had taken earlier, and felt depressed.

"Remember, My son, I chose Peter, James and John and many others based on what gifts I had given them, not what other men look at. Your disappointed heart is not unexpected, but remember that I have told you, you and My church, that I have chosen the foolish things of the world to confound the wise.

"Think of what the learned men of Peter's time said of him and the others when they went out to preach My gospel. Even

My own Son, Jesus, was not looked upon as a learned man by His peers, yet He gave the world the greatest gift mankind could ever imagine, eternal life.

"Your low test score means nothing to Me; get your mind off that and back on the dream I have placed in your heart. Proceed with your pursuit of graduate school, and I will open the doors where I wish you to go. Your advancement and promotion will be because I have ordained them to happen, not because of your own power or might.

"Receive this as a lesson in humility and rejoice that you don't have to depend on your own abilities, but upon My Spirit."

Anonymous

Even a Child...

A seven-year-old girl's first journal entry: "Why do You love us so much?"

"Because you are My child."

"Lord, is there anything You want to say to me?"

"Yes, something very, very important. That I love you very, very much."

"Is there more You want to say?"

"No."

"Thank You, Lord, for all You have spoken to me. Goodnight."

This same girl journaled for the second time the following morning.

"Dear Lord God, thank You very much for helping me journal last night. I have a question for You. Why did You say

215

let the little children come unto Me and forbid them not for of such is the Kingdom of Heaven?"

"Because I am their Savior, and I love them."

Her father joined her and they read Matthew 19:13-15. She tried to picture the scene of Jesus with the children and see herself present in the scene in whatever way she would appear. This is what she recorded.

"I am sitting on Jesus' lap. He has one hand on my shoulder and the other around my waist. He said, *'God bless you.'*

"It felt very, very good."

Charity

Be Filled with Me

Journaling frequently brings peace to those who lead a very busy life and find it hard to just sit quietly before the Lord:

"We walked along the shore together. We got in a small boat and He rowed out—the lake was calm; I ran my hand through the water—it was warm. The sun was beginning to rise. It was a perfect day. I expressed my love to Him, and He warmly received it. We rowed back to shore, beached the boat and walked along with arms around each other. He spoke to me, saying that we do have time to walk together, to run together, to laugh together, to enjoy being with one another. It is always time well spent.

"The one who takes time to be filled with Me will never be empty when others come in need. And when they reach in to take of you, they will find Me."

Carol

Share My Life

I was meditating on the Lord, when a picture of Him on the cross appeared to me.

He spoke: *"This is where death came to your sin and to the old nature."*

Then I saw the tomb. He was standing beside it in His resurrected body.

"This is where life came to you and you received a new nature."

Then I saw Him seated on His throne. There was room beside Him. I knew it was for me.

He held His hand toward me and said, *"Come up here beside Me. This is where power comes to you. You are a child of the King, and I share with you power and authority to rule. Some of My children never make it to the throne. I have a place for them here, but they do not listen for My voice, they do not look for My beckoning. They have life, My life, but they do not have it in the abundant proportions I have promised. To receive this, they must come to My throne and take unto themselves the authority and power I hold out to them. To share My life is to share My cross, My resurrection and My throne.*

"Keep coming boldly to My throne, little one."

Anonymous

The Prophetic Word Confirms the Vision

"The Spirit impressed me deeply with Revelation 1:6, 'He has made us to be a kingdom, priests to His God and Father.' 'He has formed us into a kingdom...' (AMP).

"I saw Jesus on the other side of a violently flowing river. He was tall and strong and in His right hand He held two keys which He extended toward me. I knew He wanted me to take those keys. With His left hand He reached out to me, to help me cross the river. I looked at the river—suddenly the rushing torrent rose to such height I could not see Jesus. I looked up to see Him and looked away from the water. The waters lowered and He was still there.

"Fastening my eyes upon Him, I stepped into the current and was swept under. I reached for His hand, and although I was too far away to grasp it, His hand met mine and grasped it firmly. I could see His long arm. He led me out on the other side, and as I cried, He held me close. I knew He wanted me to take the keys and use them. They represented His power and authority over death and over all the works of the enemy.

"I asked Him to speak to me about what I was seeing. He extended His right hand toward me, palm up, with the two keys lying in His palm. As I looked at them, I saw a deep scar in His palm. I knew He was reminding me that His death on the cross had won Him those keys, and if I desired to make use of them, I would have to give up self, totally. I kissed the scar in His palm and cried for what He was asking. There was such an appeal in His eyes—I knew He deeply desired this of me.

"Then He showed me that He would not relinquish the keys into my hand but that I was to place my hand in His, and His hand would guide me in the use of the keys. They would be at my disposal, but only under His direction would they be used."

The next evening at a church prayer meeting a woman spoke in prophecy to this journaler, saying that the keys were available to her and that she was to be bold in using them. The prophecy served to confirm what she had received in journaling.

Anonymous

Fly Specks in My Path

This writer felt that the Lord was setting him upon a path toward a certain goal. However, there seemed to be tremendous roadblocks in the path. The Lord answered:

"Am I Lord? Then I shall determine the circumstances, and I shall then be Lord over these as well. No one prevents what I have determined shall be done. What you see as major roadblocks are as fly specks in My path. Can you trust Me with all of that which concerns you?"

Anonymous

I Would Show You Good Things

This woman asked the Lord to reveal to her the characteristics, attitudes and motivation in her spirit, most especially those which were displeasing to Him.

"I would show you good things, and yet you would not receive them. You focus too much on those things within you which you see as displeasing to Me. I am focusing on those things which please Me. Because your heart is toward Me, these displeasing things will be leaving. I prefer you to focus on the good things and receive the joy I have in these.

"Your heart is pure toward Me. In your heart is My love. That is your motivation; that is your basic characteristic, as it is Mine. The times you feel something else rise within you is frequently satan attempting to edge his way in—but, as you trust Me and ask Me, I thrust these things from you—as long as I know it is not your heart's desire to receive or entertain a motive different than My love."

Joanna

Your Troubles Shall Not Overflow

"*Come, My child, and walk with Me. See the waters lapping at the shoreline? They will never overflow the boundaries I have set. Neither will your troubles overflow the boundaries I have set for them. The end of all this will be good. Do not worry about what you are to say or do—I shall continue to give as you need, just as I gave manna as the children of Israel needed it. What need [would you have] for faith and trust in Me if all the answers were neatly stacked where you could see them and draw from them at will? I shall provide; I shall sustain; I shall give energy. You have only to look to Me, depend on Me.*

"*Take comfort, My child—go forth in My peace this day.*"

Anoymous

I Am Your Success

"Lord, I love You so much and appreciate Your love and care for me. How can I ever thank You for showing me that if I will take time to listen, You really will speak to me?!"

"*I love you, My child, and that love is much stronger and deeper than you can understand. It is this love which will sustain you in the days ahead. When you feel discouraged, puzzled, weary, My love is always there to encompass your hurting heart. Be joyful in that knowledge!*

"*I see your anxiety when things do not happen in the lives of others as rapidly as you would like, but I say, be at peace; rest in Me. These are My concerns, you are only My instrument. It is he who wields the instrument who is responsible for the work done by the instrument. You must feel no pressure to 'succeed.' I am your success. Simply rest in Me and trust Me to do the work in the lives of others.*"

"Lord, You are so good to me! I receive everything from You!"

"Then receive My love. It is poured forth as a fountain forever. Do you not yet see how much I cherish you? O child of Mine, believe what I tell you. I cradle you in My bosom. I hold you and protect you. Nothing in this world can harm you or take away that which I have given you—love, joy, peace, rest in Me. I will teach you. Do not struggle—simply wait on Me. Trust Me in all that concerneth you. It is with joy I see your heart. I hear your requests. Consider them done."

Anonymous

You Are a Winner Through Me!

"You see yourself as such a failure, such a hopeless case and therefore you already have given up and thrown in the towel to defeat and failure. You convince yourself even before the fight that you will not win, which results in certain failure and defeat. When one goes into battle already believing that they will lose, then there is no hope or strength to conquer. Defeat is inevitable.

"But I do not see you that way! I am not convinced or persuaded of those lies and misconceptions. You are My son. Bought with My precious blood. More than a conqueror! An overcomer! A delight to the Father. You are overturning many years and generations of ungodly belief and ungodly structures that have been set up against the knowledge of God. I will help you to identify and then to pull down ungodly patterns of unbelief in your life. I will bring you to a place of utter rest in Me and to a place of great intimacy which will result in great exploits that will reach the nations. FIX your eyes on Me! I am able to do this. I am the Great I Am.

"You are no different than My disciples were. They were also steeped in great unbelief as they walked with Me and saw all that I did and yet they were still engulfed in unbelief and ungodly patterns of thought. But I brought them to a place of

221

great faith and relationship with Me. I am faithful. Great is My faithfulness to you.

"You are Mine. You are Mine just as much as the apostles were Mine. They were not more My children or more favored than you. You are just as much a child of Mine as they were. Continue to acknowledge and repent of your sin of unbelief and turn your attention and focus to Me, to My words for you and you will continue to experience a transformation in your life that will revolutionize your world that will in turn, revolutionize all those that you are called to affect.

"Trust Me like a little child would trust his father. Remember Josiah at a young age when you repeatedly told him to trust you when he was ready to jump into your arms in the water. He was so afraid to jump, but you persuaded him to trust, to jump, because you knew you would not fail him. And you did not. He jumped, then again and then again until his fear of the water was overcome. Trust was built and established. Now, trust Me and jump. I will catch you. You can do it. Jump! I cannot fail you. I will not fail you. I will catch you. You are forever safe in My arms. You will not drown. I will not fail you. Trust will be built and established."

Michael (Canada)

10

Yada—Sharing Love

Patti grew up in western New York. As a teenager, she listened to a disc jockey named Danny on the radio almost every day. He was very popular with young people, and wherever they gathered, radios were soon blaring and his voice filled the air.

After being at college and living in another part of the state for a time, we moved back to the western New York area. One day, while listening to the news on television, Patti was surprised to recognize the voice she had heard so often as a teenager. While continuing as a radio disc jockey, Danny had also become somewhat of a local television personality. Patti then had a picture she could associate with the voice. Any time she wants to hear what Danny has to say, she can easily tune the television to the proper channel where she can clearly hear and see him.

All of the formulas, principles and stories in this book have been given to help you hear and recognize the Lord's voice within your spirit. I hope you have been able to add vision to your life also and see God moving with the eyes of your heart, and that you have learned how to tune your heart to increase your receptivity. But if you stop there, you have no greater relationship with Jesus than Patti has with Danny the disc jockey.

Patti knows Danny's voice and even recognizes his face, but she doesn't know him as a person. They have never shared their thoughts or feelings. There is no love or even friendship between them. It is possible to know someone's voice without knowing them.

So we return to the beginning. Communion with His children is the deepest desire of God's heart. It is important for us to be able to recognize His voice because it greatly enhances our ability to have fellowship with Him. But our goal is not to simply know God's voice, but to know God.

Jesus told us that "this is eternal life, that [we] may know thee the only true God, and Jesus Christ whom [Thou] hast sent" (Jn. 17:3). Our salvation is not a possession but a relationship. Eternal life is not simply living forever; we must also grow in love.

The Greek word translated "know" is *ginosko*. This does not refer to the simple, casual "knowing" of an acquaintance, or even a close friend. *Ginosko* means being involved in an intimate growing relationship. It is the word used in the Septuagint in Genesis 4:1, where it says that Adam "knew" Eve and she bore a son. *Ginosko* refers to the most intimate personal relationship between a husband and wife. This is eternal life. This is the reason for which we were redeemed: That we might have a deep, intimate love relationship with the Father and Son, which grows sweeter throughout time and eternity.

The Hebrew counterpart of *ginosko* is the word *yada* and that is the word I like to use to characterize our time of loving fellowship in prayer. Prayer is not an activity we do—it is being with Him. Until we move beyond our limited perceptions of prayer as petition, supplication, praise, and thanksgiving, we will never come to the deep loving relationship for which we were created. Those aspects of prayer are important—please don't misunderstand me! But if they do not flow out of *yada*, knowing God intimately, they are in danger of becoming mere religious activities.

He Longs to Love You

When we accept Jesus as Lord of our lives, we become engaged to Him. The time we remain on earth after our conversion until the Lord returns is our betrothal period. It is our opportunity to spend lots of time together, deepening our relationship, sharing our hopes and dreams, joys and pains, successes and challenges. Paul told the Corinthian church, "I betrothed you to one husband, that to Christ I might present you as a pure virgin" (2 Cor. 11:2). When the Lord returns, we shall be part of the Church united with her Lord at the great marriage supper of the Lamb.

During our betrothal, our Fiancé longs for our company. He wants us to share whatever is on our hearts, and be comfortable enough to be able to simply sit together silently, enjoying each other's love. He spoke the following words to Patti in her journal:

"I love you. I long for you to return to Me as much as you long for someone to share your heart. I do need your love. I do love you. I long to express My love to you. Please do not reject Me. I love you. Please accept all the blessings I have showered upon you as gifts of love. I love you, My child, My darling one. You are precious to Me. You are a treasure I hold dear to My heart. Come share your life with Me."

When Jesus looked upon Jerusalem, the city He loved so much, He was hurt by the people's rejection, but He still loved without measure. He cried out: "O Jerusalem, Jerusalem…How often I wanted to gather your children together, just as a hen gathers her brood under her wings, and you would not have it!" (Lk. 13:34). Jesus still longs to draw us close to Himself, to give us security and identity, to let us feel His heart beating with love for us! How we hurt Him when we are too busy to spend time with Him. How His heart is wounded when we choose rules instead of relationship, service instead of love.

A student received this from the Lord in journaling: "My child, you feel that you have an issue with prayer. Why? It is merely a conversation with a close, intimate friend—Me. Come to Me and talk, listen, enjoy—all the things you would do with any earthly friend—although I can be more—I am your everything. Allow Me to flow through you, from you in everything you think, say and do. Talk more. Listen more. Watch more. It is easy if you look to Me for guidance—for My leading. I love you. Come. Rest in My rest. Allow Me to flow."

How delighted Jesus is when we choose *yada*! "As the bridegroom rejoices over the bride, so your God will rejoice over you" (Is. 62:5). I wonder if we can really grasp this love our Savior has for us! Listen: "You have made my heart beat faster, my sister, my bride; You have made my heart beat faster with a single glance of your eyes, with a single strand of your necklace. How beautiful is your love, my sister, my bride! How much better is your love than wine, and the fragrance of your oils than all kinds of spices! Your lips, my bride, drip honey; honey and milk are under your tongue, and the fragrance of your garments is like the fragrance of Lebanon" (Song of Sol. 4:9-11).

These are the words of a man in love! Though the Song of Solomon speaks of the love of a husband and wife, it is also a beautiful representation of the love between Christ and His bride, the Church. He loves us with an unfathomable love. He longs to express that love to us.

The Lord does not want us to come to Him only when we have a need or a question. He doesn't want us to always have an ulterior motive for seeking Him. Although fellowship makes us more productive, He does not want us to come to Him simply to increase our productivity. He wants us to come to Him because we love Him so much we can't stay away.

The Lord said to me, "I enjoy just being with you, not doing anything special together, just being together. I enjoy the fragrance of your worship. Times of solitude are peaceful to Me. It is like a quiet brook, flowing on the mountainside. I desire your presence. It is refreshing to Me. It is the fulfillment of My purposes when you choose to be with Me. It brings Me great pleasure. Do it often. Do not think that every time we come together it must be to accomplish something. Simply being together is the greatest accomplishment, just being with one another. Come, let us enjoy one another."

Taking Time to Love

"Love at first sight" is a romantic fantasy. Love does not burst full-bloom into our hearts. It begins as a tiny seed which grows into a strong and beautiful blossom if it is carefully tended. Love comes from spending time together, laughing, crying, working and playing together. There is no shortcut to true love that endures, in spite of what Hollywood would have us believe.

When the Lord called the twelve disciples, His first and primary reason was that they might be with Him (Mk. 3:14). He did not principally want their service, although that would certainly come. First and foremost He wanted them to be with Him, to be His friends, to share His joys and sorrows.

When Patti and I were dating, we spent most of our time together. Except when our class schedules didn't allow it, we were almost inseparable. We got up early to have devotions together. When time and finances permitted, we went out on dates. We talked about everything, and no part of our lives was hidden from the other.

Why, you might ask, did we act that way? Did we make a rule that we had to spend every possible waking hour together? Was there a law that forced us to write each other every day during vacations? Did some strange requirement force me to do crazy things, like driving all night to spend a few short days with her? Of course not! We loved each other. We wanted to be together. When we were apart something within us was incomplete. The more time we were together, the more we wanted to be together, until we knew that we wanted to spend the rest of our lives sharing our love.

My relationship with the Lord is the same way. There is no law that forces me to share my life with Him. We have not made a rule that I must spend a certain amount of time with Him in journaling each week. But His love draws me to Himself. When I become caught up in the busyness of life, deep inside I can hear Him calling to me to come rest in His presence.

One day He said, "I am the Alpha and Omega, the beginning and the end. I am able to do abundantly above all that you are able to think or ask. Just come to Me and I will be your strength. I will be your Lover. You must simply come to Me. It cannot be accomplished without time together. So, come to Me often, continuously. I am always here. I am always ready to listen and respond. I am a great and loving God, slow to anger and abounding in lovingkindness. You must only seek Me with all your heart and come to Me. Will you do that?"

Over and over He calls those who will hear Him to come and spend time with Him. To Patti He said, "I want you to learn to live out of My heart. You know what pleases Mark and you seek to live out of that. Know what pleases Me. Know Me and love Me. You cannot abide in Me until you know Me and love Me. And you cannot know Me and love Me until you spend time with Me. Come to Me. Take time to know Me."

As "deep calleth to deep," our spirits respond with longing for Him. "As the deer pants for the water brooks, so my soul pants for Thee, O God. My soul thirsts for God, for the living God; When shall I come and appear before God?" (Ps. 42:1,2).

As lovers seize every opportunity to be together, my heart seizes every chance to spend time with the Lover of my soul. In His gentle presence, I find peace, satisfaction and joy. "Your love is better than wine. Your oils have a pleasing fragrance, your name is like purified oil; therefore the maidens love you. Draw me after you and let us run together! The king has brought me into his chambers. We will rejoice in you and be glad; we will extol your love more than wine" (Song of Sol. 1:2-4).

Living in Relationship

Communion with the Lord is not something we do at a special time each week. Communion is a way of life that affects every part of our being. When we live in our relationship with Jesus, everything we do will be touched.

For example, how many of us believe in the necessity of every believer being a witness? How many of us have read books and taken classes designed to increase our ability to be effective witnesses? Yet how many of us feel that we often fail our Lord by not being the witnesses we should be? All too often, we pastors have brought guilt and condemnation upon our people because we have not fully understood the true concept of witnessing. Jesus did not tell His disciples, "You must go out and witness to the people of Jerusalem, Judea and Samaria." No, when Jesus spoke, "witness" was not a verb, but a noun, not something we do, but something we are. "You shall be My witnesses" (Acts 1:8; see also John 15:26,27).

What is a witness? Suppose you have gone to your corner grocery for some milk. It is late at night. Suddenly you hear a commotion at the register. As you peek around the end of the aisle, a man with a gun forces the proprietor to give him all the money from the cash register. When the thief turns to leave, you get a good look at his face. The police arrive moments later and you step forward. "I was a witness, Officer," you say. "I saw the whole thing." At the trial, you are then expected to testify to everything you saw and heard. The judge will allow nothing more or less.

Jesus said that after the Holy Spirit came upon us, we would be His witnesses. In other words, we would tell others what we have seen Him do and heard Him say. Peter and John understood what Jesus meant. They saw a lame man begging on the Temple steps. But they also saw, in their spirits, Jesus healing that man. So they spoke out of the Father's initiative and the man began walking and leaping and praising God. Then they began testifying to what they knew about Jesus. As a result, they were put in jail and brought to trial. The Council marveled at their testimony as witnesses, and began to recognize them as having been with Jesus.

That is true witnessing. It is seeing what Jesus is doing, hearing what He is saying, and then appearing on the witness stand before the world to testify to what He has said and done. If we have been with Jesus, our testimony will convince the spectators and many will be saved from eternal punishment.

Worship took on new meaning for me when I began to see it as part of my total experience of communion with the One I love. As I opened the eyes of my heart to see the reality of what I was singing, worship became a spiritual encounter. I began to see Jesus seated at the right hand of the Father, enthroned upon the praises of His people. I began to see His pleasure with our praise and the ways He ministered His love back to us. As I gave Him permission, the Holy Spirit took over and showed me spiritual realities behind the words of our songs.

One Sunday morning, Patti offered the Lord the eyes of her heart during a time of worship and He gave her a beautiful vision that continued through the rest of the service. I have asked her to share it with you, because it demonstrates so many of the principles taught in this book. It shows that as we become quiet in God's presence, tuning to vision and spontaneous expression, the active flow of the Holy Spirit can arise within us, and God can minister wondrous things to us. In this case Patti quieted herself using music, very similar to what Elisha did (2 Kgs. 3:15). I'll let her tell the story:

"This Sunday began like most Sundays. I was tired from being up several times with Joshua, the baby. Our foster son wasn't home and his sister wasn't anywhere in sight. Mark had gone to the church soon after I woke up, so I got the little ones ready alone. Company was coming for dinner so I had to start that, and the house wasn't terribly clean. I didn't have time to set my hair and when I got dressed, I looked even heavier than usual, so I had to change into something that made it less obvious.

"By the time I arrived at church, worship had started and I felt as terrible as I usually did on Sundays. When Mark asked how I was, my response was, 'I hate Sundays!' I began clapping and singing, however, offering a sacrifice of praise.

"After a while, there came a lull in the service and a spirit of quietness came upon the congregation. A voice kept repeating within me, 'Behold! Your Lover comes, riding upon a white horse, conquering and to conquer!' Being uncertain as to whether it was a message only to me or to everyone, I kept silent. In light of what followed, I can now see that the speaker was the forerunner of the Lord, going ahead to prepare me for His arrival.

"Very soon He came to me. He rode upon a white horse and He wore a white suit. As He dismounted, I ran to Him. He held me as I cried out my frustration and anger and depression. Then, with His arms around me, we turned and walked back into my morning. He showed me that the circumstances had not been as bad as my state of mind, and helped me see what could be done to prevent such mornings in the future.

"My morning healed and dealt with, we returned to the grassy meadow where we had left His horse. The congregation had returned to worship and I joined in singing.

"I sang of His steadfast love extending to the heavens, of His faithfulness, righteousness and wisdom. And I sang of finding peace in the shadow of His wings, and drinking from streams of rejoicing.

"It was my love song to my King, and as I looked into His face, I felt deep love for Him and His love returning to me.

"Next we sang 'My Glory and the Lifter of My Head,' a happy song of praise for the joy He gives to replace our sadness. As I sang and clapped, I looked at Jesus and He was dancing! I couldn't help joining in His laughter of pure delight and celebration.

"As the men began singing 'Let Us Adore,' Jesus joined in, inviting me to worship His Father with Him. We began to walk arm in arm, singing together our praise to God.

"Suddenly He was back on His horse as we arrived at a large grassy arena. A huge crowd was gathered around the empty field. I found my place in the front row of the crowd as Jesus rode victoriously around the arena. I felt that I would burst with pride and joy as we sang, 'The Lord is good, the Lord is great, and greatly to be praised!'

"We were obviously celebrating a great victory and honoring the One Who had accomplished it. He smiled at us as He rode by, His face expressing such love and nobility. We sang to Him, the Lion of Judah, the King of kings.

"Jesus ascended to a raised platform at the end of the arena. There was a canopy over this stage and colorful flags or banners at each side. I couldn't see who was performing the ceremony, but I felt that it was His Father crowning Him with a beautiful but simple golden crown. As we sang, my Lord started across the arena toward me.

"I was dressed as a medieval lady, with a long flowing dress and a tall hat streaming with ribbons. I sensed that, though I was still important as myself, I had become symbolic of the Church. He led me as His bride back to the platform to reign with Him, as the congregation sang, 'Maranatha! Let your kingdom's reign come!'

"Suddenly the song 'This Is the Day' broke forth, and I thought in disappointment, 'That doesn't fit. My vision is over.' But Jesus felt otherwise. I suddenly found us dancing together around the arena. He let me know that we were celebrating His Father's work. Jesus had won the victory but it was through the power of His Father that it was possible. Indeed, the Lord had made the day and we could rejoice and be glad in Him.

"The final song of the worship service was 'Rejoice in the Lord Always.' We returned to the platform and the crowd spilled onto the field, dancing a kind of minuet of celebration.

"Before communion I saw that the crowd had moved to a large banquet table. Jesus sat at the center as guest of honor. I was at His left hand as His bride and Roger, our elder, on His right as Master of Ceremonies. Roger spoke about an enemy we were soon to face and the victory our Lord had already achieved against him. As we took the Lord's Supper, I had to restrain myself from physically lifting the cup as a toast to Jesus, but that is what my spirit was doing. The remainder of the time was spent giving further testimonials to honor our victorious Ruler and Friend."

Faith

Faith is a natural result of a life of fellowship with God. Romans 10:17 says that faith comes from hearing the *rhema* of Christ. When Jesus speaks to us, faith is not a difficult task; it just happens naturally. Mel Tari said, in *The Gentle Breeze of Jesus,* that simple faith is nothing more than a natural result of knowing Jesus, of being close enough to Him to know what He wants to do in a certain situation. Then, in simple obedience, we do whatever He tells us.

Have you ever been privileged to witness the relationship of a couple who have enjoyed fifty years of marital love? They know each other so well that they hardly even have to ask what the other thinks or wants. She knows just how to fix his eggs and his morning coffee. He knows her favorite color dress and what restaurant to take her to. If he dies without leaving a will, she knows exactly who should get the gold watch and his books. Because they have spent so much time together, honestly sharing their whole lives, they instinctively know what the other would want to do in a situation and how they should help.

That is a life of faith built on *yada.* As we share love with Jesus, His *rhema* creates faith in our hearts and we are able to live in obedience to His Word.

One of the strongest desires that motivates Christians to learn to recognize the Lord's voice is the desire to know the will of God. We long for His guidance along every step of our lives, which is as it should be. Knowing the Lord's will is a natural outcome of being with Him. In Psalm 32:8,9, the Lord tells us, "I will instruct you and teach you in the way which you should go; I will counsel you with My eye upon you. Do not be as the horse or as the mule which have no understanding; whose trappings include bit and bridle to hold them in check...."

King David had many servants around him who watched his every move intently so that they might anticipate his needs. When he reclined at the table to eat, the servants were nearby. If he wanted fig cakes, all he had to do was glance at them and one of the servants brought them to him. When he wanted more wine, just a glimpse at it would suffice to signal them to refill his cup. His servants watched him so closely that he did not even have to speak his desires. He could indeed counsel them with his eye.

The Lord says He wants to guide us this way, too. He wants us to be so close to Him that we will immediately know His desires. He wants our focus to be so intently upon Him that all it takes is the movement of His eye to guide us. He doesn't want to guide us like one would guide a horse, with a bit in the mouth, which makes it painful to disobey, or a bridle, which removes all other options. He wants to guide us with His eye.

When we began hearing the Lord's voice, my wife and I struggled to find a balance in guidance. The Lord spoke to Patti: "Your life is full of decisions. Every single thing you do and say involves a choice, a decision. I want to make those decisions for you. Turn to Me before you make any choice. Allow My desires to fill you." She objected to His words, imagining they would mean a constant inner dialogue, which could be very draining.

He replied, "My goal is not for you to be constantly asking questions, but rather that you be constantly aware of My answers and desires. More than mental conversation, I want spiritual awareness, awareness that I live inside you, that I am a Person, that I am wise and loving and want to and can guide you better than you can guide yourself. You have sensed My restraint and often said, 'Oh, so what!' and gone ahead to fulfill your own desires. I want you to say, 'So what!' to your desires and appetites and 'Yes, Lord!' to Me."

Summary

Yada is the center of life, the very core of Christianity. All that we do finds its source and its fulfillment in our love for Jesus. Everything we do, we do out of love for our Lord. Every thought, word and deed flows out of our deep, intimate knowledge of Him. And everything we do leads us to a greater love for Him. Daily we grow in *yada* knowledge of Jesus. Daily we grow to more deeply love the Lover of our soul.

Jesus is waiting to share His love with you! He is waiting for you to come and share your life with Him. Remember and use the keys which will help you unlock the door to that sweet intimacy for which you have longed:

Key One: Tune your heart to receive the spontaneous voice of the Spirit within you.

Key Two: Quiet yourself inwardly so you are able to sense God's inner movement.

Key Three: Open the eyes of your heart, asking the Father to fill them with His dream and vision.

Key Four: Journal, writing down the spontaneous dialogue that comes to your heart.

If you encounter difficulties that seem to block your way, return to the Tabernacle or examine your life in light of Hebrews 10:22. It is very important that you maintain a meek spirit, which gladly submits to testing by the Word and the Body of Christ.

Come now to meet with your best Friend. Allow me to set the scene. Become involved in the picture I will draw for you. Read slowly, seeing, hearing and feeling the story. When you reach the end of my words, allow the Holy Spirit to carry the vision wherever He will. Say to Jesus all you want to and listen to what He wants to say to you.

Now Sit Back and Relax...

Come with me in your spirit to a mountainside in the province of Galilee. It is a beautiful summer day. The air is warm but up here on the hillside there is a gentle breeze that refreshes you. You find a comfortable position to sit in the thick grass. Occasionally you look up as you hear the call of a bird flying overhead. Below you in the distance the reflection of the sun on the Sea of Galilee sparkles and shimmers.

You are vaguely aware of the crowd gathering around you. You have chosen a spot right in the front, right there among Peter, James, John, Andrew and the others who are always with Him. For you are here to see Jesus. He's sitting up ahead, a little apart from the others. He's leaning back against a big rock and His head is bowed. You can tell He's talking to His heavenly Father by the peaceful look on His face.

As you watch Him, waiting for Him to begin speaking, you reflect on the last few days. For weeks you had been hearing about the carpenter's son from Nazareth who was going throughout the country preaching and healing. At first you hadn't paid much attention, assuming it was just another self-proclaimed "messiah" like so many before. But the rumors continued and soon you sensed that this man was not like the others. This Jesus spoke with such authority that even the scribes and Pharisees were silenced. People were being healed and demoniacs set free by the power of His word. Your interest grew as reports came in from Jerusalem, Tyre, Sidon and the Decapolis.

Then, just a few days ago, He arrived in your town. While some businesses were frantically trying to meet the demands of the huge crowd that followed Him, you closed your shop to join them.

Absently you chew on a blade of grass, remembering...

The first time you had heard Him speak was in the synagogue. He was asked to read the Scriptures. The room hushed expectantly as He walked forward. His voice was strong and clear as He read from the scroll. When He finished the day's portion, He began to teach. Such wisdom flowed from Him! The men leaned forward in eagerness to hear more and the women strained not to miss a word.

"The kingdom of God is right here in your midst," He said. "Don't keep looking for your Deliverer, for God is visiting you this very day." When He finished speaking, there were a few moments of silence. No one wanted to intrude on the spirit of holy Presence they all felt. Then a child cried and the spell was broken. The room came alive with heated discussions. Some, of course, were angry and skeptical. But then, they were always negative and critical, so you weren't surprised. Most of the people were excited and wanted to hear more....

You hear the giggle of a little girl behind you, and your thoughts turn to little Rachel. Her parents have been your friends since childhood. You knew of their sorrow when year after year passed without God giving them a child. The whole village rejoiced with them when they announced the news that her mother was with child. But their joy was tempered with sorrow when little Rachel was born, for she was blind. You watched her grow and your heart ached for her and her parents when you saw her sit by the door listening to the other children running and playing. She was such a sweet, cheerful child, always trying to make others forget their sorrows with her bright little laugh.

At your suggestion her parents had taken her to Jesus. As always there was a crowd around Him, but when your

238

neighbors saw Rachel and her parents, they moved aside, encouraging them to get closer. Finally the four of you made it to the place where Jesus was ministering.

As you stepped through the throng, a man threw down his crutches and began leaping about, praising God and hugging everyone in sight. Jesus was smiling as He watched his joy, and then His eyes rested on Rachel. His expression changed to one of incredible love and compassion. He stepped toward your little group and knelt down in front of Rachel. He spoke to her softly. You couldn't hear the words, but you saw her face break into a beautiful smile and she nodded her head. Very gently, Jesus cupped her face in His hands. He spoke softly again, then leaned forward and kissed her forehead.

At that moment, you saw the light come into her big, black eyes. Her face was alive with emotions, first amazement, then wonder and joy. The first thing she saw was Jesus' face. He was smiling at her and she grabbed Him around the neck in a big bear hug. In her excitement, she knocked Him off balance and they fell together, laughing aloud for pure joy. He scooped her up and handed her to her parents, who were so overcome with emotion that they could barely speak. But somehow, you knew He understood....

Jesus stirs and you are brought back to the present. How you wish you could talk with Him! There is so much you want to say, so many questions you want to ask. He looks directly at you and smiles. Automatically you smile back, and the desire to talk with Him grows.

The crowd is suddenly silent as He begins to speak. His words are like a gentle rain falling on the dry ground of your heart. You drink in every word, and feel your spirit beginning to come alive. Every few minutes His eyes meet yours and you know that what He is saying is meant for you. If only you could talk to Him alone! He would understand that ache in your heart. He would understand that dream you harbor deep within. If only.... But, of course, it would be impossible. Even if the crowds left, He was always surrounded by His disciples. He didn't have time for just you....

So you gaze at Him raptly, not noticing the hours pass. His words are life to you and you want to hear every one. You sense that He is almost finished speaking and your heart is gripped with a strange sadness. When He stops speaking, you must go home, alone, with all those feelings still pent up inside of you; and you dread that. You don't want to leave His presence.

He is finished now. The crowd begins to gather up their things to return to the village for the night. You notice the sun is low in the western sky, but you don't move. Not yet. This is holy ground and you want to capture this moment to savor forever.

You are aware that Jesus is speaking quietly to His disciples. They glance your way, but you hardly notice them as they begin to move away.

Suddenly you realize that everyone is gone; everyone, that is, except Jesus and you. You look around startled. Is it possible? Are you really alone with Him? He smiles at you and nods His head. He stands to His feet, His eyes inviting you to join Him. Hardly believing what is happening, you scramble to your feet. Together you walk up over the hill. At first you are a little shy, but He gently draws you out. Your heart explodes with joy and you feel that there has never been such a beautiful day. Your words begin to spill out, tumbling over one another in your eagerness to say all that is within you. He listens and understands. You knew that He would.

Now as I leave you walking along the path with Jesus, tune to the spontaneous words and impressions that begin bubbling up from within you. They are God's voice. Out of your inner stillness this vision comes alive and moves with a life of its own, birthed in the Father's initiative. Begin capturing the spontaneous flow on paper as you journal. And behold, you find that you, too, have begun communing with God. It is the dawning of a whole new day in your spiritual walk. Now let us begin.

Appendix A

Logos *and* Rhema *in the Greek New Testament*

The first person to make me aware of the distinction between *logos* and *rhema*, two Greek words translated "word" in the New Testament, was David (Paul Yonggi) Cho. I heard Dr. Cho speak at the Niagara Falls Convention Center, and he said that *rhema* is fellowship with the Holy Spirit. It is the spoken word of God in our hearts, and he said we must learn to live out of the *rhema* word and not just the written Word.

The idea excited me. It seemed right that we live out of our fellowship with the Holy Spirit, the voice of God within our hearts. I immediately went home and got out my concordances to see if I could substantiate this distinction. To my dismay I found that there appeared to be much overlap between *logos* and *rhema*, and I did not seem able to confirm the distinction made by Dr. Cho. Therefore I set the whole issue aside.

After a couple of years, the Lord brought me back to look at it another time. What amazed me the most was studying through the seventy verses where *rhema* is used in the New Testament (see Appendix B). I recommend you do it also. I was shocked to discover something I had missed before: in each of these references, *rhema* seems to refer to a spoken word, never the written word. I thought that maybe this word was distinctive after all; and that maybe I could use it, as Dr. Cho had suggested, to describe the spoken voice of God within my heart.

With that in mind I went to some Bible dictionaries and discovered that *logos* is used in the New Testament 331 times, and *rhema* is used 70 times. The *Dictionary of New Testament Theology* defines *logos* as, "Collect, count, say, intellectual, rational, reasonable, spiritual." *Rhema* is, "That which is stated intentionally; a word, an utterance, a matter, event, case." *Vine's Expository Dictionary of New Testament Words* defines *logos* as "The expression of thought. Not the mere name of an object (a) as embodying a conception or ideal; (b) a saying or a statement." *Rhema*, "Denotes that which is spoken; what is uttered in speech or writing."

The distinctions between *logos* and *rhema*, according to the *Dictionary of New Testament Theology* are, "Whereas *logos* can often designate the Christian proclamation as a whole in the New Testament, *rhema* usually relates to individual words and utterances: man has to render account for every unjust *rhema* (Matt. 12:36); Jesus answered Pilate without a single *rhema* (Matt. 27:14); the heavenly ones speak unutterable *rhemas* (2 Cor. 12:4)." The significance of *rhema* (as distinct from *logos*), according to *Vine's Expository Dictionary of New Testament Words*, "is exemplified in the injunction to take the sword of the Spirit, which is the Word (*rhema*) of God (Eph. 6:17); here the reference is not to the whole Bible as such, but to the individual Scripture which the Spirit brings to our remembrance for use in time of need, a prerequisite being the regular storing of the mind with Scripture."

Coupling these definitions with my own personal insight received by examining every use of *rhema* in the New Testament, I knew that the voice of God I was hearing within my heart was *rhema*. I found that *rhema*, His voice within, could provide the precise word I needed for use in specific counseling situations. Allow me to illustrate:

A man from our church phoned one day to ask if he could send his supervisor from work to me for counseling. I had never seen the man who was referred to me for help. I had spent fifteen years studying the *Logos*. I couldn't possibly tell him everything I knew in two hours. I needed *rhema*. So I went before the Lord and asked for His word to this man. The Lord told me three things: "The man will be heavy set, he will be wearing a red-striped shirt, and he needs to be assured of My unconditional love for him."

When the man arrived, he was heavy set and wearing a red-striped shirt! He shared his story with me: Many years ago he had accepted Jesus, but soon he began to backslide. He repented and returned to the Lord, but backslid once more. For the last several years, this had been the pattern of his life, following the Lord, backsliding, and then repenting.

Believing that he had depleted his quota of forgiveness, he was hopeless and depressed. I marveled at the goodness of God as the man became convinced of the Lord's unconditional love and forgiveness without measure. God had taken the wisdom of the ages and given me just the right word for the moment. He didn't have to give me the details about the man's appearance. I believe He did that to give me confidence and encouragement because I was quite new at seeking the Lord's voice in that way.

John the Baptist said that Jesus spoke the word (*rhema*) of God. Jesus declared, "I speak these things as My Father taught me...the things which I have seen with [or in the presence of] My Father" (Jn. 8:28,38). When Jesus spoke *rhema* words, He cut through the surface and touched the spirit, the very heart of men. When I speak out of the reasonings of my own mind, I may or may not speak to the heart. When I speak the words I have received within, my ministry is effective.

Appendix B

The Seventy Uses of Rhema *in the New Testament*

Rhema is translated "word" in the following fifty-four passages:

Matt. 4:4	Luke 24:11	Acts 2:14	Rom. 10:8 (2)
Matt. 12:36	John 3:34	Acts 5:20	Rom. 10:17
Matt. 18:16	John 5:47	Acts 6:11	Rom. 10:18
Matt. 26:75	John 6:63	Acts 6:13	2 Cor. 12:4
Matt. 27:14	John 6:68	Acts 10:22	2 Cor. 13:1
Mark 14:72	John 8:20	Acts 10:37	Eph. 5:26
Luke 1:38	John 8:47	Acts 10:44	Eph. 6:17
Luke 2:29	John 10:21	Acts 11:14	Heb. 1:3
Luke 3:2	John 12:47	Acts 11:16	Heb. 6:5
Luke 4:4	John 12:48	Acts 13:42	Heb. 11:3
Luke 5:5	John 14:10	Acts 16:38	Heb. 12:19
Luke 20:26	John 15:7	Acts 26:25	1 Pet. 1:25 (2)
Luke 24:8	John 17:8	Acts 28:25	2 Pet. 3:2
Jude 17	Rev. 17:17		

Rhema is translated "saying" in the following eight passages:

Mark 9:32	Luke 2:17	Luke 2:51	Luke 9:45 (2)
Luke 1:65	Luke 2:50	Luke 7:1	Luke 18:34

Rhema is translated "thing" in the following three passages:

Luke 2:15

Luke 2:19

Acts 5:32

Additional Verses:

Matthew 5:11 — "… shall say all manner of evil [lit., every evil *rhema*] against you falsely…."

Luke 1:37 — "With God nothing [lit., not any *rhema*] shall be impossible."

Appendix C

Understanding the Power of Rhema, *"The Spoken Word"*

Kinds of *Rhema* and Biblical Examples

Most life-giving: I speak what God is currently speaking within (i.e., my *rhema* comes forth from His *rhema*).

"The words [*rhema*] that I say…I do not speak on my own initiative, but the Father abiding in Me does His works" (Jn. 14:10).

"The words [*rhema*] which You gave me I have given to them…" (Jn. 17:8).

(See also Luke 1:38; 5:5; John 5:19,20,30; 8:26,28,38; 3:34; 6:63; Acts 10:13; 2 Corinthians 12:4; Ephesians 6:17; and Hebrews 11:3; 12:19.)

Possibly life-giving: I speak the written Word of God.

"Stand and continue to speak to the people in the temple the whole message [*rhema*] of this life" (Acts 5:20).

Neutral: I speak out of myself.

"By the mouth of two or three witnesses every word [*rhema*] may be confirmed" (Matt. 18:16).

Somewhat destructive: I speak the generalized word of satan, which I have heard in the past.

"Every evil word [*rhema*] that men shall speak, they shall render account for it in the day of judgment" (Matt. 12:36).

Most destructive: I speak what satan is currently speaking within.

"We have heard him speak blasphemous words [*rhema*] against...God" (Acts 6:11).

"The tongue is a fire...set on fire by hell" (Jas. 3:6).

Our Goal

To produce the maximum amount of life by saying only what the Father is currently speaking within us, through our fellowship with the Spirit (Jn. 14:10,16).

Appendix D

Greek New Testament Words Used to Describe Revelatory Experiences

Words Describing Dream and Vision

In the Greek New Testament, there are many different words and phrases used to describe encountering God through dream and vision, and experiencing revelation. They are as follows:

Onar—a common word for "dream." Precisely, it is a vision seen in sleep, as opposed to waking. It is used in Matthew 1:20; 2:12,13,19,22 and 27:19.

Enupniom—a vision seen in sleep. It stresses the givenness, almost surprise quality, of what is received in sleep. It is used in Acts 2:17 and Jude 8.

Horama—translated "vision." It can refer to visions of the night or sleeping experiences, as well as to waking visions. It is used in Matthew 17:9; Acts 7:31; 9:10,12; 10:3,17,19; 11:5; 12:9; 16:9,10 and 18:9.

Opasis—can signify the eye as the organ of sight, an appearance of any kind, even a spectacle; but there are also two instances where it means a supernatural vision: Acts 2:17 and Revelation 9:17. The distinction between the perception of the physical and the nonphysical is lacking in the Greek. Both "seeings" are genuine perception.

Optasia—translated "vision." It has the sense of self-disclosure, of "letting oneself be seen." It is used in the following four passages: Luke 1:22; 24:23; Acts 26:19 and 2 Corinthians 12:1.

Ekstasis—the word from which the English word "ecstasy" is derived. It literally means "standing aside from oneself, being displaced or over against oneself," and ordinarily there is a sense of amazement, confusion and even of extreme terror. It may refer to either sleeping or waking experiences. Psychologically, both the dreams of sleep and the imagery that occurs on the border of wakefulness, hypnagogic or hypnopompic imagery, fit the condition that *ekstasis* describes. Although translated "trance," it is misleading to use the word "trance" as a direct translation. It is used in Mark 5:42; 16:8; Luke 5:26; Acts 3:10; 10:10; 11:5 and 22:17.

Ginomai en pneumati—translated "to become in Spirit" (Rev. 1:10). This signifies a state in which one could see visions and be informed or spoken to directly by the Spirit. Related phrases are found in Matthew 4:1; Mark 1:12; Luke 1:41 and 4:1.

Ephistemi, paristemi—simply referring to the fact that some reality stands by in the night or in the day. It is used in Luke 1:11; Acts 10:30; 16:9; 23:11 and 27:23.

Angelos or angel—meaning an actual physical envoy, a messenger, or a divine being sent by God, and *daimon, daimonion, diabolos* or demon, devil and satan, referring to nonphysical entities or powers from satan. Both angels and demons can be encountered in dreams and visionary experiences as shown in the following references: Acts 10:3; Jude 8; and many instances in the book of Revelation.

Blepo and *eido*—meaning "to see," "to perceive." These words are used to mean "see" in the normal outer sense, yet are also used to refer to seeing in the spiritual sense as evidenced in the following passages: Revelation 1:2,11; Mark 9:9 and Luke 9:36. Obviously, because of the dual use of these words to describe both inner and outer sight, the early Church considered visionary experiences to be just as easy to perceive and observe, to be given as often, and to be equally valid as the perceptions one has of the outer physical world.

Blepo simply means physical seeing but *eido* has the additional meaning of seeing all that is there, the essential nature of a thing, perception.

Apokalupsis—translated "revelation," literally means disclosure, divine uncovering or revelation. It is used in Romans 16:25; 1 Corinthians 14:6,26; 2 Corinthians 12:1,7 and Galatians 2:2.

When considering the great variety of words New Testament Christians had to choose from to describe their visionary experiences, it is evident that they were able to very precisely define the exact type of visionary encounter they were having. Probably our poverty of vocabulary in finding one or two suitable words to clearly define our visionary experiences demonstrates the scarcity of direct spiritual encounter we all experience in the Western culture. May we restore to our vocabulary a host of suitable words to clearly define the variety of inner spiritual experiences we are having!

Appendix E

How God Uses Vision and Image *

The best approach to discovering what God has to say on an issue is to gather all the Scripture from Genesis to Revelation on that subject and then meditate on them for a time, asking the Holy Spirit to speak to you and recording the insights you receive. Using the word search option of CompuBIBLE, we have gathered on the following pages verses that deal with dream, vision, seer, look, and eyes, along with occasional contextual verses that give clearer insight.

While asking the Lord to grant you a spirit of revelation (Eph. 1:17,18) meditate on these verses, allowing God to reveal to you how He desires to use dream and vision in your life.

Following are some questions you may want to explore:

1. What is God's desired use of dream and vision in my life?

a. Does God speak through them?

b. How common should this experience be?

c. Does satan speak through dream and vision?

d. How do I test dream and vision?

* This concordance study was first published in *Seduction?? A Biblical Response* by Thomas Reid & Mark Virkler.

e. Is there anything I am to do to promote the flow of divine vision within me?

2. Does God use images as part of His encounter with us?

a. If so, how is image to be used properly? Give some examples.

b. What is the negative use of image? Give some examples.

3. Can we be trained in the use of the eyes of our hearts? Use Scripture to support your answer.

4. List other questions you may want to research also.

Index: Vision

Title: The place of dream and vision in one's spiritual life.

Range: Genesis 1:1 to Revelation 22:21

Subject: 1. dream; 2. vision; 3. seer; 4. look; 5. eyes

Note: CompuBIBLE uses parentheses to indicate words that do not appear in the original Greek, words which the King James Version shows in italics.

Mandates

Gen. 3:5 For God doth know that in the day ye eat thereof, then your eyes shall be opened, and ye shall be as gods, knowing good and evil.

Gen. 3:6 And when the woman saw that the tree (was) good for food, and that it (was) pleasant to the eyes, and a tree to be desired to make (one wise), she took of the fruit thereof, and did eat, and gave also unto her husband with her; and he did eat.

Gen. 3:7 And the eyes of them both were opened, and they knew that they (were) naked; and they sewed fig leaves together, and made themselves aprons.

Num. 12:6 And he said, Hear now my words: If there be a prophet among you, I the Lord will make myself known unto him in a vision, (and) will speak unto him in a dream.

1 Sam. 28:6 And when Saul inquired of the Lord, the Lord answered him not, neither by dreams, nor by Urim, nor by prophets.

1 Sam. 28:15 And Samuel said to Saul, Why hast thou disquieted me, to bring me up? And Saul answered, I am sore distressed; for the Philistines make war against me, and God is departed from me, and answered me no more, neither by prophets, nor by dreams: therefore I have called thee, that thou mayest make known unto me what I shall do.

Ps. 89:19 Then thou spakest in vision to thy holy one, and saidst, I have laid help upon (one that is) mighty; I have exalted (one) chosen out of the people.

Hos. 12:10 I have also spoken by the prophets, and I have multiplied visions, and used similitudes, by the ministry of the prophets.

Joel 2:28 And it shall come to pass afterward, (that) I will pour out my spirit upon all flesh; and your sons and your daughters shall prophesy, your old men shall dream dreams, your young men shall see visions...

Acts 2:17 And it shall come to pass in the last days, saith God, I will pour out of my Spirit upon all flesh: and your sons and your daughters shall prophesy, and your young men shall see visions, and your old men shall dream dreams...

John 5:19 Then answered Jesus and said unto them, Verily, verily, I say unto you, The Son can do nothing of himself, but what He seeth the Father do: for what things soever He doeth, these also doeth the Son likewise.

John 5:20 For the Father loveth the Son and showeth him all things that himself doeth: and he will show him greater works than these, that ye may marvel.

John 8:38 I speak that which I have seen with my Father: and ye do that which ye have seen with your father.

Opened Eyes

There is a place and a need to have the eyes of our hearts opened by the Spirit, so we can see the vision of God. The Scriptures clearly state that not everyone has opened eyes. We must recognize this lack and need, and seek God that He would open the eyes of our hearts.

Gen. 21:19 And God opened her eyes, and she saw a well of water; and she went, and filled the bottle with water, and gave the lad drink.

Num. 22:31 Then the Lord opened the eyes of Balaam, and he saw the angel of the Lord standing in the way, and his sword drawn in his hand: and he bowed down his head, and fell flat on his face.

Num. 24:2 And Balaam lifted up his eyes, and he saw Israel abiding (in his tents) according to their tribes; and the spirit of God came upon him.

Num. 24:3 And he took up his parable, and said, Balaam the son of Beor hath said, and the man whose eyes are open hath said:

Num. 24:4 He hath said, which heard the words of God, which saw the vision of the Almighty, falling (into a trance), but having his eyes open...

Num. 24:15 And He took up his parable, and said, Balaam the son of Beor hath said, and the man whose eyes are open hath said:

Num. 24:16 He hath said, which heard the words of God, and knew the knowledge of the most High, (which) saw the vision of the Almighty, falling (into a trance), but having his eyes open...

Deut. 29:2 And Moses called upon all Israel, and said unto them, Ye have seen all that the Lord did before your eyes in the land of Egypt unto Pharaoh, and unto all his servants, and unto all his land;

Deut. 29:3 The great temptations which thine eyes have seen, the signs, and those great miracles:

Deut. 29:4 Yet the Lord hath not given you a heart to perceive, and eyes to see, and ears to hear, unto this day.

1 Sam. 3:1 And the child Samuel ministered unto the Lord before Eli. And the word of the Lord was precious in those days; (there was) no open vision.

1 Sam. 3:2 And it came to pass at that time, when Eli (was) laid down in his place, and his eyes began to wax dim, (that) he could not see;

1 Sam. 3:3 And ere the lamp of God went out in the temple of the Lord, where the ark of God (was), and Samuel was laid down (to sleep);

1 Sam. 3:4 That the Lord called Samuel: and he answered, Here (am) I.

1 Sam. 3:5 And he ran unto Eli, and said, Here (am) I; for thou calledst me. And he said, I called not; lie down again. And he went and lay down.

1 Sam. 3:6 And the Lord called yet again, Samuel. And Samuel arose and went to Eli, and said, Here (am) I; for thou didst call me. And he answered, I called not, my son; lie down again.

1 Sam. 3:7 Now Samuel did not yet know the Lord, neither was the word of the Lord yet revealed unto him.

1 Sam. 3:8 And the Lord called Samuel again the third time. And he arose and went to Eli, and said, Here (am) I; for thou didst call me. And Eli perceived that the Lord had called the child.

1 Sam. 3:9 Therefore Eli said unto Samuel, Go, lie down: and it shall be, if he call thee, that thou shalt say, Speak, Lord; for thy servant heareth. So Samuel went and lay down in his place.

1 Sam. 3:10 And the Lord came, and stood, and called as at other times, Samuel, Samuel. Then Samuel answered, Speak; for thy servant heareth.

1 Sam. 3:15 And Samuel lay until the morning, and opened the doors of the house of the Lord. And Samuel feared to skew Eli the vision.

2 Kings 6:15 And when the servant of the man of God was risen early, and gone forth, behold, an host compassed the city both with horses and chariots. And his servant said unto him, Alas, my master! how shall we do?

2 Kings 6:16 And he answered, Fear not: for they that (be) with us (are) more than those that (be) with them.

2 Kings 6:17 And Elisha prayed, and said, Lord, I pray thee, open his eyes, that he may see. And the Lord opened the eyes of the young man; and he saw: and, behold, the mountain (was) full of horses and chariots of fire round about Elisha.

Job 33:15 In a dream, in a vision of the night, when deep sleep falleth upon men, in slumberings upon the bed;

Job 33:16 Then he openeth the ears of men, and sealeth their instruction.

Ps. 119:18 Open thou mine eyes, that I may behold wondrous things out of thy law.

Isa. 42:18 Hear, ye deaf; and look, ye blind, that ye may see.

Isa. 42:19 Who (is) blind, but my servant? or deaf, as my messenger (that) I sent? who (is) blind as (he that is) perfect, and blind and the Lord's servant?

Isa. 42:20 Seeing many things, but thou observest not; opening the ears, but he heareth not.

Isa. 44:18 They have not known nor understood: for he hath shut their eyes, that they cannot see; (and) their hearts, that they cannot understand.

Jer. 5:21 Hear now this, O foolish people, and without understanding; which have eyes, and see not; which have ears, and hear not...

Lam. 2:9 Her gates are sunk into the ground; he hath destroyed and broken her bars: her king and her princes (are) among the Gentiles: the law (is) no (more); her prophets also find no vision from the Lord.

Matt. 13:15 For this people's heart is waxed gross, and (their) ears are dull of hearing, and their eyes they have closed; lest at any time they should see with (their) eyes, and hear with (their) ears, and should understand with (their) heart, and should be converted, and I should heal them.

Matt. 13:16 But blessed (are) your eyes, for they see: and your ears, for they hear.

Mark 8:18 Having eyes, see ye not? and having ears, hear ye not? and do ye not remember?

John 12:40 He hath blinded their eyes, and hardened their heart; that they should not see with (their) eyes, nor understand with (their) heart, and be converted, and I should heal them.

Acts 28:27 For the heart of this people is waxed gross, and their ears are dull of hearing, and their eyes have they closed; lest they should see with (their) eyes, and hear with (their) ears, and understand with (their) heart, and should be converted, and I should heal them.

Rom. 11:8 (According as it is written, God hath given them the spirit of slumber, eyes that should not see, and ears that they should not hear;) unto this day.

Rom. 11:10 Let their eyes be darkened, that they may not see, and bow down their back alway.

2 Cor. 4:18 While we look not at the things which are seen, but at the things which are not seen: for the things which are seen (are) temporal; but the things which are not seen (are) eternal.

Looking to See

Scripture places great emphasis on lifting up our eyes and looking to see.

Gen. 18:1 And the Lord appeared unto him in the plains of Mamre: and he sat in the tent door in the heat of the day;

Gen. 18:2 And he lift up his eyes and looked, and, lo, three men stood by him: and when he saw (them), he ran to meet them from the tent door, and bowed himself toward the ground...

Gen. 31:10 And it came to pass at the time that the cattle conceived, that I lifted up mine eyes, and saw in a dream, and, behold, the rams which leaped upon the cattle (were) ringstraked, speckled, and grisled.

Gen. 31:11 And the angel of God spake unto me in a dream, (saying), Jacob: and I said, Here (am) I.

Gen. 31:12 And he said, Lift up now thine eyes, and see, all the rams which leap upon the cattle (are) ringstraked, and grisled: for I have seen all that Laban doeth unto thee.

Exod. 3:1 Now Moses kept the flock of Jethro his father in law, the priest of Midian: and he led the flock to the backside of the desert, and came to the mountain of God, (even) to Horeb.

Exod. 3:2 And the angel of the Lord appeared unto him in a flame of fire out of the midst of a bush: and he looked, and, behold, the bush burned with fire, and the bush (was) not consumed.

Exod. 3:3 And Moses said, I will now turn aside, and see this great sight, why the bush is not burnt.

Exod. 3:4 And when the Lord saw that he turned aside to see, God called upon him out of the midst of the bush, and said, Moses, Moses. And he said, Here (am) I.

Exod. 3:5 And he said, Draw not nigh hither: put off thy shoes from off thy feet, for the place whereon thou standest (is) holy ground.

Exod. 3:6 Moreover he said, I (am) the God of thy father, the God of Abraham, the God of Isaac, and the God of Jacob. And Moses hid his face; for he was afraid to look upon God.

Exod. 16:9 And Moses spake unto Aaron, Say unto all the congregation of the children of Israel, Come near before the Lord: for he hath heard your murmurings.

Exod. 16:10 And it came to pass, as Aaron spake unto the whole congregation of the children of Israel, that they looked toward the wilderness, and, behold, the glory of the Lord appeared in the cloud.

Exod. 16:11 And the Lord spake unto Moses saying...

Josh. 5:13 And it came to pass, when Joshua was by Jericho, that he lifted up his eyes and looked, and, behold, there stood a man over against him with his sword drawn in his hand: and Joshua went unto him, and said unto him, (Art) thou for us, or for our adversaries?

Josh. 5:14 And he said, Nay; but (as) captain of the host of the Lord am I now come. And Joshua fell on his face to. the earth, and did worship, and said unto him, What saith my lord unto his servant?

Josh. 5:15 And the captain of the Lord's host said unto Joshua, Loose thy shoe from off thy foot; for the place whereon thou standest (is) holy. And Joshua did so.

1 Chron. 21:16 And David lifted up his eyes, and saw the angel of the Lord stand between the earth and the heaven, having a drawn sword in his hand stretched out over Jerusalem. Then David and the elders (of Israel, who were) clothed in sackcloth, fell upon their faces.

Dan. 10:1 In the third year of Cyrus king of Persia, a thing was revealed unto Daniel, whose name was called Belteshazzar; and the thing (was) true, but the time appointed (was) long: and he understood the thing, and had understanding of the vision.

Dan. 10:5 Then I lifted up mine eyes, and looked, and behold a certain man clothed in linen, whose loins (were) girded with fine gold of Uphaz:

Dan. 10:6 His body also (was) like the beryl, and his face as the appearance of lightning, and his eyes as lamps of fire, and his arms and his feet like in colour to polished brass, and the voice of his words like the voice of a multitude.

Dan. 10:7 And I Daniel alone saw the vision: for the men that were with me saw not the vision; but a great quaking fell upon them, so that they fled to hide themselves.

Dan. 10:8 Therefore I was left alone, and saw this great vision, and there remained no strength in me: for my comeliness was turned in me into corruption, and I retained no strength.

Dan. 10:9 Yet heard I the voice of his words: and when I heard the voice of his words, then I was in a deep sleep on my face, and my face toward the ground.

Dan. 10:10 And, behold, a hand touched me, which set me upon my knees and (upon) the palms of my hands.

Dan. 10:11 And he said unto me, O Daniel, a man greatly beloved, understand the words that I speak unto thee, and stand upright: for unto thee am I now sent. And when he had spoken this word unto me, I stood trembling.

Dan. 10:12 Then said he unto me, Fear not, Daniel: for from the first day that thou didst set thine heart to understand, and to chasten thyself before thy God, thy words were heard, and I am come for thy words.

Dan. 10:13 But the prince of the kingdom of Persia withstood me one and twenty days; but, lo, Michael, one of the chief princes came to help me; and I remained there with the kings of Persia.

Dan. 10:14 Now I am come to make thee understand what shall befall thy people in the latter days: for yet the vision (is) for (many) days.

Dan. 10:15 And when he had spoken such words unto me, I set my face toward the ground, and I became dumb.

Dan. 10:16 And, behold, (one) like the similitude of the sons of men touched my lips: then I opened my mouth, and spake, and said unto him that stood before me, O my lord, by the vision my sorrows are turned upon me, and I have retained no strength.

Ps. 5:3 My voice shalt thou hear in the morning, O Lord; in the morning will I direct (my prayer) unto thee, and will look up.

Ps. 25:15 Mine eyes (are) ever toward the Lord; for he shall pluck my feet out of the net.

Ps. 123:1 Unto thee lift I up mine eyes, O thou that dwellest in the heavens.

Ps. 123:2 Behold, as the eyes of servants (look) unto the hand of their masters, (and) as the eyes of a maiden unto the hand of her mistress; so our eyes (wait) upon the Lord our God, until that he have mercy upon us.

Ps. 141:8 But mine eyes (are) unto thee, O God the Lord: in thee is my trust; leave not my soul destitute.

Isa. 8:17 And I will wait upon the Lord, that hideth his face from the house of Jacob, and I will look for him.

Isa. 17:7 At that day shall a man look to his Maker, and his eyes shall have respect to the Holy One of Israel.

Isa. 17:8 And he shall not look to the altars, the work of his hands, neither shall respect (that) which his fingers have made, either the groves, or the images.

Isa. 40:26 Lift up your eyes on high, and behold who hath created these (things), that bringeth out their host by number: he calleth them all by names by the greatness of his might, for that (he is) strong in power; not one faileth.

Ezek. 1:1 Now it came to pass in the thirtieth year, in the fourth (month), in the fifth (day) of the month, as I (was) among the captives by the river of Chebar, (that) the heavens were opened, and I saw visions of God.

Ezek. 1:4 And I looked, and, behold, a whirlwind came out of the north, a great cloud, and a fire infolding itself, and a brightness (was) about it, and out of the midst thereof as the color of amber, out of the midst of the fire.

Ezek. 2:9 And when I looked, behold, a hand (was) sent upon me; and, lo, a roll of a book (was) therein...

Ezek. 8:3 And he put forth the form of a hand, and took me by a lock of mine head; and the spirit lifted me up between the earth and the heaven, and brought me in the visions of God to Jerusalem, to the door of the inner gate that looketh toward the north; where (was) the seat of the image of jealousy, which provoketh to jealousy.

Ezek. 8:4 And, behold, the glory of the God of Israel (was) there, according to the vision that I saw in the plain.

Ezek. 8:5 Then said he unto me, Son of man, lift up thine eyes now the way toward the north. So I lifted up mine eyes the way toward the north, and behold northward at the gate of the altar this image of jealousy in the entry.

Ezek. 8:7 And he brought me to the door of the court; and when I looked, behold a hole in the wall.

Ezek. 10:1 Then I looked, and, behold, in the firmament that was above the head of the cherubims there appeared over them as it were a sapphire stone, as the appearance of the likeness of a throne.

Ezek. 10:9 And when I looked, behind the four wheels by the cherubims, one wheel by one cherub, and another wheel by another cherub: and the appearance of the wheels (was) as the colour of a beryl stone.

Ezek. 44:1 Then he brought me back the way of the gate of the outward sanctuary which looketh toward the east; and it (was) shut.

Ezek. 44:4 Then brought he me the way of the north gate before the house: and I looked, and, behold, the glory of the Lord filled the house of the Lord: and I fell upon my face.

Ezek. 44:5 And the Lord said unto me, Son of man, mark well, and behold with thine eyes, and hear with thine ears all that I say unto thee concerning all the ordinances of the house of the Lord, and all the laws thereof; and mark well the entering in of the house, with every going forth of the sanctuary.

Dan. 12:5 Then I Daniel looked, and, behold, there stood other two, the one on this side of the bank of the river, and the other on that side of the bank of the river.

Zech. 1:18 Then lifted up mine eyes, and saw, and behold four horns.

Zech. 2:1 I lifted up mine eyes again, and looked, and behold a man with a measuring line in his hand.

Zech. 4:2 And said unto me, What seest thou? and I said, I have looked, And behold a candlestick all (of) gold, with a bowl upon the top of it, and his seven lamps thereon, and seven pipes to the seven lamps, which (are) upon the top thereof...

Zech. 5:1 Then I turned, and lifted up mine eyes, and looked, and behold a flying roll.

Zech. 5:5 Then the angel that talked with me went forth, and said unto me, Lift up now thine eyes, and see what (is) this that goeth forth.

Zech. 5:9 Then lifted I up mine eyes, and looked, and, behold, there came out two women, and the wind (was) in their wings; for they had wings like the wings of a stork: and they lifted up the ephah between the earth and the heaven.

Zech. 6:1 And I turned, and lifted up mine eyes, and looked, and, behold, there came four chariots out from between two mountains; and the mountains (were) mountains of brass.

Acts 7:55 But he, being full of the Holy Ghost, looked up steadfastly into the heaven, and saw the glory of God, and Jesus standing on the right hand of God...

Rev. 4:1 After this I looked, and, behold, a door (was) opened in heaven: and the first voice which I heard (was) as it were of a trumpet talking with me; which said, Come up hither, and I will shew thee things which must be hereafter.

Rev. 6:8 And I looked, and behold a pale horse: and his name that sat on him was Death, and Hell followed with him. And power was given unto them over the fourth part of the earth, to kill with sword, and with hunger, and with death, and with the beasts of the earth.

Rev. 14:1 And I looked, and, lo, a Lamb stood on the Mount Sion, and with him an hundred forty (and) four thousand, having his Father's name written in their foreheads.

Rev. 14:14 And I looked, and behold a white cloud, and upon the cloud (one) sat like unto the Son of man, having on his head a golden crown, and in his hand a sharp sickle.

Rev. 15:5 And after that I looked, and, behold, the temple of the tabernacle of the testimony in heaven was opened....

Seers

Prophets were also called seers. They were people who saw in the spiritual world the vision of Almighty God. This was a common title and office in Scripture and needs to be restored to the life of the Church. We need to again train prophets who are seers. In the New Covenant the veil has been torn, and now we all have access directly before the throne room of Almighty God. We all may prophesy (1 Cor. 14:31).

2 Sam. 15:27 ...Zadok...a seer...

2 Sam. 24:11 ...Gad, David's seer...

1 Chron. 25:5 ...Heman the king's seer...

1 Chron. 29:29 ...Samuel the seer...

2 Chron. 9:29 ...Iddo the seer...

2 Chron. 19:2 ...Hanani the seer...

2 Chron. 29:30 ...Asaph the seer...

2 Chron. 35:15 ...Jeduthun the king's seer

Amos 7:12 ...Amos...thou seer...

1 Sam. 9:9 (Beforetime in Israel, when a man went to inquire of God, thus he spake, Come, and let us go to the seer: for (he that is) now (called) a Prophet was beforetime called a Seer.)

1 Sam. 9:10 Then said Saul to his servant, Well said; come, let us go. So they went unto the city where the man of God (was).

1 Sam. 9:11 (And) as they went up the hill to the city, they found young maidens going out to draw water, and said unto them, Is the seer here?

Responsibilities of Seers

The responsibilities of seers included consulting and advising kings, exhorting the people, delivering the Word of God to the people, and recording the Word of God.

2 Sam. 24:11 For when David was up in the morning, the word of the Lord came unto the prophet Gad, David's seer, saying,

2 Sam. 24:12 Go and say unto David, Thus saith the Lord, I offer thee three (things); choose thee one of them, that I may (do it) unto thee.

2 Kings 17:13 Yet the Lord testified against Israel, and against Judah, by all the prophets, (and by) all the seers, saying, Turn ye from your evil ways, and keep my commandments (and) my statutes, according to all the law which I commanded your fathers, and which I sent to you by my servant the prophets.

1 Chron. 9:22 All these (which were) chosen to be porters in the gates (were) two hundred and twelve. These were reckoned by their genealogy in their villages, whom David and Samuel the seer did ordain in their set office.

1 Chron. 17:3 And it came to pass the same night, that the word of God came to Nathan, saying,

1 Chron, 17:4 Go and tell David my servant, Thus saith the Lord, Thou shall not build me an house to dwell in....

1 Chron. 17:15 According to all these words, and according to all this vision, so did Nathan speak unto David.

1 Chron. 21:9 And the Lord spake unto Gad, David's seer, saying,

1 Chron. 21:10 Go and tell David, saying, Thus saith the Lord, I offer thee three (things): choose thee one of them, that I may do (it) unto thee.

1 Chron. 26:28 And all that Samuel the seer, and Saul the son of Kish, and Abner the son of Ner, and Joab the son of Zeruiah, had dedicated; (and) whosoever had dedicated (any thing, it was) under the hand of Shelomith, and of his brethren.

1 Chron. 29:29 Now the acts of David the king, first and last, behold, they (are) written in the book of Samuel the seer, and in the book of Nathan the prophet, and in the book of Gad the seer...

2 Chron. 9:29 Now the rest of the acts of Solomon, first and last, (are) they not written in the book of Nathan the prophet, and in the prophecy of Ahijah the Shilonite, and in the visions of Iddo the seer against Jeroboam the son of Nebat?

2 Chron. 12:15 Now the acts of Rehoboam, first and last, (are) they not written in the book of Shemaiah the prophet, and of Iddo the seer concerning genealogies? And (there were) wars between Rehoboam and Jeroboam continually.

2 Chron. 16:7 And at that time Hanani the seer came to Asa king of Judah, and said unto him, Because thou hast relied on the king of Syria, and not relied on the Lord thy God, therefore is the host of the king of Syria escaped out of thine hand.

2 Chron. 16:8 Were not the Ethiopians and the Lubims a huge host, with very many chariots and horsemen? yet, because thou didst rely on the Lord, he delivered them into thine hand.

2 Chron. 16:9 For the eyes of the Lord run to and fro throughout the whole earth, to shew himself strong in the behalf of (them) whose heart (is) perfect toward him. Herein thou hast done foolishly: therefore from henceforth thou shalt have wars.

2 Chron. 16:10 Then Asa was wroth with the seer, and put him in a prison house; for (he was) in a rage with him because of this (thing). And Asa oppressed (some) of the people the same time.

2 Chron. 29:25 And he set the Levites in the house of the Lord with cymbals, with psalteries, and with harps, according to the commandment of David, and of Gad the king's seer, and Nathan the prophet: for (so was) the commandment of the Lord by his prophets.

2 Chron. 32:32 Now the rest of the acts of Hezekiah, and his goodness, behold, they (are) written in the vision of Isaiah the prophet, the son of Amoz, (and) in the book of the kings of Judah and Israel.

2 Chron. 33:18 Now the rest of the acts of Manasseh, and his prayer unto his God, and the words of the seers that spake to him in the name of the Lord God of Israel, behold, they (are written) in the book of the kings of Israel.

2 Chron. 33:19 His prayer also, and (how God) was intreated of him, and all his sins, and his trespass, and the places wherein he built high places, and set up groves and graven images, before he was humbled: behold, they (are) written among the sayings of the seers.

2 Chron. 35:15 And the singers the sons of Asaph (were) in their place, according to the commandment of David, and Asaph, and Heman, and Jeduthun the king's seer; and the porters (waited) at every gate; they might not depart from their service; for their brethren the Levites prepared for them.

Ezek. 40:2 In the visions of God brought he me into the land of Israel, and set me upon a very high mountain, by which (was) as the frame of a city on the south.

Ezek. 40:4 And the man said unto me, Son of man, behold with thine eyes, and hear with thine ears, and set thine heart upon all that I shall chew thee; for to the intent that I might skew (them) unto thee (art) thou brought hither: declare all that thou seest to the house of Israel.

Ezek. 40:6 Then came he unto the gate which looketh toward the east, and went up the stairs thereof, and measured the threshold of the gate, (which was) one reed broad; and the other threshold (of the gate, which was) one reed broad.

Hab. 2:2 And the Lord answered me, and said, Write the vision, and make (it) plain upon tables, that he may run that readeth it.

Hab. 2:3 For the vision (is) yet for an appointed time, but at the end it shall speak, and not lie: though it tarry, wait for it; because it will surely come, it will not tarry.

Rev. 1:10 I was in the Spirit on the Lord's day, and heard behind me a great voice, as of a trumpet...

Rev. 1:11 Saying, I am Alpha and Omega, the first and the last: and, What that seest, write in a book...

Rev. 1:14 His head and (his) hairs (were) white like wool, as white as snow; and his eyes (were) as a flame of fire...

Appendix F

Dreams and Visions Throughout Church History

Not only are dreams and visions prevalent in every dispensation of the Bible, they have also been a consistent part of Church history. In order to give you a clearer view of the Church's experience with dreams and visions throughout the last 2000 years, I offer the following examples.

Augustine

Rather than ignoring dreams as the contemporary Church has done, Augustine took the entire Twelfth Book in his *De Genesi ad Litteram* to explain his understanding of dreams and visions.

Polycarp

The book *Martyrdom of Polycarp* tells of Polycarp praying not long before his martyrdom, and being informed of what was shortly to happen through a symbolic vision. He saw the pillow under his head catch fire and realized that this image of destruction signified his own impending capture and death.

Justin Martyr

In his writings, Martyr said that dreams are sent by spirits. He believed that dreams are sent by both evil spirits and God.

Irenaeus

As Irenaeus refuted gnostic speculation in his writings, he indicated his clear view concerning dreams and the life of the Christian. In his principal work, *Against Heresies*, Irenaeus commented appreciatively and intelligently on the dream of Peter in the tenth chapter of Acts; he believed that the dream itself was a proof of the authenticity of Peter's experience. Again, he stressed the legitimacy of Paul's dream at Troas. He also inferred from the dreams of Joseph in Matthew that Joseph's dreaming showed how close he was to the real God. In still another place, he explained that although God is Himself invisible to the eye directly, He gives us visions and dreams through which He conveys the likeness of His nature and glory.

Clement

In discussing the nature and meaning of sleep, Clement urged: "Let us not, then, who are sons of the true light, close the door against this light; but turning in on ourselves, illumining the eyes of the hidden man, and gazing on the truth itself, and receiving its streams, let us clearly and intelligibly reveal such dreams as are true…Thus also such dreams as are true, in the view of him who reflects rightly, are the thoughts of a sober soul, undistracted for the time by the affections of the body, and counseling with itself in the best manner…Wherefore always contemplating God, and by perpetual converse with Him inoculating the body with wakefulness, it raises man to equality with angelic grace, and from the practice of wakefulness it grasps the eternity of life" (*Stromata*, or *Miscellanies*).

Origen

In his great answer to the pagans, *Against Celsus*, Origen defended the visions of the Bible, saying: "We, nevertheless, so far as we can, shall support our position, maintaining that, as it is a matter of belief that in a dream impressions have been brought before the minds of many, some relating to divine things, and others to future events of this life, and this either with clearness or in an enigmatic manner, a fact which is manifest to all who accept the doctrine of providence: so how is it absurd to say that the mind which could receive impressions in a dream should be impressed also in a waking vision, for the benefit either of him on whom the impressions are made, or of those who are to hear the account of them from him?"

Having satisfied his parallel between dreams and visions, Origen then went on to discuss the nature of dreams. In *Contra Celsus*, Origen further declared that many Christians had been converted from their pagan ways by this kind of direct breakthrough into their lives in waking visions and dreams of the night. He made it clear that many such instances of this sort of conversion were known.

Tertullian

Tertullian devoted eight chapters of his work *A Treatise on the Soul*, or *De Anima*, to his study of sleep and dreams. He believed that all dream, and evidenced it by the movement of sleeping infants. He believed that dreams occur from four sources: demons, God, natural dreams that the soul creates, and finally "the ecstatic state and its peculiar conditions" or, in other words, the unconscious. Furthermore he states, "And thus we — who both acknowledge and reverence, even as we do the prophecies, modern visions as equally promised to us, and consider the other powers of the Holy Spirit as an agency of the Church for which also He was sent, administering all gifts in all, even as the Lord distributed to every one...."

Thascius Cyprian, Bishop of Carthage in 250 A.D.

In a letter to Florentius Pupianus he said, "Although I know that to some men dreams seem ridiculous and visions foolish, yet assuredly it is to such as would rather believe in opposition to the priest, than believe the priest." In another letter he wrote that God guides the very councils of the Church by "many and manifest visions." He commended the reader, Celerinus, because his conversion to the Church had come through a vision of the night.

Lactantius, chosen by Constantine the Great to tutor his son.

In his *Divine Institutes*, he included a chapter, "The Use of Reason in Religion; and of Dreams, Auguries, Oracles, and Similar Portents," in which he cited examples to show that through dreams, a knowledge of the future is occasionally given to pagans as well as to Christians. His example of a logical fallacy is that of a man who has dreamed that he ought not believe in dreams.

Constantine

Lactantius writes of the heavenly vision that gave Constantine his great victory in 300 A.D. The story begins with Constantine being in desperate need and calling on God for help. "Accordingly he called on Him with earnest prayer and supplications that He would reveal to him Who He was, and stretch forth His right hand to help him in his present difficulties. And while he was thus praying with fervent entreaty, a most marvelous sign appeared to him from heaven, the account of which it might have been hard to believe had it been related by any other person. But since the victorious emperor himself long afterwards declared it to the writer of this history, when he was honored with his acquaintance and society, and confirmed his statement by an oath, who could hesitate to accredit the relation especially since the testimony of after-time has established its truth? He said that about noon, when the day was already beginning to decline, he saw with his own eyes the trophy of a cross of light in the heavens, above the sun, and bearing the inscription, CONQUER BY THIS. At this sight he himself was struck with amazement, and his whole army also, which followed him on this expedition, and witnessed the miracle.

"He said, moreover, that he doubted within himself what the import of this apparition could be. And while he continued to ponder the reason on its meaning, night suddenly came on; then in his sleep the Christ of God appeared to him with the same sign which he had seen in the heavens, and commanded him to make a likeness of that sign which he had seen in the heavens, and to use it as a safeguard in all engagements with his enemies.

At dawn of day he arose, and communicated the marvel to his friends: and then, calling together the workers in gold and precious stones, he sat in the midst of them, and described to them the figure of the sign he had seen, bidding them represent it in gold and precious stones. And this representation I myself have had an opportunity of seeing" (*The Life of Constantine I*, 28-30).

Socrates

One dream Socrates mentioned was that of Ignatius of Antioch. Ignatius had a vision of angels who sang hymns in alternate chants, and so introduced the mode of antiphonal singing (*Ecclesiastical History*, Vol. 35 and 36, by Theodoret).

Athanasius, Bishop of Alexandria from 328 to 373

In his great masterpiece of Christian apology, *Against the Heathen*, he wrote: "Often when the body is quiet, and at rest and asleep, man moves inwardly, and beholds what is outside himself, traveling to other countries, walking about, meeting his acquaintances, and often by these means divining and forecasting the actions of the day. But to what can this be due save to the rational soul, in which man thinks of and perceives things beyond himself?

"…For if even when united and coupled with the body it is not shut in or commensurate with the small dimensions of the body, but often, when the body lies in bed, not moving, but in death-like sleep, the soul keeps awake by virtue of its own power, and transcends the natural power of the body, and as though traveling away from the body while remaining in it, imagines and beholds things above the earth, and often even holds converse with the saints and angels who are above earthly and bodily existence, and approaches them in the confidence of the purity of its intelligence; shall it not all the more, when separated from the body at the time appointed by God Who coupled them together, have its knowledge of immortality more clear?" (II.31.5 and 33.3)

Gregory of Nyssa

In his major philosophical work, *On the Making of Man*, Gregory deals directly with the meaning and place of sleep and dreams in man's life. He believed that when man is asleep the senses and the reason rest, and the less rational parts of the soul appear to take over. Reason is not, however, extinguished, but smolders like a fire "heaped with chaff" and then breaks forth with insights that modern dream research calls "secondary mentation."

He went on to say that "while all men are guided by their own minds, there are some few who are deemed worthy of evident Divine communication; so, while the imagination of sleep naturally occurs in a like and equivalent manner for all, some, not all, share by means of their dreams in some more Divine manifestation...." His reasoning was that there is a natural foreknowledge that comes in an unknown way through the nonrational part of the soul — the "unconscious," according to modern depth psychology — and it is through this part of the soul that God communicates Himself directly.

Gregory then enumerated the other meanings that dreams can have, offering quite a complete outline of the subject. He suggested that dreams can provide mere reminiscences of daily occupations and events. Or, they can reflect the condition of the body, its hunger or thirst, or the emotional condition of the personality. Dreams can also be understood in medical practice as giving clues to the sickness of the body. Indeed, far from stating a superstitious belief, Gregory laid out quite well the principle upon which today's analytical study of dreams is based.

Gregory also told, in a sermon entitled "In Praise of the Forty Martyrs," of a dream that occurred while he was attending a celebration in honor of the soldiers who had been martyred. In the dream, the martyrs challenged Gregory for his Christian lethargy, and it had a profound effect upon his life.

It is clear that philosophically, practically and personally, Gregory of Nyssa believed the dream could be a revelation of depths beyond the human ego.

Basil the Great

In his commentary on Isaiah, Basil states, "The enigmas in dreams have a close affinity to those things which are signified in an allegoric or hidden sense in the Scriptures. Thus both Joseph and Daniel, through the gift of prophecy, used to interpret dreams, since the force of reason by itself is not powerful enough for getting at truth" (S. Basilii Magni, *Commentarium in Isaiam Prophetam*, Prooemium 6f., J.-P. Migne, Patrologiae Graecae, Paris, 1880, Vol. 30, Col. 127-30).

That Basil believed in continuing to consider dreams is indicated by the letter he wrote to a woman in which he interpreted the dream she had sent him. He suggested to her that her dream meant she was to spend more time in "spiritual contemplation and cultivating that mental vision by which God is wont to be seen."

Gregory of Nazianzen

In his second book of poems, Gregory writes: "And God summoned me from boyhood in my nocturnal dreams, and I arrived at the very goals of wisdom" (S. Gregorii Theologi, *Carminum*, Liber II, 994-950). In another place he told that this nocturnal vision was the hidden spark that set his whole life aflame for God. In one of his poems, he spoke of the ability of demons to also speak through one's dreams. "Devote not your trust too much to the mockery of dreams, nor let yourself be terrified by everything; do not become inflated by joyful visions, For frequently a demon prepares these snares for you" (*Carminum*, Liber I, 608-9, lines 209-12).

St. John Chrysostom

In his commentary on Acts, volume one, he states, "To some the grace was imparted through dreams, to others it was openly poured forth. For indeed by dreams the prophets saw, and received revelations." According to Chrysostom, dreams are sent to those whose wills are compliant to God, for they do not need visions or the more startling divine manifestations, and he mentioned Joseph, the father of Jesus, and Peter and Paul as examples of this truth (*Homilies on Matthew*, IV. 10f., 18; v. 5).

Synesius of Cyrene

Synesius wrote an entire book on dreams. He said, "One man learns...while awake, another while asleep. But in the waking state man is the teacher, whereas it is God who makes the dreamer fruitful with His own courage, so that learning and attaining are one and the same. Now to make fruitful is even more than to teach" (Augustine Fitzgerald, *The Essays and Hymns of Synesius of Cyrene*, London, Oxford University Press, 1930, p. 332 [from *Concerning Dreams*]).

Synesius laid out a sound reason for discussing dreams and then enumerated the blessings to be gained from studying them. For the pure soul who receives impressions clearly, a proper study of dreams gives knowledge of the future with all that this implies. Important information is also provided about bodily malfunction and how it can be corrected. Far more important, this undertaking brings the soul to consider immaterial things and so, even though it was begun merely to provide knowledge of the future, it turns the soul to God and develops a love of Him. Synesius also told how dreams had helped him in his writings and in his other endeavors, and how they often gave hope to men who had been oppressed by the difficulties of life.

He made fun of people who relied on the popular dream books, insisting that only by constantly checking dreams with experience could they be understood. Their essential nature is personal, and they must be understood by the dreamer in terms of his own life. Some of them seem to be direct revelations of God, but there are also many dreams that are obscure and difficult to interpret. He suggested that anyone who is serious in studying them should keep a record so that he knows his sleeping life as well as his waking one.

He even saw the connection between mythology and dreams, and explained his belief that the myth is based upon the dream; a true interest in mythology helps a man find the more vital meaning in his own dreams. Finally, Synesius showed the reason for his belief that dreams give hints about eternal life. As the sleeping state is to the waking one, so the life of the soul after death is to the dream life, and thus this state gives some idea of the kind of life that is led by the soul after death.

Ambrose

In Ambrose's famous letter to Theodosius calling for his repentance, he declared that God in a dream forbade him to celebrate communion before the Emperor unless he repented. These are his dramatic words: "I am writing with my own hand that which you alone may read.... I have been warned, not by man, nor through man, but plainly by Himself that this is forbidden me. For when I was anxious, in the very night in which I was preparing to set out, you appeared to me in a dream to have come into the Church, and I was not permitted to offer the sacrifice.... Our God gives warnings in many ways, by heavenly signs, by the precepts of the prophets, by the visions even of sinners He wills that we should understand, that we should entreat Him to take away all disturbances...that the faith and peace of the Church...may continue" (St. Ambrose, Letter LI 14).

Augustine tells how God revealed to St. Ambrose in a dream the hidden location of two martyred saints, who were then retrieved and given a proper consecration (St. Ambrose, Letter

XXII; St. Augustine, *The Confessions*, IX [VII] 16; *The City of God*, XXII 8).

In St. Ambrose's more theological writings, Ambrose showed that an angel who speaks through a dream is functioning at the direction of the Holy Spirit, since angelic powers are subject to and moved by the Spirit.

Augustine

As has already been mentioned in number one of this series, Augustine wrote widely concerning the place and understanding of dreams in the Christian's life. His study of perception was as sophisticated as any in the ancient world. He saw reality as consisting of outer objects to which we react with our bodies, and the impressions of this sense experience, impressions that are "mental" in nature. We then have the inner perception of this sense experience, and finally the mental species in its remembered form. It is the action of the ego that unites these perceptions to the object.

In one place, he calls the faculty of imagination the bridge that mediates the object to consciousness, thus presenting almost the same thinking as that worked out by Synesius of Cyrene. Augustine saw man as possessing an outward eye that receives and mediates sense impressions, and an inward eye that observes and deals with these collected and stored "mental" realities that are called "memory."

In addition to the realities that come from outer perception and from inner perception of "memories," autonomous spiritual realities (angels and demons) can present themselves directly to the inner eye. These are of the same nature as the stored "mental" or psychic realities that are perceived inwardly. Augustine writes that men in sleep or trance can experience contents that come from memory "or some other hidden force through certain spiritual commixtures of a similarly spiritual substance" (St. Augustine, *On the Trinity*, XI. 4.7).

These autonomous realities are nonphysical; yet they can either assume a corporeal appearance and be experienced through the outward eye, or they can be presented directly to the consciousness through the inner eye in dreams, visions and trances. Thus, through dreams, man is presented with a whole storehouse of unconscious memories and spontaneous contents; he is given access to a world that the fathers called "the realm of the spirit."

Just as angels have direct contact with man's psyche and present their messages before the inner eye, so also do demons. "They persuade [men], however, in marvelous and unseen ways, entering by means of that subtlety of their own bodies into the bodies of men who are unaware, and through certain imaginary visions mingling themselves with men's thoughts whether they are awake or asleep" (*The Divination of Demons*, V. 9, N.Y., Fathers of the Church, Inc., 1955, Vol. 27, p. 430).

In addition to presenting a theory of dreams and visions, Augustine also discussed many examples of providential dreams in the course of his writings. One of the most important of them was the famous dream of his mother Monica, in which she saw herself standing on a measuring device while a young man whose face shone with a smile approached her. She was crying, and when he asked why, she told of her sorrow that her son had turned away from Christ. He told her to look, and suddenly she saw Augustine standing on the same rule with her and she was comforted. Realizing the significance of the symbolism, she was able to go on praying for him with patience and hope; her dreams and visions are also mentioned in several other places in *The Confessions* (*The Confessions*, III. 19; V. 17; VI. 23; VIII. 30).

Jerome

In his early life, Jerome was torn between reading the classics and the Bible until he had this dream. "Suddenly I was caught up in the spirit and dragged before the judgment seat of the Judge; and here the light was so bright, and those who stood around were so radiant, that I cast myself upon the ground and did not dare to look up.

"Asked who and what I was I replied: 'I am a Christian.' But he who presided said: 'Thou liest, thou are a follower of Cicero and not of Christ. For "where thy treasure is, there will thy heart be also."' Instantly I became dumb, and amid the strokes of the lash—for He had ordered me to be scourged — I was tortured more severely still by the fire of conscience, considering with myself that verse, 'In the grave who shall give thee thanks?'

"Yet for all that I began to cry and to bewail myself, saying: 'Have mercy upon me, O Lord: have mercy upon me.' Amid the sound of the scourges this cry still made itself heard. At last the bystanders, falling down before the knees of Him who presided, prayed that He would have pity on my youth, and that He would give me space to repent of my error. He might still, they urged, inflict torture on me, should I ever again read the works of the Gentiles....

"Accordingly I made an oath and called upon His name, saying: 'Lord, if ever again I possess worldly books, or if ever again I read such, I have denied Thee.' Dismissed then, on taking this oath, I returned to the upper world, and to the surprise of all, I opened upon them eyes so drenched with tears that my distress served to convince even the incredulous. And that this was no sleep nor idle dreams, such as those by which we are often mocked, I call to witness the tribunal before which I lay, and the terrible judgment which I feared...I profess that my shoulders were black and blue, that I felt the bruises long after

I awoke from my sleep, and that thenceforth I read the books of God with a zeal greater than I had previously given to the books of men" (St. Jerome, Letter XXII, *To Ekustochium*, 30).

Jerome's studies also gave him good reason to value dreams and visions. In commenting on Jeremiah 23:25ff, he shared Jeremiah's concern, indicating that dreaming is a kind of prophesying that God can use as one vehicle of revelation to a soul. It can be a valuable revelation from God if a man's life is turned toward Him. But dreams can become idolatrous when they are sought and interpreted for their own sake by one who is serving his own self-interest instead of God. The value of the dream depends upon the person who seeks it and the person who interprets it. Sometimes God sends dreams to the unrighteous, like those of Nebuchadnezzar and Pharaoh, so that the servants of God may manifest their wisdom. Thus it is the duty of those who have the word of the Lord to explain dreams (S. Eusebii Hieronymi, *Commentariorum in Jeremiam Prophetam*, IV. 23).

This word could not be sought, however, by pagan practices. In commenting on Isaiah 65:4, Jerome went along with the prophet and condemned people who "sit in the graves and the temples of idols where they are accustomed to stretch out on the skins of sacrificial animals in order to know the future by dream, abominations which are still practiced today in the temples of Aescylapius (*Commentariorum in Isaiam Prophetam*). Later, however, in the discussion of Galatians, he brought up specifically the dream in the sixteenth chapter of Acts in which Paul "was given the true light (*lucam vero*)" (*Commentariorum in Epistolam ad Galatos*, 11).

Jerome made no distinction at all between the vision and the dream. He clearly valued them both. Yet in the end, he fixed the ground firmly that would justify a growing fear of these experiences. In translating Leviticus 19:26 and Deuteronomy

18:10 with one word different from other passages, a direct mistranslation, Jerome turned the law: "You shall not practice augury or witchcraft [i.e. soothsaying]" into the prohibition: "You shall not practice augury nor observe dreams." Thus by the authority of the Vulgate, dreams were classed with soothsaying, and the practice of listening to them with other superstitious ideas.[1]

From here we enter the 1000-year period known as the Dark Ages, and little more is said until the writings of Thomas Aquinas.

Thomas Aquinas

Aquinas was greatly influenced by Aristotle and sought to reduce Christianity into Aristotle's worldview. This worldview left no room for direct spiritual encounter. Therefore dreams and visions were played down, along with experiences of angels and demons, healing, tongue-speaking and miracles. In the end, Aquinas' life contradicted what he had written. He did come into direct relationship with God through a triple dream experience and ceased to write and dictate. When he was urged to go on, he replied: "I can do no more; such things have been revealed to me that all I have written seems as straw, and I now await the end of my life" (*Great Books of the Western World*, Vol. 19 [Thomas Aquinas], Chicago, Encyclopedia Britannica, Inc., 1952, p. vi).

This was the turning point for the Church's view of dreams and their ability to carry revelation from Almighty God into the believer's life. Although the Church has flip-flopped back and forth somewhat in its opinion of the value of dreams, the pervading view today is much in line with the rationalism of our day, and very much out of line with the teachings of Scripture and the early Church fathers. One appears strange if he believes that God would actually communicate today to His children through the medium of dreams and visions.

Abraham Lincoln

Abraham Lincoln dreamed about his impending death just days before his assassination.

There are many more modern examples that could be quoted, but that is not our purpose at this time. There are entire books on the market today giving a Christian philosophical and theological base for interpreting dreams. There also are testimonial books concerning the variety of dreams and visions being experienced in the Church today.

As we have seen over and over again, dreams and visions are considered interchangeable, and so, even though much of this research deals primarily with dreams, it should be viewed in a wider scope to include visions as well.

It is time for the Church to return to a biblical understanding of dreams and visions and revelation.

Footnotes

[1] The word *annan* occurs ten times in the Old Testament. In most cases in the current versions, it is simply translated "soothsayer" or "soothsaying."

More Powerful Resources from Mark and Patti Virkler

Available through
Communion With God Ministries
3792 Broadway St., Cheektowaga, NY 14227
www.cwgministries.org
1-800-466-6961
716-681-4896

Communion With God
Ministries

49 Lies I Rejected When I Renounced Phariseeism
Am I Being Deceived?
Apprenticed to Leadership
Appropriating Covenant Blessings audio/video
Christian Leadership University Catalog
Christian Restoration Fellowship International Catalog
Christianity and the New Age audio
Counseled by God: **book, study guide, teacher's guide, audio/
video series**
Creative Management Seminar audio/video series
Dialogue With God
Dynamic Five Fold Team Leadership
Ethical Network Marketing
Experiencing God: Lamad Encounter Groups
Flow of Life, The
Four Keys to Hearing God's Voice audio/video
Foundations of Life, The
Fulfill Your Financial Destiny
Gifted to Succeed
Go Natural! - Eden's Health Plan: **book, workbook, teacher's
guide, audio/video series**
Great Mystery, The

Health Mastery Through Muscle Response Testing
Hear God Through Your Dreams
How Do You Know?
How to Hear God's Voice: book, seminar workbook, teacher's guide, teen edition, audio/video series
"How to Receive the Baptism in the Holy Spirit" booklet
Naturally Supernatural: book, audio series
Pharisee's Struggle with the Holy Spirit, The audio
Prayers That Heal the Heart: book, seminar guide, audio/video series
Restoring Health Care as a Ministry
Revelation Knowledge audio
Rivers of Grace – Raising children by the Spirit rather than the law
Sense Your Spirit
Sound Doctrine Through Revelation Knowledge
Spirit Born Creativity: book, teacher's guide, audio/video series
Spirit-Anointed Teaching Seminar audio series
Supernatural Church, The
Through the Bible: book, teacher's guide, handbook of answers
Twenty Key Biblical Principles for Management
Tools for the Workman: book, teacher's guide
Wading Deeper Into the River of God
What Do Left-brainers Receive? audio
Why Christian Home Education?
Worshipping with Sign Language: songbook, video series

Tracts and Articles

Contributing Strands Worksheet
Overcoming Blocks and Hindrances to Hearing God's Voice
You Can Hear God's Voice

All of these, as well as many other **free downloadable books** and articles, are available online at:

www.cwgministries.org

Visit us on the web today!

Can you *possibly* learn it all from this one book?

What if hearing God's voice was truly second nature?

You **can** attain that level of mastery by expanding your learning experience into a three-month home study college course from Christian Leadership University

When you meditate on revelation truths in the context of a Christian Leadership University course, you are required to fully integrate the life-changing principles. Nothing is left to chance. You will learn what you are supposed to learn and your life will be transformed by the power of the Holy Spirit.

Don't just dabble in the voice of God!

REN103 Communion with God (3 credits)
Course materials include this book *(Dialogue With God)*; *How to Hear God's Voice (*also by Mark Virkler); the How to Hear God's Voice audio CD series; and an extensive course syllabus. The complete 10-hour audio series will draw you into a classroom experience with others who are learning to hear from God right alongside you. You are guaranteed to have a great time as Mark shares his story with passion, including the all-too-familiar trials and often hilarious misconceptions and mistakes that are an integral part of the journey. You should invest about one hour a day for 12 weeks to complete this course. You will be assigned an instructor who is available to you by internet, phone and regular mail. Certain required assignments will be submitted to your instructor for grading.

Christian Leadership University Catalog:
www.cluonline.com

Enroll at: www.cluonline.com/apply
1-800-466-6961